COLD WAR PEACEMAKER

The Story of Cowtown and the Convair B-36

DON PYEATT and DENNIS R. JENKINS

specialtypress
PUBLISHERS AND WHOLESALERS

Specialty Press
39966 Grand Avenue
North Branch, MN 55056 USA
(651) 277-1400 or (800) 895-4585
Fax: (651) 277-1203
www.specialtypress.com

ISBN 978-1-58007-127-7
Item Number SP127

Library of Congress Cataloging-in-Publication Data

Pyeatt, Don.
  Cold War peacemaker: the story of Cowtown and the Convair B-36 / by Don Pyeatt and Dennis R. Jenkins.
      p. cm.
  Includes bibliographical references and index.
  ISBN 978-1-58007-127-7
  1. B-36 bomber--History. 2. Convair transport planes--History. I. Jenkins, Dennis R. II. Title.
    UG1242.B6P94 2010
    623.74'63--dc22
                                    2009024080

Printed in China
10 9 8 7 6 5 4 3 2 1

On the Front Cover:
A classic study of a B-36F. Note that the small Convair line number has been scratched off the nose – the censors mutilated the original negative to delete this number and deny the Soviets information. (Frank F. Kleinwechter Collection)

On the Back Cover (top):
Interestingly, this B-36B does not have any cannon installed in its nose turret, although the nose gun sight can clearly be seen projecting from the glazed area beneath the empty turret. The photo was taken on 14 May 1950 at Fairfield-Suisun, California. Note the early faired-type ECM antennas on the forward fuselage. (Frank F. Kleinwechter)

On the Back Cover (bottom):
The Last B-36J (52-2827) during its private dedication ceremony at the Pima Air & Space Museum in Tucson, Arizona, in October 2009. After many years in Fort Worth, the airplane was finally moved to Pima and carefully restored to a mostly accurate appearance. (Don Pyeatt)

On the Front Flap:
This RB-36H (51-5743) paid a visit to Cheyenne, Wyoming, during October 1954. The six large pusher propellers were a trademark of the B-36. (P. Paulson via Dave Menard Collection)

On the Back Flap:
Air Force Plant 4 in Fort Worth. This photo was taken during the early 1950s and shows 33 B-36s on the ramp around the facility. Given the lack of cars in the parking lots surrounding the mile-long building, it is likely a Sunday morning. (Jack Kerr via Frank Kleinwechter Collection)

On the Title Page:
A Featherweight III B-36 J (52-2222) during what appears to be an open house at Mountain Home AFB. The airplane wears a late version of the 7th Bomb Wing (Heavy) shield – the 7th BW motto translates to 'Death from Above." (B.J. Brown)

Distributed in the UK and Europe by
Crécy Publishing Ltd
1a Ringway Trading Estate
Shadowmoss Road
Manchester M22 5LH England
Tel: 44 161 499 0024
Fax : 44 161 499 0298
www.crecy.co.uk
enquiries@crecy.co.uk

CONTENTS

PREFACE

Superlatives are a minimal linguistic component used to describe the Convair B-36 "Peacemaker" intercontinental bomber. The size and power of the airplane can only be described with words like "huge" and "enormous." Given the normal reaction of people who first viewed the prototype, many had taken to calling it the "Jesus" airplane.[1] The B-36 commanded awe from all who saw and heard it, and journalists not often at a loss for words described it in news articles as the "Superduper Fortress"[2] and even the "Super-Super-Superfortress."[3] Everything about the B-36 was larger than life and hard to describe.

The story of the B-36 is unique in American aviation history. It survived near-cancellation on six separate occasions during an extremely protracted development program. It was the symbol of a bitter inter-service rivalry between the newly formed Air Force and the well-established Navy over who would control delivery of atomic weapons during the early years of the Cold War. The nuclear mission brought with it the lion's share of funding and prestige, things both services wanted to keep largely for themselves. As a result of the bickering, the aircraft was the subject of numerous Congressional hearings, a multitude of newsreels, and countless newspaper and magazine articles.

The B-36 was operational for only ten years, and there were always questions as to whether it could accomplish its assigned strategic bombardment mission. Nobody denied the aircraft was slow, although sometimes it was hard to ascertain just how slow it really was in comparison to other aircraft of the era. Nobody advertised the weaknesses of their aircraft, and published performance figures were often misleading, or in some cases, pure fabrication. However, the B-36 flew so high that it probably did not really matter, at least initially. Few fighters of its era could climb as high, and surface-to-air missiles were just being developed. It was probably not until the last few years of its service life that the B-36 was particularly vulnerable.

The aircraft also had very long legs, a necessary attribute for the first truly intercontinental bomber. It is hard to imagine a modern aircraft remaining airborne for two days without refueling, but it was not particularly unusual for the B-36 to do so; it took a long time to fly 10,000 miles at 250 mph.

Then there were the problems. Despite its seemingly obsolete appearance, the B-36 pushed 1940s state of the art further than any other aircraft of its era. Its sheer size brought structural challenges, while its high-altitude capabilities brought more problems; the thin air could not adequately cool the engines while, ironically, everything else on the airplane froze because of the low temperature. Sophisticated defensive and bombing systems presented development, maintenance, and operational headaches. Insufficient training for ground crews and severe spare parts shortages exacerbated the problems. Nevertheless, in the end, the B-36 did its job – for the initial years of the Cold War, the "Big Stick" was the major deterrent available to the Free World.

Curious about the quotation marks around the name "Peacemaker"? Convair had proposed the name for the B-36, but several religious groups opposed its adoption, and in the end, the B-36 spent its career without an official moniker. Peacemaker is generally used, but was never sanctioned by the Air Force.

Consolidated Vultee Aircraft Corporation produced the B-36 at its plant in Fort Worth, Texas, adjacent to Carswell Air Force Base. With Carswell as the primary training base for B-36 operations and its proximity to the manufacturing plant, Fort Worth became a destination for many prominent military and political leaders, visiting heads of state, and celebrity figures from around the world. Fort Worth became the focus of the world's media attention – and the nemesis of our country's perceived enemy, the Soviet Union.

Within these pages we attempt to provide a glimpse of the era of the B-36. This story concentrates on the 7th and 11th Bombardment Wings, mostly because they were in Fort Worth and we had long-standing relationships with many of these veterans. However, similar stories undoubtedly took place at the other wings and cities where the Peacemaker served. We encourage you to research the local history in your areas of interest.

Acknowledgments

No book can be produced in a vacuum and, more so than most, this one is the product of tremendous cooperation from a great many people. Much of the unique content of this book is largely attributable to Mike Moore, Karen Hagar, and Diana Vargas at Lockheed Martin Aeronautics Company in Fort Worth (the former Convair). As always, Walter J. Boyne, Jay Miller, Terry Panopalis, and Mick Roth supplied information and photographs. Many B-36 enthusiasts also contributed from their personal collections: Max

Campbell, Ed Calvert, Richard Freeman, Richard Marmo, Wendell Montague, Bill Plumlee, George Savage, Joe Trnka, Bert Woods, and John W. "Zimmy" Zimmerman. Ray Wagner and A. J. Lutz at the San Diego Air & Space Museum graciously allowed access to their extensive photo archive – easily one of the best in the world when researching Convair subjects.

A very special acknowledgment is extended to C. Roger Cripliver and Frank F. Kleinwechter, Jr., both of whom passed away during development of this book. The authors of most authoritative books about the B-36 have sought historical and photographic materials from Roger and Frank for very good reasons. Roger Cripliver made his career at Government Aircraft Plant 4 in Fort Worth beginning in 1945 after serving in World War II with the U.S. Army Air Force's Central Flight Training Command as a flight-line crewmember, instructor, crew chief, flight engineer, and airplane inspector. He became known as *de facto* historian for Plant 4 through all of its phases. After his death, his extensive collection of historic Convair documents and photographs were bequeathed to the History of Aviation Collection, Special Collections Department, McDermott Library, The University of Texas at Dallas. Across the runway from Convair, Frank F. Kleinwechter, Jr., after serving in World War II, served his country again in the Strategic Air Command (SAC) at Carswell AFB. Frank was one of very few who were fortunate to have clearance to carry a camera during missions and on the flight line. Frank photo-documented the entire B-36 era at Carswell, including the aircraft's early propaganda flights and later missions to Europe and North Africa. After retirement from SAC, he served as historian for the 7th Bomb Wing B-36 Association from its beginning until his death. Frank's extensive collection of 7th Bomb Wing memorabilia was being moved to the Fort Worth Public Library at the time of his death and continues as this book goes to press.

DEDICATION

Charles "Roger" Cripliver
8 August 1918–25 January 2007

Lt.Col. Frank Frederick Kleinwechter, Jr., USAF (ret)
16 October 1920–28 March 2008

Both Roger and Frank were consummate gentlemen and will be sorely missed by all who knew them.

Others who graciously contributed include: James Baldwin, Kimzy Bertalotto, Jr., Bob Bradley (formerly of Convair, San Diego), Mark Cleary (45th SW/HO), Joe Carver (Air Force Historical Research Agency), George Cully, Doug Davidge, Scott Deaver, Archie Difante (Air Force Historical Research Agency), Robert F. Dorr, Ben Fey (Convair retiree), James Foss (P&W), Lt.Col. Richard "Dick" George (USAF retired), John Gourley, Wesley Henry (National Museum of the U.S. Air Force), Teresa Vanden-Heuvel (AMARC Public Affairs), Ellen LeMond-Holman (Boeing St. Louis), Marty Isham, Joe Jopling (Convair retiree), Doug Kirkpatrick, Mike Lombardi (Boeing Historical Archives), Gary T. McNeece (Fairchild Heritage Museum), David Menard, Claude S. Morse (AEDC/ACS), J'Nell Pate (Fort Worth historian), Bill Norton, Stan Piet (Glenn L. Martin Museum), Wayne Reece, Greg W. Roberts (P&W), Frederick N. Stoliker, Brett Stolle (National Museum of the U.S. Air Force), Sheila Stupcenski (P&W), Warren F. Thompson, and Ben Whitaker.

Don Pyeatt
Fort Worth, Texas

Dennis R. Jenkins
Cape Canaveral, Florida

Frank F. Kleinwechter, Jr. (Photo by Don Pyeatt)

C. "Roger" Cripliver. (Photo by Don Pyeatt)

COLOR PHOTOGRAPHY

Surprisingly few color photographs remain of the B-36, and fewer still that are of sufficient quality to publish. Partly, this is because color film was unusual, and expensive, during the 1950s, so most people used black & white films. Of the color photographs that were taken, many have faded or color-shifted to an extent they are no longer usable.

In many way, however, it does not matter. The B-36 was not a particularly colorful airplane – most of them remained in their natural metal finish their entire careers, although a few received white "high altitude camouflage" in their waning years. The exceptions were only a handful of B-36Bs that received high-visibility arctic-red empennages and wingtips, and two Kirtland test airplanes that were resplendent in a bizarre red, white, and blue scheme.

Regardless, the next few pages contain some of the more interesting color images, although many have color-shifted and we did not attempt to over-restore them. Enjoy.

"Development of the Bomber: DH-4 to B-36" by John McCoy. The evolution of the bomber in the United States began with the deHavilland DH-4, although most of those in U.S. service were actually manufactured by Dayton-Wright or Fisher Body (General Motors). The DH-4 saw extensive use in World War I. Next is the Martin-Curtiss NBS-1, which equipped Army bombing squadrons during the mid-1920s. The NBS-1 used two of the same Liberty engine that the DH-4 had used a decade earlier. The first monoplane shown above is the Martin B-10, which began to enter service in the mid-1930s. It was quickly outclassed by the next aircraft shown – the famous Boeing B-17 Flying Fortress, which along with the Convair B-24 Liberator (not shown) saw extensive use during World War II. Boeing did not rest on its laurels, and by the end of the war had introduced the B-29 Superfortress, the product of one of the most amazing manufacturing programs ever undertaken. At the bottom of the illustration is the Convair B-36, the largest piston-engined bomber ever produced. (U.S. Air Force – DVIC Photo DF-SC-84-08873)

A mixed formation of B-36As and B-36Bs shows the effect of the red arctic markings – the airplane stands out considerably better than its natural metal finish companions. (National Archives via the Stan Piet Collection)

The B-36 was the first strategic bomber to routinely conduct training flights over the Arctic Circle, and SAC painted a handful of them with bright red markings in case they made forced landings. (San Diego Air & Space Museum Collection)

A group of red-tail B-36Bs along with at least one non-red-tail aircraft. Note the variation in markings on the forward fuselage – some aircraft have buzz numbers, others do not. This was not DayGlo paint as is often reported; just bright red. (San Diego Air & Space Museum Collection)

A red-tail B-36B-1-CF (44-92033) seen behind the fence at Carswell AFB. The Strategic Air Command (SAC) did not approve of photographing strategic bombers, limiting the opportunities for crew members to snap pictures such as this one. (Frank Kleinwechter via Don Pyeatt)

The XB-36 (42-13570) differed in many details from the production airplanes that would follow. In addition to the "airline" type canopy over the pilots and the massive 110-inch main landing gear, the bomb bay and gun turret arrangement were significantly different. Nevertheless, the overall size and shape of the airplane is familiar to anyone who has seen a B-36. (Convair)

Lacking any other method of transporting the B-58 static test article from Fort Worth to Wright-Patterson AFB, Convair elected to use this B-36F-1-CF (49-2677). The inboard propellers were removed and the landing gear remained down in flight. (Convair)

Geometric tail codes were used during part of the B-36's career. The Triangle J code signified the 7th BW at Carswell AFB. The 8th Air Force insignia was also painted on the tail. This photo was taken on 26 May 1950. (Frank Kleinwechter via Don Pyeatt)

A Featherweight III airplane from the 11th BW during 1956. Note the flush blister cover and lack of a nose turret. The solid bombardier's panel indicates this aircraft was equipped with the Y-3 periscopic bombsight. (John Hoffman via Warren Thompson

The B-36 was a popular attraction during open houses, with an RB-36D (44-92089) shown here at Carswell on 20 May 1950. At this point there were no squadron color markings on the aircraft. (Frank Kleinwechter via Don Pyeatt)

This B-36B-1-CF (44-92033) shows off the red arctic markings that were used by the Project GEM aircraft. The undersides of the horizontal stabilizer are not completely red – this is different than most of the aircraft where the entire stabilizer and elevator were painted. Note the short-lived buzz number on the forward fuselage (BM was assigned to the B-36 fleet). (Lockheed Martin)

The standard (shiny) aluminum and (dull) magnesium natural metal finish used by most of the B-36 fleet during its career. There was little to externally differentiate most B-36 models after the jet pods were added. (Tony Landis Collection)

The single XC-99 used aluminum skin instead of the largely magnesium skin used by the bomber. A variety of small markings were applied to the vertical stabilizer over the years, and for a while, a small XC-99 logo adorned the forward fuselage. Later in its career, the top of the cockpit area was painted white to combat the heat of the sun. (San Diego Air & Space Museum Collection)

In February 1949, a B-36A-5-CF (44-92010) was on display at Andrews AFB, Maryland, with what many believe was its closest rival – a Northrop YB-49 flying wing. Note the North American B-45 and Boeing B-47 in the background. (Thomas TIlley via Ron Kaplan)

The Boeing Superfortress (this is a B-29B-55-BA, 44-84027) seemed like a large aircraft until it was parked next to the XB-36. The B-36 had a wing span that was 60 percent greater than the Boeing airplane. (Frank Kleinwechter Collection)

The JRB-36F (49-2707) led an interesting career, being the initial testbed for the Project FICON parasite fighter project, and also for the Tom-Tom wingtip coupling experiments. Here, an RF-84F (51-1849) prepares to hook up to the bomber. (Lockheed Martin)

Unquestionably the most colorful B-36s were a pair of EB-36Hs (51-5726 shown) from Kirtland AFB. These were used as high-altitude photo targets for ground-based cameras on the Atlantic Missile Range at Cape Canaveral. (AFRL/Phillips Research Site History Office)

The NB-36H-20-CF (51-5712) was one of the more colorful B-36s. Before its first flight the airplane had "Crusader" written in the blue stripe on the forward fuselage, but this was removed sometime during flight tests for unexplained reasons. (Convair)

The crew of the NB-36H discuss the upcoming flight before boarding the airplane. The airplane was designated XB-36H from 11 March 1956 until 6 June 1956 and this is what was originally painted where NB-36H is displayed above. (Lockheed Martin)

Only the first (49-2676) of two all-jet YB-60s actually flew, and proved to be much slower than the contemporary Boeing XB-52 Stratofortress. Most of the wing structure was, surprisingly, identical to the B-36F it was converted from. (Convair)

The pair of YB-60s used the same nacelles, pylons, and engines as the Boeing XB-52, and was considered an inexpensive alternative in case the B-52 was unreasonably delayed. Despite its sleek appearance, the YB-60 was not nearly as fast as the Boeing airplane since it had not been designed for high-speed flight and still used a thick wing and empennage. (Convair)

Heading home from Hawaii after Operation REDWING. Originally, a B-36 was going to drop the TX-51 device during Shot Cherokee as part of Operation REDWING, but a last-minute analysis indicated the B-36 was too slow to escape the thermal effects of the expected yield of the weapon. (Kimzy Bertalotto, Jr. via Wayne Reece)

One of the B-36Js (52-2824) used as atomic sampler aircraft in Hawaii with the 327th Bomb Squadron from the 92nd Bomb Wing. Four B-36s from the squadron deployed from 14 April to 15 July 1956 as part of Operation REDWING. Note the large sampler box protruding from the forward sighting blister. This held filters that collected radioactive particles. (Kimzy Bertalotto, Jr. via Wayne Reece)

Although a B-52 dropped the primary weapon during Operations REDWING, one of these B-36Js dropped a low-yield TX-28 during Shot Osage on 17 June 1956. The 3,150-pound device had a 70-kiloton yield when it detonated at 670 feet altitude. The B-36s were also used to drop diagnostic canisters in support of Shot Cherokee. (Kimzy Bertalotto, Jr. via Wayne Reece)

A brand-new B-36D-45-CF (44-92080) on the field at San Diego. This airplane had originally been built as a B-36B-20-CF in Fort Worth and was converted to a D-model in San Diego. The aircraft was redelivered to the Air Force in late 1951, but was written off on 29 January 1952 when it landed short at Fairchild AFB, killing seven crewmembers. (San Diego Air & Space Museum Collection)

Miss Featherweight, a B-36H-1-CF (50-1086) at Eglin AFB, Florida, on 10 October 1955. A pair of 22,000-pound T-14 Gland Slam bombs are sitting beside the airplane waiting to be loaded for a test over the Eglin bombing range. (Frank Kleinwechter via Don Pyeatt)

The last B-36J (52-2827) at the Pima Air & Space Museum in Tucson, Arizona, shortly after it was moved from its long-time home in Fort Worth. After years of trying, Fort Worth conceded it could not properly display the airplane. (Bob Adams Collection)

The last B-36J after it was restored and placed on display at Pima. The restoration has a few inaccuracies such as the sighting blisters (this was a Featherweight III airplane) and the masked-off white belly paint (instead of freehand). (Bob Adams Collection)

Maintenance on the B-36 was never easy. Here a technician inspects the top of the rudder, which was almost 47 feet above the ground. Note the open turret bay on the fuselage. (National Museum of the United States Air Force Collection)

The end of the line. This B-36H (51-5737) arrived at Davis-Monthan AFB, Arizona, in January 1958. Unlike modern aircraft that frequently languish in the boneyard for years, the B-36s were reduced to ingots within months. (Frank Kleinwechter via Don Pyeatt)

CHAPTER 1

COWBOYS TO COCKPITS
AVIATION COMES TO FORT WORTH

This late 1940s view of Carswell AFB shows 29 pre-jet B-36s on the Air Force ramp, including 10 with red arctic colors. Lake Worth is in the upper right of this photo, and Air Force Plant No. 4 is along the top. The seven B-36As parked at an angle on the left portion of the Convair ramp are waiting to be remanufactured into RB-36Es. (Photo by Jack Kerr via Frank Kleinwechter, scan and digital processing by Don Pyeatt)

"The more highly scientific war enginery becomes, the more the game of war will be one that can be played only by the most scientific and enlightened Nations. More and more will home and country be defended by machinery and less by blood. Fewer and fewer men will be obliged to engage in the trade of war, and more and more will be able to devote themselves to peaceful pursuits. Less and less will war be the arbiter of Nations, for the difficulty and the expense will become so prohibitive that wars will no longer pay."

— From the *New York Herald*, 6 September 1908, "Man's Amazing Tomorrow" by military inventor Hudson Maxim

The awe-inspiring size of the XB-36 is seen in this 27 May 1949 photo of a Convair C-87 (transport version of the B-24) flying alongside the new super-bomber. (National Archives)

Despite a troubled gestation period, checkered with multiple attempts to alternately accelerate development and terminate the program, the XB-36 (42-13570) was finally rolled-out of the Consolidated Vultee plant in Fort Worth on 8 September 1945. Ironically, the manufacturing facility, officially designated Government Aircraft Plant 4,[1] and the bombers it built during World War II, were partly responsible for the XB-36 not being completed during the war; the B-24 Liberator and B-32 Dominator enjoyed higher priorities until victory was assured.

Once the XB-36 had been shown to the public, the Air Force, Consolidated, and many subcontractors wasted no time placing full-page advertisements in publications worldwide to extol the capabilities of the B-36. Large photographs of the XB-36 were published in newspapers, magazines, and newsreels in many countries. Radio news programs were replete with stories of the B-36 and its unheard-of capabilities.

"Big, Big, BIG B-36 Makes B-29 Look Like Tin Lizzie" screamed one headline.[2] To keep the media frenzy alive, and the Soviets nervous, Consolidated then announced the B-36 would carry its own defensive jet fighters – as many as four – inside its massive bomb bays.[3] The relentless propaganda campaign was an unqualified success. The Army Air Forces effectively used the B-36 to intimidate the Soviet Union – and ironically, the U.S. Navy – even before the first operational airplane had been delivered. The B-36 arrived on the world's stage much like the great ape in the 1933 movie epic *King Kong*.

After the first B-36s were delivered in 1948, the Air Force continued the propaganda blitz as it began showing off its new aircraft at air shows and political events, and by making low-level passes over many American cities. Coupled with severe cutbacks in the defense budget resulting from the postwar economic slump, this publicity placed the B-36 at the center of a very public debate regarding whether the newly formed Air Force, or the traditional flag-bearing Navy, would control the burgeoning U.S. nuclear arsenal – and the massive funding it

Typical of full-page ads from Convair was this September 1945 example that was published worldwide in major newspapers and magazines soon after the first flight of the XB-36. (Don Pyeatt Collection)

brought. Despite a less-than-ideal entry into operational service, the Air Force continued to showcase the B-36 at every opportunity.

The 20 January 1949 inauguration of President Harry S. Truman was the largest in U.S. history, even more lavish and outlandish than that of W. Lee (Pappy) O'Daniel's 1939 inauguration as governor of Texas. The Republican-controlled Congress, confident that Thomas E. Dewey would win the 1948 presidential election, approved $80,000 ($700,000 in 2009 dollars) for inauguration festivities. After Truman's surprise victory, the Democrats claimed possession of the funds and proceeded to spend every bit of it. During the event, described modestly as a spectacle by the media, 40,000 people marched in a seven-mile-long parade of floats and performers, a mounted posse from Missouri, a herd of mules, and entire regiments of uniformed soldiers and armored vehicles. An estimated one million people attended the event. Hundreds of railroad sleeper cars were pressed into service as hotel rooms for a few of those who trekked to the capitol for the event. Above the pageantry flew a cover of military aircraft piloted by 400 cadets from Randolph and Barksdale AFBs, plus 100 Women in the Air Force (WAF) pilots from Lackland AFB.[4] Capping it all was a rumbling cacophony that was heard all the way to Moscow, caused by a low-level overflight of five ground-shaking B-36s (essentially the entire fleet at that time) from the 7th Bomb Wing at Carswell AFB in Fort Worth.[5] All other events of that day paled in the shadows and sounds of the B-36 armada.

The continuing barrage of B-36 propaganda resulted in intense, worldwide interest for anything related to the new airplane. Presidents, heads of state, politicians, journalists, entertainers, and various other publicity seekers soon learned that a connection with the bomber guaranteed an instant, free, and far-reaching spotlight in the world press. Prominent and not-so-prominent people alike began appearing in Fort Worth to tour the Consolidated plant and the adjacent Carswell AFB. Engineering and materiel vendors calling on Consolidated often resulted in more than 60 plant visits per day and prompted the company to create a reception area to handle the onrush.

Comedian Bob Hope tours the flight line during a January 1951 performance at Carswell AFB. Hope was one of many celebrities that wanted to see the new bomber. (Frank F. Kleinwechter)

Cowtown

A visitor arriving in Fort Worth during the 1940s may have envisioned the destination to be a modern, progressive city composed of sparkling new buildings inhabited by aeronautical engineers, scientists, and government workers. That vision was not to be realized. Stepping from a steam-powered train onto the wooden passenger platform at Fort Worth's railroad station, a visiting dignitary would have seen a large banner proclaiming "Welcome to Cowtown – Where the West Begins." Other visitors, arriving at the municipal airport, would exit a Douglas DC-3 into an eye-tearing stench that permeated

One of the B-36s (upper left corner) in a formation of five of the new bombers from the 7th Bombardment Wing at Carswell AFB that overflew the inauguration of Harry S. Truman on 20 January 1949. The photo was taken from the nose of a following B-36. (Frank F. Kleinwechter Collection)

Prince Bernhard of Netherlands during a visit to Consolidated and Carswell AFB 6 March 1950. From left, Gen. Roger M. Ramey, Commander, 8th Air Force, Prince Bernhard, and Brig. Gen. Clarence S. Irvine, Commander, Carswell AFB. (Don Pyeatt Collection)

Fort Worth Meacham Field in the 1940s. Note the Douglas transports operated by American, Delta, and Braniff airlines and the American Airlines maintenance hangar. (via Dave Pearson)

the city, and often the entire county. The visitor could not know that the sickening pall, emanating from close-by cattle feed lots and meat-packing plants, was a lingering reminder to locals of what was responsible for the Consolidated plant's existence in their town.

A limousine and driver often met visitors of national or international preeminence. Those of special importance were taken downtown to the Fort Worth Club[6] where they were greeted by the city's business and political leaders, followed by a reception that included a banquet and an open bar. Special guests would also meet the president of the club, Amon G. Carter, owner and publisher of the *Fort Worth Star-Telegram*, and also the city's most active booster

through his position with the Chamber of Commerce. Carter would often add to the hospitality of the Fort Worth Club by taking guests to his Shady Oak Farm for an evening of fun, food, and drinks. Mr. Carter entertained the world's best-known celebrities, dignitaries, corporate and banking heads, and entertainers. Heads-of-state and various world leaders, including presidents Roosevelt, Truman, and Eisenhower, were often guests of Carter at Shady Oak Farm. The lavish parties were always of a western theme where Carter would convince the guests to dress as cowboys and Indians for a long night of revelry.

Carter would award certain visitors a hand-made hat named "The Shady Oak," made especially by the John B. Stetson Company of St. Joseph, Missouri, and sold to Carter through the local Washer Brothers and Peters Hats stores. Recipients were required to sign their hats and surrender them to Carter while being photographed wearing the western-cut Shady Oak. Carter skillfully played his own notoriety during these events to booster investments in Fort Worth and readership of his newspaper.

Fort Worth, during the 1940s, was a very unusual place indeed. It was a city whose western veneer gave no indication it was home to an ultra-modern aircraft factory and military installation. The events that prepared Fort Worth to become home to the B-36 are an integral part of the airplane's history.

Before the B-36: Wars, Cattle, Railroads, and Oil

Fort Worth began amidst military conflicts and because of its militarily strategic location. At the close of the U.S. and Mexican War, Maj. Ripley A. Arnold

The 33rd President of the United States, Harry S. Truman, wearing a Shady Oak hat presented to him by Amon Carter, looking out the hatch of a B-36A (44-92010) at Carswell AFB. Among his legacies, Truman used executive orders to begin the desegregation of the U.S. armed forces. (Tony Landis Collection)

Amon G. Carter, the cowboy tycoon, in April 1936, wearing his western "duds" during Fort Worth's Texas Centennial celebration, a year-long celebration of the 100th anniversary of independence from Mexico. Carter is wearing one of his trademark Stetson Shady Oak hats. (Fort Worth Star-Telegram Collection)

Oddly, considering a sprawling Texas city is named for him, William Jenkins Worth is buried 1,500 miles away on an island of land between Fifth and Broadway at 25th Street in New York City's borough of Manhattan. A 50-foot-tall obelisk marks the location, surrounded by skyscrapers. (Dennis R. Jenkins)

Before commercial aviation arrived in Fort Worth, Bowen Motor Coaches, started by two brothers in 1925, became part of Trailways Association in 1938. The Bowen brothers were among the original incorporators of Texas Air Transport, an early component of American Airways Inc. (Dave Pearson Collection)

established a north-south "picket line" of ten Army posts between the Rio Grande River and the Red River, along a treaty line marking the border of Indian Territory. The treaty notwithstanding, the posts protected settlers and cattle drovers along the nearby Chisholm Trail from forays of still-warring Native Americans. One post in North Texas was named Fort Worth in honor of Mexican-American War Army hero Maj. Gen. William Jenkins Worth (1794–1849). The post was established on 6 June 1849 and was named Fort Worth on 14 November 1849. Its namesake died that same year without ever having been to the fort that bore his name. Worth's grave is in New York City at Fifth Avenue and Broadway, marked by a 50-foot-tall granite obelisk.[7]

The Texas and Pacific Terminal at Main and Front Streets in Fort Worth opened on 16 December 1889. The red brick building was designed by architect O. H. Lang. It served Fort Worth until 1931, when a new terminal opened. (Portal to Texas History)

Fort Worth continued to attract settlers due to the safety provided by the Army's presence. After peace treaties were negotiated with the Native Americans, the closing of the fort on 17 September 1853 proved to be a financial boon to the settlers who bought the abandoned Army buildings and converted them to shops, banks, and offices. The settlement's location near the famous Chisholm Trail made it a rest and recreation stop for cattle drovers, as saloonkeepers and brothel operators learned to coexist with the farmers who lived nearby. Three years later the town became the Tarrant County seat and attracted lawyers, land agents, surveyors, and other professionals.

The next 25 years would see Fort Worth grow slowly with the arrival of an ice plant, blacksmith shop, general stores, banks, feed lots, and cattle-related businesses. The entertainment district settled into an area south of the courthouse and was known as Hell's Half Acre because of the almost nightly gun battles and knife fights that erupted in the saloons. As the cattle business grew, so did Hell's Half Acre, and Fort Worth became widely known as "The Paris of the Plains."

The town's primary industries were cattle, agriculture, and entertainment until the American Civil War (1861–1865) nearly drained the town of its most productive men, and long-time residents moved east, away from the then-unprotected Indian Territory. The town was dying and its only hope for survival was the Texas and Pacific Railway that was inching its way from Dallas.

A national economic depression, the Panic of 1873, halted the railroad's progress only 26 miles away and threatened to seal Fort Worth's fate. Realizing the consequences looming ahead, the townspeople united in 1876 and, with picks, hammers, and shovels, the remaining track was completed by gamblers, farmers, lawyers, and cowboys working side-by-side while prostitutes and ladies of high social standing delivered food and water to the workers in horse-drawn carts. The Texas and Pacific arrived in Fort Worth on 19 July 1876, causing an immediate population and economic boom as the town began transforming into a livestock-trading center. Twelve additional railroads eventually arrived, making Fort Worth the transportation hub of the southwestern United States.

With the shocking realization of the town's near-death still fresh in their minds, local business leaders united to ensure that Fort Worth's growth would no longer be left to chance. In 1882, the predecessor of the Fort Worth Chamber of Commerce – the Fort Worth Board of Trade – was established. Three years later, in 1885, the Fort Worth Club was founded. Thirty-five years later those two organizations, and the same 26 miles of rail lain six years earlier, would bring aviation to Fort Worth.

The first major accomplishment of the Board of Trade and the Fort Worth Club was to convince, in 1902, the Armour and Swift companies to build hog, cattle, and sheep slaughtering and processing plants near the stock pens and feed lots. This was accompanied by a Board of Trade campaign to change Fort Worth's nickname and reputation from "The Paris of the Plains" to "The Queen City of the Plains."

Armour and Swift, both out-of-state companies, were established only three miles north of the Fort Worth city limits in a one-half-square-mile area. In February 1911, this area was incorporated by the owners of the packing-houses as Niles City. Fort Worth received no taxes from the meat processors and profits made by the companies were sent to the home states of each, but Fort Worth benefited greatly from a population and retail sales expansion as immigrant workers moved into town to work at the packing plants. Up to 5,000 people worked at the plants at one time.

However, events far removed from Fort Worth soon proved to be of even greater importance. The achievement of manned heavier-than-air flight on 17 December 1903 at Kitty Hawk, North Carolina, and the arrival in Fort Worth of Amon G. Carter in May 1905, signaled the beginning of the end of Fort Worth's livestock dependence. The end would be a long time in the making, however, requiring two world wars and the creation of a newspaper and political empire.

Amon Giles Carter[8] was born on 11 December 1879, in Crafton, Texas, 60 miles northwest of Fort Worth in rural Wise County. His family soon moved to nearby Bowie where he lived as a child and earned money for his family by selling chicken sandwiches to train passengers. He quit school at the age of 11, and eventually overcame the poverty of his childhood to become a newspaper and oil baron. Much later, at the age of 71, he received an honorary diploma from a high school that bore his name, Amon G. Carter-Riverside High School. He was also bestowed two honorary doctorates; one from Texas Tech

During the early 1900s, the Armour and Swift packing houses were major employers in the Fort Worth area and each had major national advertising campaigns for products manufactured in Niles City. (Portal to Texas History)

Armour and Swift operated meat processing plants near the Stockyards, which dominated much of the north side of the Fort Worth area. The meat industry was a defining characteristic of Fort Worth for many years and the meat packing complexes dominated the landscape. Today, what remains of the Stockyards is a tourist attraction with restaurants and souvenir shops. (Fort Worth Public Library)

in Lubbock and the other from Texas Christian University in Fort Worth. He became friends with heads of state, political figures, corporate leaders, and entertainment icons from around the world. Carter eventually ruled, like a doting father, the business and political climates of all of West Texas from Fort Worth to Amarillo to El Paso. Illustrating the point, in 1936, the *Amarillo Globe* wrote, "West Texas is bound on the north by Colorado and Oklahoma, on the west by New Mexico, on the south by Mexico and on the east by Amon Carter."

Driving Carter's life was a deep love for his adopted hometown of Fort Worth, selfless philanthropy, a near-obsession with aviation, and an acquired disdain for neighboring Dallas, only 30 miles to the east. Being a product of a small, north Texas town, Carter had no use for the Eastern dandies he perceived were running Dallas. While explaining his vendetta to Dallas mayor R. L. Thornton, Carter once said, "It's really a constructive thing. If I want to get some of my people off their asses, all I do is remind them that 'you don't want those Dallas bastards to get ahead of you, do you?'"[9]

Soon after arriving in Fort Worth in May 1905 from San Francisco, Carter assisted Col. Louis J. Wortham[10] and three others in forming a newspaper, the *Star*, to compete with the already established *Telegram*. Carter became the *Star*'s advertising manager while Wortham, who represented Tarrant County in the House of the Texas Legislature, became the managing editor and one of Carter's early political mentors. On 1 January 1909, Carter purchased the *Telegram* and merged it with the *Star* to create the *Fort Worth Star-Telegram*, which grew to become one of the most influential U.S. newspapers of its time.[11]

Carter learned that he could promote both his influence and his newspaper by flamboyantly boostering Fort Worth and small towns in the vast areas of West Texas. Publicly upstaging and embarrassing neighboring Dallas, by literally stealing its industries, assured Carter of a constant supply of headlines for the *Fort Worth Star-Telegram*.[12]

Roland Garros, center, with John B. Moisant's bright red "Statue of Liberty" Bleriot, moments before Fort Worth's first public airplane flight. (Fort Worth Star-Telegram Collection, The University of Texas at Arlington Library)

To further draw public attention to Fort Worth and away from "Big-D" (which he would write as "Big d"), Carter created the popular image of Texans – big cars, Cuban cigars, western clothes, and ten-gallon Stetson hats. He wore six-shooters during public events and began all his speeches by shouting "Texas forever! Fort Worth now and hereafter!" He boldly emblazoned "Where the West Begins" on the masthead of his newspaper and the City of Fort Worth adopted the phrase as its official motto. Sage comedian Will Rogers, Carter's closest friend, once jokingly said, "Fort Worth is where the West begins, and Dallas is where the East peters out." Carter eagerly adopted Roger's version of the motto as his own.

The other far-removed event was the 17 December 1903 flight of the Wright Brothers and the beginnings of powered, heavier-than-air flight. The development of radiotelegraphy at about the same time enabled news organizations to relay almost-daily stories about early aviators to readers around the world. The achievement of human flight rapidly captivated the imagination of all of mankind and flying clubs soon formed in towns large and small by people wanting to learn more about the physics of flight. Many clubs built rudimentary gliders to enable members to experience the exhilaration of flight.

Dallas took an early lead over Fort Worth in the emerging arena of aviation. In January 1910, the Dallas Chamber of Commerce hired Otto Brodie and a group of aviators from Los Angeles to conduct the first public demonstration of heavier-than-air machines in North Texas. The sold-out event was held in March at the Texas State Fair Grounds and brought a great deal of attention to Dallas. Later that year, Dallas hired the Moisant International Aviators, a touring group of French and American pilots, to perform at the Fair Grounds in January 1911. When news of the upcoming event reached Fort Worth, several members of the Fort Worth Flying Club traveled to Dallas and contacted one of the managers of the touring airmen, H. F. McGarvie, to inquire about the possibility of an airshow at Fort Worth immediately following the Dallas event. McGarvie agreed, but only if Fort Worth could pledge $10,000 plus expenses before the end of the Dallas show. The club members rushed back to Fort Worth to promote the event to city leaders.

Early in the morning of 8 January 1911, a committee of the Fort Worth Board of Trade, established by Louis Wortham and headed by W. G. Turner,[13] met with McGarvie to finalize plans for the flying exhibition. Afterward, McGarvie and the committee inspected a former racetrack one mile northwest of downtown to determine its suitability for the event and then traveled to Dallas to meet the flyers and arrange rail transportation of the airplanes to Fort Worth.[14] The following day, the Board of Trade and the Fort Worth Manufacturer's League each pledged $5,000 to guarantee the event. Amon Carter, a member of the committee that arranged the aerial

A commercial airport, pipelines, and refineries provided the final infrastructure components that Consolidated would be searching for only 15 years – and a new world war – later.

Political and Economic Imperatives

Playing on post-World War I oppression and a severe economic depression, Adolph Hitler turned Germany's despair into a plundering machine of mass murder. Soon after gaining control of Germany's feeble government, Hitler launched blitzkrieg assaults on neighboring countries. The German takeover of Czechoslovakia on 15 March 1938 and Poland on 1 September 1939 served as a dramatic announcement of Hitler's primary goal – complete control of all of Europe. Stunned by the rapid fall of Poland, the governments of Great Britain, France, Australia, and New Zealand, acting in concert as the Allied Powers, declared war on Germany on 2 September 1939.

While proclaiming its neutrality, the United States pledged unlimited support and began providing vast amounts of war materiel to the Allied Powers. Knowing that involvement in the war in Europe could not be avoided, President Franklin D. Roosevelt called on all American manufacturing companies to rapidly increase war materiel production.

Describing American military airpower as "utterly inadequate," on 12 January 1939, Roosevelt requested Congress to provide $300 million for the purchase of 3,000 aircraft for the Army. Germany had developed formidable airpower and anti-aircraft capabilities that made their homeland seemingly invincible. The Allies understood the only way to penetrate those defenses was with overwhelming numbers of aircraft and the inevitable heavy losses of airplanes and crews. As a result of those projec-tions, the President ordered manufacturers to prepare for the production of 50,000 airplanes, nearly tripling their output, and to rush designs of new aircraft to replace the already obsolete airplanes that were then being produced.

American aircraft manufacturers, then operating as a low-volume cottage industry, were not equipped for the high-volume production that would be required to meet Roosevelt's demands and were soon overwhelmed by orders for new warplanes. To ensure that Roosevelt's aircraft production requirements would be achieved, the federal government established the Defense Plant Corporation (DPC) under Section 5d of the Reconstruction Finance Corporation Act of 1940 to provide funds to private companies to enable them to build or expand war plants.[25] Fearing a possible attack by Japan, Roosevelt proclaimed a "Zone of the Interior" that was 200 miles within the coasts and borders of the United States. The War Department ordered all new defense plants built inland.

Because of the rapidly increasing demand for defense products, Chambers of Commerce in central U.S. cities immediately began aggressive campaigns to attract new factories. Economic desperation was the driving force behind these efforts since, by 1939, the Great Depression had extracted a terrible toll on the country. City leaders knew that a sudden influx of large amounts of war funding would solve many of their economic problems.

Nowhere were economic considerations more urgent than in Fort Worth, which was again struggling to survive. Between 1930 and 1940, the southwestern Great Plains region of the United States suffered a severe drought (causing that area to be known as the Dust Bowl) that added to the agonizing conditions of the Great Depression. Fort Worth was virtually decimated by these events. In a go-for-broke effort orchestrated by the Chamber of Commerce, Fort Worth's business and political leaders

George Newman signing the first Fort Worth B-24 over to Tom Girdler. A former steelman, Girdler became chairman of the Consolidated board two weeks after Pearl Harbor. He would soon move to Detroit to assist the automakers setting up their aircraft production operations. (Lockheed Martin)

George Newman, Amon Carter (missing his Shady Oak hat), and Harry Woodhead at a Fort Worth Chamber of Commerce dinner. Woodhead was president of Consolidated and Newman was a former test pilot who would become the vice president in charge of Plant 4 at the age of 34. (Lockheed Martin)

united to attract a large war materiel factory to avert a seemingly inevitable economic collapse.

Assigned by the Chamber president as political affairs liaison, Amon Carter directed a public relations blitz at two aircraft manufacturers known to be considering building new factories. A particularly aggressive campaign was launched to entice Consolidated Aircraft Corporation of San Diego, California, or Vultee Aircraft Company of Downey, California – or both – to build aircraft manufacturing plants in Fort Worth.[26] The Fort Worth City Council, all city departments, and numerous industry leaders were poised to respond immediately to any request from the Chamber of Commerce for legal actions, tax abatements, or infrastructure improvements that would lead to winning a major war materiel plant.

Before the onset of World War II, Amon Carter was already a famous man. His contrived "feud" with neighboring Dallas and his swaggering cowboy persona became known and admired worldwide. As a result of his notoriety and generosity, Carter knew many people who would ultimately decide the future of aviation in Fort Worth. Franklin Roosevelt's daughter, Anna, and his son, Elliot, both lived in Fort Worth and FDR became a frequent visitor to the city and to the Fort Worth Club. However, of all of Carter's friends, other than Roosevelt, perhaps the two most crucial in bringing World War II aviation industries to Fort Worth were Reuben H. Fleet and Jesse H. Jones.

Carter became acquainted with Consolidated Aircraft owner Reuben Hollis Fleet. (6 March 1887–29 October 1975) during his frequent flights on Pan American World Airways Clippers. Fleet was educated at Culver Military Academy in Indiana, which had been founded by his

Amon Carter was a frequent passenger on the Pan Am Boeing 314 Clippers. On one flight, he met Maj. Reuben H. Fleet, the founder of the Consolidated Aircraft Corporation. This relationship proved key to bringing Plant 4 to Fort Worth. (National Archives College Park Collection)

First Day Cover mailed to Amon Carter, Jr., at Culver Military Academy by Amon G. Carter on 19 November 1936 during the first airmail flight from La Loche to Ile a la Crosse, Canada. While at Culver Academy, Carter Jr. was a classmate and close friend of Reuben Fleet's son, Sandy. (Don Pyeatt Collection)

uncle. Fleet's aviation career began in 1917 when he earned his pilot's wings at McCook Field, an Army training base near Dayton, Ohio. After World War I ended, Fleet was appointed to establish a national airmail system for the Army. Fleet founded Consolidated Aircraft Corporation on 29 May 1923 in East Greenwich, Rhode Island, by acquiring Gallaudet Aircraft Corporation and the rights to produce aircraft designed by Dayton-Wright Company. By merging profitable elements of multiple companies, Fleet became the first aircraft industrialist to "consolidate" the components into a single, more efficient company. Consolidated's business grew to become the primary supplier of training aircraft for the military. Fleet's company soon outgrew its East Greenwich facility and moved to an abandoned Curtiss-Wright aircraft factory in Buffalo, New York, in 1926. Because of the rapid growth of the company, and for personal reasons, Fleet moved his entire company to San Diego in 1932.[27]

In 1925, the Fort Worth Chamber of Commerce named Jesse Holman Jones (5 April 1874–1 June 1956), owner of the *Houston Chronicle* and finance chairman for the Democratic National Convention, an honorary citizen. During the decade of the 1920s, Jones' construction company built many of the downtown buildings in Dallas, Fort Worth, Houston, San Antonio, and New York. During that time, Jones was often an overnight guest of Amon Carter at the Fort Worth Club. In 1939, Jones was appointed by Roosevelt to head the Reconstruction Finance Corporation and, in 1940, the Defense Plant Corporation. Jones was responsible for buying or building anything military leaders deemed necessary during World War II. Roosevelt gave Jones discretionary power to spend up to $500 million without approval of the President or the Congress. The freedom to spend large sums of government money with little or no oversight earned for Jones the reputation of being the "fourth branch of the government" and later caused an infuriated Lyndon B. Johnson to refer to

Jones as "Jesus H. Jones." Carter and Jones were active in Texas politics and were always boosters of the state through their memberships in the Texas Chamber of Commerce.[28]

Wooing Consolidated

Of particular interest to Fort Worth was Consolidated Aircraft Corporation of San Diego, California – known locally as CONSAIR – which had two products that would prove essential to the war effort. The first was the PBY Catalina, an amphibious patrol airplane that would be widely used by the U.S. Navy and many other countries. The other was the B-24 heavy bomber – named Liberator by Rueben Fleet's wife Dorothy – that would become the most-produced bomber of the war.[29] Anticipating heavy demand for both, Consolidated began searching for a site adjacent to an inland lake to build a new assembly plant.

Thirty miles east of Fort Worth, Dallas was one of many inland cities hoping to attract new war industries. The Dallas Chamber of Commerce was also attempting to convince various aircraft manufacturers to build new plants in their city. Consolidated was of special interest to Dallas because of the possibility that a site on Mountain Creek Lake might be attractive for the production of PBYs.

Site surveyors from Consolidated arrived in Dallas in November 1939, and a site located west of Hensley Reserve Airfield, on Mountain Creek Lake, seemed to meet all of Consolidated's requirements. The land was owned by the City of Dallas and was leased to the War Department. Consolidated obtained an option on the site through the Dallas Chamber of Commerce that was contingent on a pending merger of Consolidated and the Hall Aluminum Aircraft Company.[30]

Learning of Consolidated's interest in Dallas, Amon Carter hired an engineering firm to perform a study of the Mountain Creek Lake site and a comparative study of two Fort Worth sites, Lake Worth and Eagle Mountain Lake. The study revealed that fluctuations in the water levels would prevent use of Mountain Creek Lake for launching seaplanes during dry periods, thus making the site worthless to Consolidated. On the other hand, the study concluded that the water level of the two Fort Worth lakes could be maintained at any desired level by a series of dams that had recently been constructed on the Trinity River. Carter mailed the report to Consolidated.[31]

While the Consolidated/Hall merger was being negotiated, James H. "Dutch" Kindelberger, president of North American Aviation in Inglewood, California, arrived in Dallas to search for a site to build a new assembly plant.

Jesse H. Jones was the owner of the Houston Chronicle *and the head of the government's Reconstruction Finance Corporation. Considered one of the most powerful men the country, Jones was instrumental in building the defense plants that enabled the industrial mobilization during World War II.* (National Oceanic and Atmospheric Administration)

Downtown Fort Worth in April 1948. Some of the downtown Fort Worth buildings built by Jesse Jones' construction company between 1919 and 1921 include (right to left) the Worth Hotel and Worth Theater, Fort Worth Club, Hollywood Theater and Electric Building. These buildings surround Amon Carter's Star-Telegram *building.* (Don Pyeatt Collection)

Ironically, Kindelberger chose the same Mountain Creek Lake location selected by Consolidated. When the Consolidated/Hall merger failed, the Dallas Chamber of Commerce requested Consolidated to release the city from its site agreement and leased the site to North American instead.[32] Ultimately, North American used the site to build AT-6 trainers and P-51 fighters during World War II. The factory was later taken over by Vought for the production of Naval jet fighters and attack aircraft.

At the same time, the National Defense Council (NDC) was attempting to ensure a steady supply of parts for all aircraft manufacturers. Drawing on a plan first proposed during World War I, the NDC wanted to use automobile factories to produce aircraft parts. Consolidated would be teamed with Ford for the B-24, North American with General Motors for the B-25, and Martin with Chrysler for the B-26.[33] With the entire domestic automobile manufacturing capacity converted to aircraft and military vehicle production, there would be no civilian automobiles produced until the war was over.

In addition to using the automobile manufacturers, the NDC wanted to build several large government-owned contractor-operated (GOCO) manufacturing facilities that would be leased to various aircraft manufacturers. This idea eliminated investment risks for the companies and permitted a rapid increase of aircraft production. The Plant Site Board was created within the War Department to evaluate potential locations for the new aircraft factories. Working closely with local Chambers of Commerce, the Plant Site Board conducted extensive site selection studies focusing on local labor, housing, and infrastructure availability. However, to no one's surprise, politics also played a large role in selecting locations for these plants. Roosevelt had already promised Oklahoma Governor William H. "Alfalfa Bill" Murray and Texas Governor W. Lee "Pappy" O'Daniel that aircraft assembly plants would be built in their states.[34] On 16 May 1940,

The Consolidated Model 32, the XB-24 (39-680), at Lindbergh Field in San Diego on 26 December 1939, three days prior to its first flight. Chief test pilot William B. Wheatley was at the controls and George Newman, Jack Kline, and Bob Keith were also on board. (National Archives College Park Collection)

Roosevelt authorized the military to order the 50,000 airplanes he had previously instructed the manufacturers to plan for.[35] Then, in August and September 1940, Congress authorized the President to call up the National Guard and approved the nation's first peacetime draft.

On 22 November 1940, Amon Carter received a special-delivery letter from William B. "Bill" Wheatley, Consolidated's chief test pilot. Wheatley explained that the company needed to ferry 200 PBYs from San Diego to England and had an immediate need for a layover point in the middle of the country. He told Carter to expect a letter from Edgar Gott, a Consolidated vice president, detailing requirements for the temporary base.

Carter mustered the resources of the Chamber of Commerce to meet Consolidated's requirements for food and lodging for the flight crews, and to provide fuel and build moorings for the aircraft. The following day, on 27

The Navy's PBY, designed by CAPT Dick Richardson and Isaac M. "Mac" Laddon, was one of the most successful naval patrol bombers of World War II. The XP2Y-1 (left) was initially equipped with three Wright R-1820-E1 Cyclone engines, but the upper engine was removed after its first test flight on 10 January 1929. The PBY-2 (right) was powered by two Pratt & Whitney R-1830-54 Twin Wasp engines and was more representative of the more than 4,000 PBYs built between 1936 and 1945. (Consolidated Aircraft)

Perhaps the most famous product out of the North American plant in Dallas was the Mustang, such as this P-51D-25-NT (44-84948). Dallas built 1,750 razorback P-51Cs, 1,454 bubble-canopy P-51Ds, and 1,337 similar P-51Ks at the same time they were producing AT-6 trainers. (Fred Johnsen Collection)

November, Gott was informed the facilities (which adjoined the proposed Lake Worth plant site) would be ready on 30 November, only eight days after receiving Wheatley's letter. This responsiveness on the part of Fort Worth later played a large role in Consolidated's site selection decision.

On 29 December 1940, Roosevelt proclaimed the United States would be "the arsenal of democracy" and offered massive military aid to the United Kingdom and Soviet Union. The Plant Site Board then instructed aircraft manufacturers to perform site surveys in Board-approved cities to determine locations suitable for construction of plants that would be funded by the Defense Plant Corporation and leased back to the manufacturer. Maj. Gen. George H. Brett, Chief of the Army Air Corps, ordered Reuben Fleet to immediately select one primary and one alternate location from a vetted list of cities where Consolidated would build B-24s and PBYs.

Although Fort Worth was not an approved location, Amon Carter was determined to bring the B-24 plant to Fort Worth. He immediately convinced the Chamber of Commerce to hire *Fort Worth Star-Telegram* reporters to prepare a missive for Consolidated and government officials praising Fort Worth as an ideal location.[36] Wielding enormous political power through his personal relationships within the U.S. government, Carter, along with Cyrus R. Smith,[37] cajoled relentlessly in Washington for a decision favorable to Fort Worth. After being pressured by Carter, Vice President John Nance Garner opined, "That man wants the entire government of the United States to run for the exclusive benefit of Fort Worth, and, if possible, to the detriment of Dallas."[38]

Charles A. Van Dusen, Consolidated's production manager, and Thomas F. Bowmar, head of San Diego's Chamber of Commerce,[39] accompanied Reuben Fleet on a tour of approved plant sites in Dallas, Houston, New Orleans, and Tulsa, but not before making a stop in Fort Worth.[40] After Fleet returned to San Diego, Brett telegrammed[41] him for an immediate decision. Fleet responded that Fort Worth was his choice.[42]

Brett again telegrammed Fleet, reminding him that Fort Worth was not an approved site and instructed him to select Tulsa instead. Fleet informed Brett that Consolidated had evaluated the Fort Worth location, was satisfied with it, and insisted the location be approved. Brett tersely told Fleet that he could select any location he wanted, as long as it was Tulsa. They argued at length by telegram until Brett agreed to discuss the matter with the Plant Site Board. Surprisingly, during that meeting, representatives from Dallas urged the selection of Fort Worth over Tulsa. Dallas, owing Consolidated a favor for releasing them from the Mountain Creek Lake lease and hoping the new North American plant would receive subcontracts for B-24 parts, was eager for Consolidated to locate nearby. Not persuaded by Fleet or Dallas, Brett

Forty Navy PBYs sitting on Lake Worth to escape a Gulf Coast storm. On 22 November 1940, Consolidated's chief test pilot, William B. Wheatley, asked Amon Carter to prepare an area capable of supporting 200 PBY patrol planes during a delivery flight from San Diego to England. The rapid ability to prepare Lake Worth as a PBY stopover location played a large role in Consolidated's decision to build a bomber plant in Fort Worth. (Portal to Texas History)

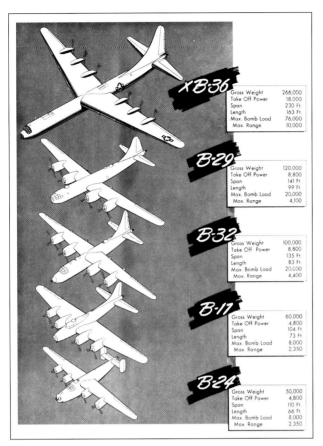

XB-36	
Gross Weight	266,000
Take Off Power	18,000
Span	230 Ft.
Length	163 Ft.
Max. Bomb Load	76,000
Max. Range	10,000

B-29	
Gross Weight	120,000
Take Off Power	8,800
Span	141 Ft.
Length	99 Ft.
Max. Bomb Load	20,000
Max. Range	4,100

B-32	
Gross Weight	100,000
Take Off Power	8,800
Span	135 Ft.
Length	83 Ft.
Max. Bomb Load	20,000
Max. Range	4,400

B-17	
Gross Weight	60,000
Take Off Power	4,800
Span	104 Ft.
Length	73 Ft.
Max. Bomb Load	8,000
Max. Range	2,350

B-24	
Gross Weight	50,000
Take Off Power	4,800
Span	110 Ft.
Length	66 Ft.
Max. Bomb Load	8,000
Max. Range	2,350

The size of strategic bombers increased tremendously during World War II. Government Aircraft Plant 4 was designed to build aircraft much larger than the 50,000-pound B-24 Liberator, and subsequently manufactured the 100,000-pound B-32 Dominator and the 266,000-pound XB-36. (San Diego Air & Space Museum Collection)

announced on 21 December 1940 that Tulsa would be the location of Consolidated's new plant.[43]

When Amon Carter learned of this announcement, he responded with a tirade of profanities that was heard throughout the offices of the *Fort Worth Star-Telegram*. He telegrammed President Roosevelt, telling him that to reject Fort Worth, "is almost a crime against national defense." He insisted that Fort Worth had the best site, climate, size, labor supply, and infrastructure that included an operational airfield and an adjoining lake for Consolidated's seaplanes.[44] After Roosevelt responded that he could not reverse the decision, Carter instructed his team of Chamber of Commerce members to pack immediately for a trip to Washington. Before leaving home, the Chamber filed a formal objection with the War Department.

Upon arriving in Washington, the Texans contacted Senator Morris Sheppard (D-TX), chairman of the Senate Military Affairs Committee, who arranged a hearing with the War Department. Concurrently, Carter was at the White House pleading his case with Roosevelt, who

promised Carter a one-week delay of a final decision while the War Department considered Fort Worth's objections. Carter ended the meeting by asking FDR to consider Tulsa as an alternate site for Douglas Aircraft's bomber plant.

The strategy worked, and on 3 January 1941, the War Department announced that bomber assembly plants would be built in Fort Worth, Kansas City, Omaha, and Tulsa. The Fort Worth plant would be known as Government Aircraft Plant 4 and would be operated by Consolidated.[45] Three days later, War Department and Army Air Corps officials inspected and approved the Fort Worth location at Lake Worth.

On 8 March 1941, the War Department awarded contracts for construction of aircraft plants at Fort Worth, Kansas City, and Tulsa. The Austin Company of Cleveland, Ohio, was awarded a $10,511,400 contract to build Government Aircraft Plant 4, and the L. J. Miles Company of Fort Worth was awarded a contract to build the adjoining Tarrant Field Airdrome.[46] In a subsequent press release, Consolidated stated the Fort Worth plant would be sufficiently large to produce an aircraft that would dwarf the 50,000-pound B-24. The purported aircraft, designated B-32, was incorrectly described as having a wingspan of 195 feet and weighing 200,000 pounds.[47] One month later, on 11 April 1941, the Army Air Corps requested preliminary design proposals from Boeing and Consolidated for an intercontinental bomber capable of delivering a 10,000-pound bomb load to a target 5,000 miles distant and returning non-stop to bases within the continental United States. These requirements dictated an aircraft much larger than the B-32.

Groundbreaking ceremonies for Government Aircraft Plant 4 were held during a rainstorm on 18 April 1941. The inhospitable weather could not hide a beaming smile on Amon Carter's face as he handed a sterling-silver shovel to Brig. Gen. Gerald C. Brant, commander of the Gulf Coast Air Training Center at Randolph Field, San Antonio. Brant took the spade and, gesturing at Carter, announced that a recommendation he had received only moments earlier for an Army Air Corps flight-training base adjacent to the plant would be forwarded to Washington. Barely audible over the sound of the heavy rain were the words of Brant as he pushed the silver spade into the muddy ground, "We're digging Hitler's grave today."[48] Construction of the plant and airfield began three days later, on 21 April 1941.

On 20 June 1941, the U.S. Army Air Corps was reorganized as the U.S. Army Air Forces. Two days later, Germany launched Operation Barbarossa by attacking Soviet Russia in a bold attempt to capture Russia's oil fields, industrial plants, and what Hitler perceived to be a "subhuman" Slavic population that could easily be enslaved to further Germany's war machine. This further strengthened the will of the United States to stop Germany before it reached Great Britain, and ultimately, the North

American continent. Operation Barbarossa also added a new measure of urgency to building aircraft plants and developing improved aircraft designs.

While the war was raging in Europe, Japanese warplanes attacked the U.S. naval base at Pearl Harbor, Hawaii, on 7 December 1941. Despite internal warning the Japanese were planning for war, the attack came as a complete surprise to the military and the general public. The next day the United States declared war on Germany and Japan. Any pretense of neutrality was abandoned, and the largest arms buildup in history began.

The United States, reeling from the massive blow to its naval fleet at Hawaii, immediately instituted a defensive posture at home while calling all reserve units to active duty and preparing for a general mobilization of its armed forces. Civilian defense plans went into effect and emergency supplies were issued to major cities and towns. Gas masks were issued to local Civil Defense centers, extra pumpers and hoses were delivered to fire departments, and blood drives were hurriedly organized. Food, fuel, and materials rationing were expanded, and the government mandated purchase of spare tires and other items from civilians and private businesses. Managers of war materiel companies that were not producing their quotas were replaced with government employees.

Upon entering the war in Europe, the United States joined the United Kingdom and their ideological opposite, the Soviet Union, in armed opposition of Germany. Soviet Premier Joseph Stalin was a murderous tyrant much like Adolph Hitler, but regardless of the awkward dichotomy of national values, the United States and the United Kingdom could not permit Nazi Germany to control the vast resources of communist Russia.

Within days of the declaration of war, the War Department selected Fort Worth as a site for one of many flight-training bases to be established throughout the conti-

Tarrant Field was the primary heavy-bomber training facility during World War II. More than 4,000 students were trained to operate the B-24 at the base. (Don Pyeatt Collection)

nental United States. The base would be built on the east side of Tarrant Field Airdrome as previously recommended to Brig. Gen. Brant by Amon Carter.

Construction of the Fort Worth flight-training base began on 7 January 1942 and on 5 May 1942, the War Department announced that headquarters of the Army Air Forces Flying Training Command would immediately occupy four floors of the Texas & Pacific Railway Station in Fort Worth under the command of Maj. Gen. Barton K. Yount. The new headquarters would direct all Army Air Forces flight-training operations in the United States. They had a staff of 75 officers and approximately 300 enlisted personnel, and the command was made responsible for training 30,000 new pilots before the end of the year. On 28 June 1942, Tarrant Field Airdrome was assigned to the Army Air Forces Flying Training Command.[49]

Other branches of the military also established bases in Fort Worth during the course of the war. A U.S. Marine PBY amphibious training base was established at Eagle Mountain Lake, and the city's municipal airport became a

The Japanese attack on Pearl Harbor on 7 December 1941 was largely responsible for the initial approval of the B-36 program, and also furthered the fate of Fort Worth as a center for aircraft manufacturing. (National Archives)

The Fort Worth municipal airport served as a Navy base during World War II. These Grumman TBF Avenger torpedo bombers are at Naval Auxiliary Air Facility Meacham waiting to be ferried to the East Coast and eventually to Europe. (National Archives)

mid-continent transient base of the U.S. Navy Ferry Command. Known as Naval Auxiliary Air Facility Meacham, this airfield was used as a stop for ferrying new aircraft to European combat zones and to train ferry pilots, including many women.

Since most aircraft and pilots were being sent to combat zones, a shortage of training aircraft and flying instructors initially impeded operations at Tarrant Field. Nevertheless, several early model B-24s were assigned to the base. As one of the first B-24 Transition Schools, maintenance proved nearly impossible due to lack of replacement parts. To make matters worse, a B-29 Transition School was also in operation at the field until it was moved to Del Rio, Texas. Tarrant Field Airdrome was renamed Fort Worth Army Air Field in May 1943 with no change to its mission.

Construction of Government Aircraft Plant 4 was completed in less than nine months, and the facility was turned over to Consolidated Vultee on 1 January 1942. Five weeks later, a $6.5 million expansion was approved that extended the length of the assembly building to nearly one mile and the plant's workforce increased to 25,000 people. While the factory was being built, thousands of local workers were hired and trained. Many were local farmers whose mechanical skills were limited to repairing tractors and hay-baling machines. In addition to training a large workforce, there was the problem of transportation to and from the plant. With automobile and bus production halted for the duration of the war and with gasoline rationing in effect, public transportation was the only practical means for employees to get to work. A local bus company, the Fort Worth Transit Company, converted unused automobile transport trailers into makeshift buses by removing the top levels from the car haulers and replacing them with plywood enclosures and seats. These

tractor-trailer contrivances transported thousands of workers to and from the plant from all parts of Fort Worth and surrounding counties.[50]

With parts manufactured by Ford Motor Company and transported to Fort Worth by train, and powered by fuel from nearby oil fields and refineries, the first B-24 built at Government Aircraft Plant 4 was finished one day less than one year after the 18 April 1941 groundbreaking ceremony.[51]

Top of page and above: *By the time that Plant 4 was completed, the main assembly hall extended almost one mile, making it the longest aircraft plant in the country. The hall was a clear-span, with no support columns to interfere with assembly. Two sets of railroad tracks ran through the plant, allowing material to be unloaded easily directly into the manufacturing facility.* (Lockheed Martin)

It only took 8.5 months from groundbreaking until the initial plant was completed, although several additions to the main hall and a couple of outlying buildings came later. There were also many acres of concrete to pour for the taxiways and ramps that surrounded the plant. Note the amount of scaffolding (above right) required to complete the main building. (Lockheed Martin)

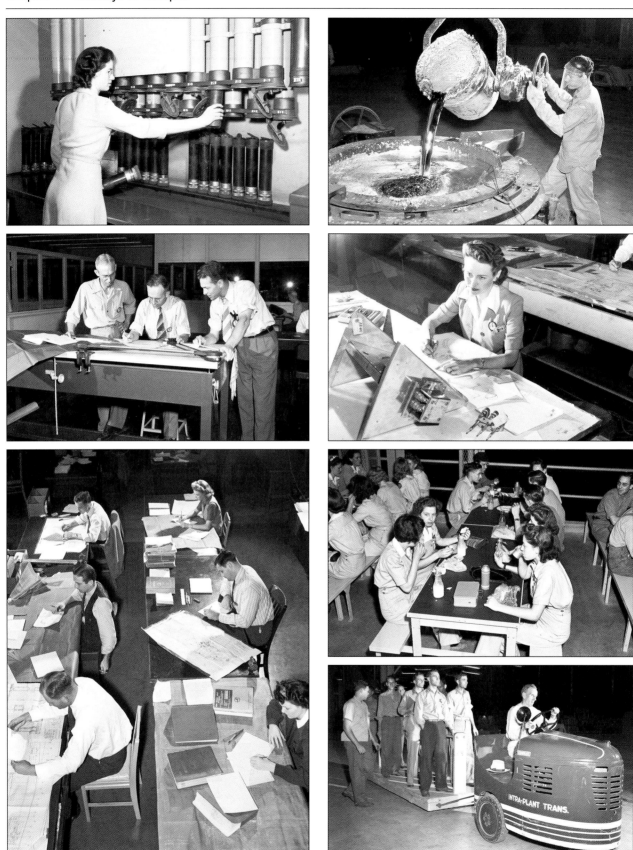

Various scenes in and around Plant 4 during the 1940s and early 1950s. In an age before computers, drafting was still a ink-and-paper affair and pneumatic tubes carried messages around the plant. Note the intra-plant transportation tug. (Lockheed Martin)

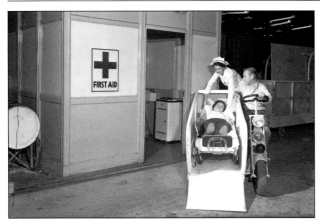

More scenes around Plant 4, including several of the large billboards that were on the periphery of the property. Even then, armed guards kept watch over the entrances. The motorcycle ambulance (top left) was an interesting touch. (Lockheed Martin)

The last Fort Worth B-24 (44-44501) rolled through the doors of the assembly building on 26 December 1944. A few months earlier, on 9 August 1944, the War Department had announced that Government Aircraft Plant 4 would switch production to the new B-32 Dominator. After a short ceremony commemorating the last of the 2,743 B-24s and 291 C-87s built at the plant, employees resumed work on the new B-32s already filling the production line.

Although the B-32 was not nearly as large as the 200,000-pound, 195-foot-wingspan aircraft that was forecast during the bomber plant's groundbreaking, it was nonetheless an impressive aircraft. At 60,000 pounds empty and with a wingspan of 135 feet, it was considerably larger than the B-24 and only slightly smaller than the Boeing B-29 Superfortress. In August 1945, a reporter with local radio station KGKO who had been given a ride in a B-32, said on-air, "You don't get a close-up view of a B-32 all at once, it's just too big for that. You have to stand back at a distance to see all of it. And, even then, it is difficult to believe at first that such a mammoth feat of engineering can really fly."[52] Little did the reporter realize that the B-32 would pale in comparison to the next bomber that would be manufactured at Government Aircraft Plant 4.

The B-32 had the distinction of being the first U.S. warplane delivered to training bases before it was delivered to combat squadrons. In January 1945, Fort Worth Army Air Field became a Very Heavy Bombardment Transition School using the first TB-32s that emerged from Government Aircraft Plant 4. These TB-32s provided "hands-on" training for air and ground crews. Many training procedures developed for the B-24 were retained

One of thousands of women working at Plant 4 during World War II, Elsie Lois Booth makes the perfect picture of "Rosie the Riveter" while working on a Fort Worth B-24. The button that reads "40" identifies what part of the plant she was cleared to work in. (Consolidated)

and expanded for the B-32, and the base's proximity to the factory allowed Consolidated to work on B-32 problems and gave the Transition School access to training aids developed by Consolidated engineers. Fort Worth Army Air Field soon gained a reputation for being one of the best aviation training schools in the Army Air Forces.

In April 1942, Lt. Col. J. A. Hilger of Houston, second in command of the Doolittle raid on Japan, accepted the first B-24 manufactured in Fort Worth. Amon Carter, in his usual Shady Oak hat, christened the airplane the City of Fort Worth using a bottle of Lake Worth water. The airplane was purchased with local war bond sale funds. Notice the aircraft's serial number has been scratched-out by censors. (Consolidated)

The B-24 was also operated by the U.S. Navy under the PB4Y designation, complete with white undersides on some examples. All aircraft were built to identical specifications on the right-hand assembly line. Aircraft requiring modifications were towed from the end of the line and re-entered the building in the left-hand line to be fitted with special modifications. (Consolidated)

The C-87 Liberator Express (44-52987 shown) was a passenger and cargo version of the B-24D with seats for 25 passengers. Plant 4 built 291 of the aircraft. (Consolidated)

Maj. Gen. Harold L. George, Commander of the Air Transport Command, visits with Amon G. Carter at Plant 4. George was the recipient of many Convair C-87s. (U.S. Air Force)

A B-24J-15-CF (42-99805) sits in front the what will become the Experimental Building at Plant 4. The Experimental Building was built specifically to manufacture the XB-36. (Consolidated)

B-24Js and C-87As await delivery at Plant 4 during late 1943 or early 1944. The nearest airplane, a C-87A-CF (43-30563), suffered a landing accident at Jorhat, India, on 3 September 1944. (Consolidated)

After the war in Europe ended on 8 May 1945, B-32 production was deeply cut along with B-24 and B-32 training requirements. Transition training soon ceased and Fort Worth Army Air Field became a Combat Crew Training School. Despite the cutbacks, on 17 July 1945 the Southwestern Division of the Army Corps of Engineers issued a contract for a $2.23 million upgrade to the field's runway and taxiways "to make the field ready for B-29, B-32, and [C-82] Flying Boxcar aircraft." The Corps evidently knew something nobody else did – when they rebuilt the runway, it was stressed to handle aircraft much larger than those listed. In the end, it was one of three runways in the world capable of supporting the B-36.[53]

On the same day the runway contract was awarded, the Allied Powers met at Potsdam, Germany, to divide the former German territories among the victors. Many discussions at the conference centered on the fate of the capital city of Berlin. Located completely within territory captured by the Soviets, Berlin would later prove to be the progenitor of yet another world conflict.

Near the end of the Potsdam Conference, Harry Truman confided to Joseph Stalin the existence of a new weapon of unimaginable power that might be used to end the war in the Pacific.[54] Stalin urged Truman to "use whatever force is necessary."[55] Truman then issued to Japan an ultimatum of unconditional surrender and a threat of "prompt and utter destruction" if it did not agree. Japan responded with a list of surrender conditions and, after the United States rejected those conditions, atomic bombs were dropped on Hiroshima and Nagasaki, effectively ending the war in the Pacific.

The last Fort Worth B-24J (44-44501) shows the signatures of many plant employees. Further down the line are a group of TB-32s showing that both types were being produced, at least for a while, simultaneously. (Lockheed Martin)

One month later, on 8 September 1945, a media frenzy began as the XB-36 was rolled out from the Experimental Building at Government Aircraft Plant 4. News reports of the mammoth bomber continued as a series of realignments began at the adjoining Fort Worth Army Air Field. These events would ensure the B-36 and Fort Worth were inextricably related for the next decade.

This TB-32-10-CF (42-108500) was representative of the unarmed trainer versions of the Dominator – note the lack of nose and tail turrets. This airplane was flown to Kingman, Arizona, and eventually scrapped. (National Archives)

Although the B-32 was a much larger airplane than the B-24, the assembly lines looked much the same. Consolidated had high hopes for the Dominator but, ultimately, only 114 of the bombers were produced and most never saw combat. Presaging the evolution of the B-36 design, the first XB-32 emerged with twin vertical stabilizers, but production aircraft used a single, much taller, tail. A similar evolution took place at the very end of B-24 production. (Lockheed Martin)

The new runway at Fort Worth Army Air Field under construction in August 1945. The runway terminated at the edge of Lake Worth. Plant 4 is at the upper right, with a variety of B-32s on the ramp, and the Army base is out of the photo at the upper left. The $2.23 million upgrade to the field's runway and taxiways was intended "to make the field ready for B-29, B-32, and [C-82] Flying Boxcar aircraft." The Corps of Engineers evidently knew something nobody else did – when they built the runway, it was stressed to handle aircraft much larger than those listed. In the end, it was one of three runways in the world capable of supporting the XB-36. This photo was taken less than a month after construction began. (Roger Cripliver Collection)

Shown in the lull between the B-32 and B-36 programs, Plant 4 is at the top and the Air Force base at the bottom. (Convair)

An overhead view of the runways, with the Air Force base at the bottom with B-29s on the ramp. (Lockheed Martin)

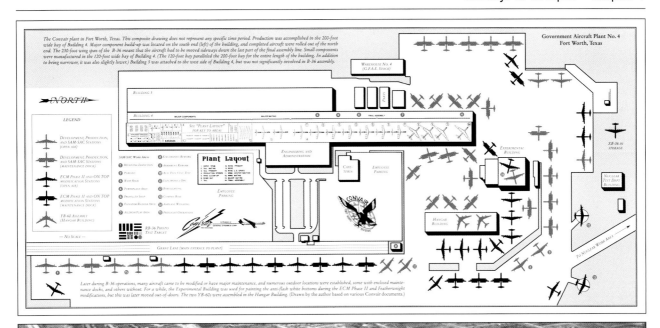

Photo and drawing: *Plant 4 in 1954, showing the large quantity of B-36s that were generally at the plant undergoing maintenance or modification. The XB-36 is in the field at the extreme right, and both YB-60s are visible on the ramp.* (Frank F. Kleinwechter Collection)

Consolidated History

What follows are extremely brief histories of the companies related to Consolidated and Convair. These histories are courtesy of the National Air and Space Museum and www.pilotfriend.com, with a little embellishment and correction where it seemed appropriate. You will undoubtedly note that the story may be more confusing than enlightening.

In the early days, it seems that almost everybody either did, or would, work for just about everybody else at some time. Then the creation of a couple of large holding companies meant that everybody bought or sold just about everybody else. Legislation and the pressures of World War II eventually gave rise to the holding companies disbanding and the establishment of mostly independent aircraft manufacturers. Later, a downturn in government business led to a new series of mergers that has left only a handful of players, and many of the legendary names disappeared. Hopefully, this brief history gives a sense of how dynamic the aviation industry has been during its 100-year history.

AVCO Corporation: T. Higbeen Embry and John Paul Riddle created the Embry-Riddle Company in Cincinnati that sold and maintained aircraft, operated a flying school, and ran an air-taxi service. In 1927, the company was awarded an Air Mail contract, but by late 1928 needed additional funds to continue. The Curtiss Aeroplane and Motor Company approached Embry-Riddle with an offer of financial support if Embry-Riddle stopped selling Fairchild aircraft and instead became a Curtiss dealer. Not wanting to lose a successful partner, Fairchild countered the offer and created the Aviation Corporation holding company to finance Embry-Riddle and other aviation companies in the Great Lakes area. Thanks to the aviation craze created by Charles Lindbergh's 1927 trans-Atlantic flight, AVCO had no problem raising more than $35 million, a significant sum of money at the time.

By the end of 1929, AVCO had bought its parent company, Fairchild, along with Embry-Riddle, and acquired interests in more than 90 aviation-related companies, including at least 13 airlines. On 1 February 1930, AVCO formed American Airways, which took control of all the airlines in the company except Embry-Riddle. In April 1932, Errett L. Cord sold two airlines to AVCO and became a member of the board of directors. This brought the Airplane Development Corporation into AVCO, which established the Aviation Manufacturing Corporation in early 1934 to manage the Airplane Development Corporation (really Vultee, and later Consolidated-Vultee), the Lycoming Manufacturing Company, and Stinson Aircraft.

The Air Mail Act of 1934 forced the reorganization of holding companies such as AVCO. Embry-Riddle was spun off and eventually emerged as the Embry-Riddle Aeronautical University. The airlines were spun off as American Airlines. The airframe and engine manufacturers were retained within the newly renamed Avco Manufacturing Corporation, which became the Avco Corporation in 1959. In December 1984, Avco was purchased by Textron and renamed Avco Systems Textron, becoming Textron Defense Systems in 1985. Over the years, Avco had gradually sold most of its aircraft interests until, by 1985, it was primarily a financial institution centered around the insurance business.

Vultee Aircraft Corporation: Gerard "Jerry" Vultee and Vance Breese had started the Airplane Development Corporation in early 1932 after American Airlines showed great interest in their six-passenger V-1 design. Soon after, Errett Cord bought all 500 shares of stock in the company and Airplane Development Corporation became a Cord subsidiary in 1934. AVCO then established the Aviation Manufacturing Corporation (AMC) in 1934 through the acquisition of Cord's holdings including the Airplane Development Corporation. The timing was fortuitous, since the Air Mail Act of 1934 forced the large holding companies to split up their assets into airline companies and aircraft companies. AMC was liquidated on 1 January 1936 and Vultee Aircraft Division was formed as an autonomous subsidiary of AVCO in November 1937. Vultee acquired control of AVCO's Stinson Aircraft Corporation subsidiary in October 1939, creating the Stinson Division of Vultee.

Maj. Reuben H. Fleet (1887–1975). (Justin C. Gruelle, 1958)

Vultee Aircraft, Inc. was established in November 1939, acquiring the assets of Aviation Manufacturing Corporation – including Lycoming and Stinson – but remaining an AVCO subsidiary. Ultimately, Vultee purchased a controlling interest in Consolidated Aircraft Corporation from Maj. Reuben H. Fleet in November 1942, forming Consolidated-Vultee Aircraft Corporation on 17 March 1943.

Consolidated Aircraft Corporation: Reuben H. Fleet graduated as Military Aviator No. 74 in 1917, and ultimately was tasked with setting up the first air mail between New York and Washington D.C. before becoming the Army Air Service's chief aviation contracting officer, part of the Engineering Division, based at McCook Field. The post-war budget cuts convinced Fleet to resign from the Army on 30 November 1922, On 29 May 1923, Fleet founded the Consolidated Aircraft Corporation to build Dayton-Wright TW-3s in a building leased from the Gallaudet Aircraft Corporation in East Greenwich, Rhode Island. Fleet soon took over Gallaudet Aircraft and acquired the rights to Dayton-Wright Company designs from General Motors, which had since left the aviation business. One of his first acts was to hire Isaac M. "Mac" Laddon, who had been in charge of designing heavy aircraft for the Army. Consolidated went on to a long line of successful designs and lucrative contracts for seaplanes for the Navy. Starting with their XPY-1 of 1928, the string of successes culminated in one of the most numerous and successful seaplanes, the PBY Catalina.

In February 1929, Fleet formed Fleet Aircraft in Buffalo, New York. Consolidated purchased Fleet Aircraft in August 1929, but continued production under the Fleet name. At the same time, Consolidated acquired Thomas-Morse Aircraft Corporation as a subsidiary. Fleet moved his company to San Diego, California, in 1932 where it was locally known as CONSAIR. In November 1941, under increasing pressure to retire, Fleet sold his 34 percent stock holding to Vultee Aircraft, a subsidiary of AVCO, for $10 million. Vultee subsequently purchased a controlling interest in Consolidated and formed the Consolidated-Vultee Aircraft Corporation, still within AVCO.

Consolidated-Vultee Aircraft Corporation: Vultee purchased a controlling interest in Consolidated Aircraft Corporation in November 1942, forming Consolidated-Vultee Aircraft Corporation on 17 March 1943. Both companies had been operating independently for more than a year under the AVCO umbrella. The new company was known internally as CVAC or Convair, although this name was not trademarked or otherwise official. On 12 April 1946, Reuben Fleet resigned from the Consolidated-Vultee board, finally ending his involvement with the company he built.

The company flourished during World War II and caught the interest of multimillionaire investor Floyd B. Odlum. In 1946, Odlum began buying AVCO stock through his Atlas Corporation, and on 4 September 1947, Odlum swapped his AVCO stock for the Consolidated-Vultee aviation operations in San Diego, Fort Worth, and Detroit. Atlas Corporation took control of Consolidated-Vultee in November 1947. Odlum was primarily interested in making money, and subsequently negotiated a merger between Consolidated-Vultee and the Electric Boat Company, a submarine manufacturer. The two firms officially merged on 29 April 1954 to create General Dynamics Corporation, with an Electric Boat division and a Convair division, the name finally becoming official and a registered trademark. The Convair Division would operate over the next quarter century primarily as an independent company under the General Dynamics corporate umbrella. In 1985, the Convair space efforts were split off to form General Dynamics Space Systems Division. In 1993, the General Dynamics Space Division (in effect, the San Diego operations) was sold to Martin Marietta, and the fixed-wing aircraft business (in effect, Fort Worth operations) was sold to Lockheed. In 1994, the Aerostructures unit was sold to McDonnell Douglas and, in 1996, the Convair Division ceased to exist.

As we said, more confusing than enlightening.

Floyd B. Odlum (1892–1976). (Library of Congress)

CHAPTER 2

CONSOLIDATED B-36
A TRUE INTERCONTINENTAL BOMBER

The first B-36B (44-92043) to be converted into a jet-augmented D-model at San Diego makes its initial flight on 6 December 1950. Note that the outboard propeller on the left wing is feathered. (San Diego Aerospace Museum Collection)

For the first two decades after it was built, Government Aircraft Plant 4 was intrinsically linked to the production of heavy bombers. The Army Air Forces accepted its first Fort Worth B-24 on 1 May 1942 and the last on 30 December 1944. During this time, Fort Worth built 3,034 Liberators and its derivatives, with a peak production of 200 per month. By the end of the war, 114 larger B-32s had been added to the number of heavy bombers produced in Fort Worth. The next airplane would be much larger.[1]

The first widespread attempts at bombardment came from German Zeppelins and British DH-4s during World War I, but the technology of the day did not allow a truly meaningful demonstration. This had changed by the time the next world war began, and the Americans and British used the concept to great advantage over Europe and Japan.

In the Pacific, the ultimate statement of strategic bombing took place on 6 August 1945 when a Boeing B-29 Superfortress dropped a Mk I "Little Boy" atomic bomb on Hiroshima; more than 4 square miles of the city were destroyed, killing 66,000 people and injuring another 69,000. Three days later, another B-29 dropped a Mk III[2] "Fat Man" on Nagasaki, destroying 1.5 square miles of the city, killing 39,000 people and injuring 25,000 more.

As devastating as these attacks were, the damage and casualties paled in comparison to the fire bombing campaign that had been conducted against Kobe, Nagoya, Osaka, and Tokyo. For instance, during one ten-day period during the summer of 1945, B-29s dropped incendiaries that burned more than 32 square miles of urban-industrial centers in those cities. By early August, these attacks had destroyed more than 50 percent of the urban areas in Japan and killed more than a million people. Nevertheless, it is the atomic bombs that will forever be remembered.

Despite the relative success of aerial bombardment during World War II, it was not obvious at the beginning that the campaign would be possible, much less successful. During the early days of 1941, it appeared Great Britain might quickly fall to the German onslaught and leave the United States without any bases outside the Western Hemisphere. Consequently, the United States decided to develop an aircraft that could attack targets in Europe from airfields in North America. The Army Air Corps (the Army Air Forces were not formally established until 20 June 1941) drafted requirements for a very-heavy bomber with a 450-mph top speed at 25,000 feet, a 275-mph cruising speed, a service ceiling of 45,000 feet, and a maximum range of 12,000 miles at 25,000 feet. The aircraft needed to carry 10,000 pounds of bombs over a radius of 5,000 miles or a maximum load of 72,000 pounds over a much shorter distance. Given the available technology, they were ambitious requirements.[3]

During the early 1940s, the concept of aerial refueling was not considered practical for an operational aircraft, although numerous, generally successful, experiments had

The ultimate statement of strategic bombing came when Boeing B-29 Superfortresses dropped atomic bombs on Hiroshima, Japan, (above) on 6 August 1945 and a similar attack on Nagasaki (top) on 9 August. (National Archives)

Regardless its contribution to strategic airpower, the B-29 is also the symbol of what is probably the most impressive industrial mobilization in history. It involved Boeing plants at Renton, Washington, and Wichita, Kansas, a Bell plant at Marietta, Georgia ("Bell-Atlanta"), and a Martin plant at Omaha, Nebraska ("Martin-Omaha"). In addition, thousands of subcontractors were involved in the project, which ultimately produced 3,970 airplanes prior to V-J Day. (Mike Machat Collection / Wings-Airpower History Collection)

In addition to conventional 500–2000-pound bombs and early atomic weapons, the B-29 was also capable of carrying the 43,000-pound T-12 bombs that were developed in the closing days of World War II. (National Archives College Park Collection)

been conducted beginning as early as 1918.[4] This meant that the new bomber, of necessity, would be very large, if for no other reason than to accommodate the required fuel. However, experience constructing very large aircraft was effectively limited to the Boeing XB-15 and the Douglas XB-19 flying laboratories, both of which were considerably smaller and slower than the aircraft envisioned by the Army.[5]

Requests for preliminary designs were released to Boeing Aircraft Co. and Consolidated Aircraft Corp. on 11 April 1941. The eventual winner of the design competition would receive $135,445 for the studies, while the losing bidder would get $435,623. On 3 May 1941, preliminary design data was submitted by Boeing for their Models 384 and 385 and Consolidated for the "Model 35 Multi-Engine Long Range Bombardment Type Airplane." The results were not encouraging since neither manufacturer could meet all of the requirements.[6]

A meeting between Assistant Secretary of War (Air) Robert A. Lovett, Chief of the Army Air Forces Maj. Gen. George H. Brett, and ranking officers of the Air Staff was held on 19 August 1941 in an attempt to accelerate the bomber project, mainly by relaxing the requirements. This was a relative concept, and the revised specifications were still a tall order – a cruising speed between 240 and 300 mph, a 40,000-foot service ceiling, a range[7] of 10,000 miles, and an effective combat radius of 4,000 miles with a 10,000-pound load. Despite the reduction from the earlier specifications, this was still four times the combat radius of the Boeing B-17 Flying Fortress while carrying more than twice the bomb load. Given their experience with the XB-19, Douglas was added to the list of potential bidders and all three companies submitted proposals in early September 1941.[8]

The Army Air Forces decided the Consolidated design was the most promising, largely because, "although it represented progressive engineering, it contained no

Boeing designed the XB-15 (Model 294) in 1934 to see if it was possible to build a heavy bomber with a 5,000-mile range. At the time the XB-15, shown here near Wright Field on 28 March 1938, was the largest aircraft in the United States. The airplane set a number of load-to-altitude records, including a 31,205-pound flight to 8,200 feet on 30 July 1939. The airplane finished its career as the XC-105 carrying cargo around the Caribbean during World War II. (National Archives College Park Collection)

The cockpit of the Douglas XB-19, like the 212-foot-span airplane itself, was large. This is the view looking aft, showing the flight engineer at the back and the radio operator at the left. (Mike Machat Collection / Wings-Airpower History Collection)

The XB-19 was the largest bomber built for the Army Air Corps until the XB-36 in 1946. Like the XB-15, the Douglas airplane was only a testbed and not a prototype production aircraft. (Mike Machat Collection / Wings-Airpower History Collection)

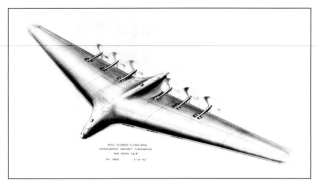

Consolidated knew that Jack Northrop was working on the B-35 flying wing at the same time the XB-36 was being designed. The engineers in San Diego conducted several flying-wing studies, such as this 1942 effort. In the end, they decided that a conventional wing-fuselage airplane better met the requirements for a very heavy bomber. (San Diego Air & Space Museum Collection)

unusual engineering features that might make its construction doubtful." Consolidated estimated the development and manufacture of two experimental very-long-range bombers would cost $15 million. On 15 November 1941, the Army issued contract W535-ac-22352 for two XB-36 experimental aircraft to be built at the Consolidated facility in San Diego, California. The first airplane was to be delivered in May 1944 and the second in November. Although the aircraft was generally similar to the original Model 35, there were sufficient differences for Consolidated to assign the aircraft a new model number – 36 – conveniently the same as the official designation.[9]

XB-36

Isaac Machlin "Mac" Laddon, an executive vice president who had been chief engineer on the PBY flying boat, had managed the Consolidated proposal effort. The

manager of the Engineering Department, Harry A. Sutton, and manager of Preliminary Design, Ted P. Hall, led the design of the XB-36.

The aircraft would be powered by six new 28-cylinder Pratt & Whitney "X-Wasp" air-cooled radial engines (which became the R-4360 Wasp Major), each driving a 19-foot-diameter, 3-blade Curtiss-Wright propeller in a pusher configuration. The 10,000-mile range was a challenge – the aircraft would spend almost 2 days in the air – so six fuel tanks with a capacity of 21,116 gallons were incorporated into the 230-foot wing that had an area of 4,772 square feet. The 163-foot-long fuselage had four bomb bays with a maximum capacity of 72,000 pounds. Forward and aft pressurized crew compartments were connected by an 80-foot-long, 25-inch-diameter tube that ran through the bomb bays. Defensive armament consisted of five 37mm cannon and ten .50-caliber machine guns distributed between two retractable turrets on top of the fuselage, two on the bottom, and a radar-directed tail turret, although the actual configuration remained in a state of flux for several years and the XB-36 emerged unarmed.

It took 3 pounds of fuel to carry each pound of empty weight, so Consolidated embraced advanced hydraulic and electrical systems in an attempt to reduce (or at least control) weight. Engineers also believed that conventional 1,500-psi hydraulic systems were inadequate to effectively move the large landing gear and flaps required for the new aircraft. With assistance from Wright Field, Convair developed the 3,000-psi hydraulic system that would remain a standard for the aircraft industry until the Bell V-22 Osprey pioneered (with great difficulty) a 5,000-psi system in the late 1990s. A new 400-cycle, 208-volt, 3-phase alternating current (AC) electrical system was also adopted to replace the direct current (DC) systems used by other aircraft. This permitted the use of lighter-weight motors; for instance, a 16-hp AC motor weighed only 23 pounds, compared to 100 pounds for an equivalent DC motor. There

Like its two immediate predecessors, the original XB-36 design had twin vertical stabilizers. A 1941 model (left) shows four-blade propellers. The mockup (above) was constructed in San Diego, and was moved to Fort Worth when the Army decided to use Plant 4 for production. Note the large non-retractable turrets on top of the fuselage and the cut-back engine nacelles. (left: Convair; above: Clarence Edward Calvert Collection)

was also less chance of the AC motors arcing at high altitudes, and they were considered generally more reliable.[10]

Despite the innovations, when the XB-36 mockup was inspected on 20 July 1942, weight estimates were much higher than anticipated, mostly because the X-Wasp engine was significantly heavier than expected; the six engines comprised a full one-third of the empty weight of the airplane. The result was that the airplane could not meet the 10,000-mile requirement and fell short of its speed and altitude goals. The Mockup Committee agreed to delete "less necessary" equipment such as some crew comfort and survival items, providing a minor weight reduction, although the projected range was still considerably less than desired. Nevertheless, the Army finally approved the mockup in September 1942.[11]

On 1 August 1942, two weeks after the XB-36 mockup inspection, Consolidated suggested shifting the B-36 program from San Diego to the new Government Aircraft Plant 4 in Fort Worth. The move was suggested mostly to make space available in the San Diego plant for increased B-24 and PBY construction. The government agreed this was prudent, freeing up space in San Diego and concentrating the engineering staff at the plant that would eventually produce the bomber. The move was approved less than a week later on 6 August.[12]

Eventually, at the peak of B-36 production, Government Aircraft Plant 4 would occupy 546 acres and include 4,000,000 square feet of enclosed space and 8,500,000 square feet of paved ramp areas. An on-site environmental chamber could simulate altitudes as high as 60,000 feet and temperatures of –100 degrees F. The plant employed more than 31,000 people producing one B-36 per week (the average production for most of the run). There were 57 major subcontractors (excluding Convair's San Diego plant) and 1,553 suppliers located in 36 states and the District of Columbia. A total of 2,500 machine tools and 126,500 production tools were used,

and the assembly line integrated 8,500 separate subassemblies and 27 miles of wiring.[13]

The XB-36 wooden mockup was broken down, packed onto rail cars and, along with 200 engineers, began the 1,205-mile trek east to Texas. The mockup was reconstructed in the Experimental Building at Fort Worth, the same location that would build the first prototype. The move to Texas was completed about 30 days after being approved, but development was set back several months as the team adjusted to its new surroundings. After the move, Richard C. "Sparky" Sebold and Herbert W. Hinckley assumed leadership of the program, but wartime production demands at Fort Worth for the B-24 Liberator, C-87 Liberator Express, AT-22 (the flight engineer trainer version of the C-87), and later for the B-32 Dominator, again slowed development of the B-36.[14]

Before construction had even begun on the XB-36, Consolidated asked the Army to order the B-36 into production, claiming that two years could be saved if preliminary work on production aircraft could be accomplished in parallel with the experimental models. However, the Army believed that the majority of its efforts should be toward aircraft that could support the march across the Pacific and declined the offer, ordering Consolidated to concentrate on building B-24s and developing the B-32.

Another Consolidated request in the summer of 1942 fared somewhat better when the Army agreed to the development of an XC-99 cargo version of the XB-36. Originally, Consolidated had wanted to use the XC-99 to test the XB-36 engines, landing gear, and flight characteristics. The company believed the cargo airplane could be ready to fly much sooner than either of the XB-36s because armament and other military equipment was not required. However, the Army stipulated that one of the two bombers had to be completed at least three months ahead of the cargo aircraft. Consolidated accepted the government's conditions and a $4.6 million contract was approved by year's end.[15]

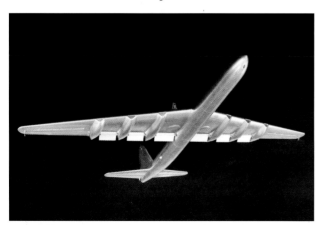

This model of the XB-36 was tested in the National Advisory Committee on Aeronautics (NACA) wind tunnel at the Langley Aeronautical Laboratory to verify the effectiveness of the trailing edge flaps. (National Archives College Park Collection)

The partially complete XB-36 is rolled out of the Experimental Building. Note the location and configuration of the two upper turret bays, particularly the aft bay. This configuration was unique to the XB-36. (San Diego Air & Space Museum Collection)

The clean shape of the XB-36 was the result of a careful design meant to minimize drag, a key consideration to achieving the intercontinental range the Army required. Note the large radio mast behind the cockpit. (Convair)

The XB-36 made its 37-minute maiden flight on 8 August 1945 piloted by Beryl A. Erickson and G. S. "Gus" Green, assisted by seven other crewmembers. The main wheels had not been fitted with their doors. (San Diego Air & Space Museum Collection)

On 17 March 1943, Consolidated Aircraft Corp. merged with Vultee Aircraft, Inc., becoming Consolidated Vultee Aircraft Corporation. This name was often truncated to "Convair," although this did not become official until 29 April 1954, when Consolidated Vultee Aircraft Corporation became the Convair Division of the General Dynamics Corporation. In between those years, Fort Worth usually referred to itself internally as CVAC, although San Diego continued to use CONSAIR.[16]

While Consolidated wrestled with weight increases and various developmental troubles, world events boosted the importance of the B-36. By the spring of 1943, China appeared nearly defeated by Japan, and neither the B-17 nor B-24 had sufficient range to operate over the vast distances of the Pacific. The B-29 had entered production, but was proving troublesome in initial service. The parallel development of the B-32, generally considered "insurance" in case the B-29 failed, was not progressing well, largely because of a low priority in the national production scheme. Neither of these types could reach Japan from the continental United States, and extremely bloody battles would need to be won before the Mariana Islands could become bases for B-29 or B-32 operations. Speeding up B-36 development might allow attacking the Japanese Home Islands from bases in Alaska and Hawaii.

After various consultations, Secretary of War Henry L. Stimson waived the customary procurement procedures and authorized the Army to order the B-36 into production without waiting for the two experimental aircraft. A letter of intent[17] for 100 production B-36s was signed on 23 July 1943 at an estimated cost of $175 million – slightly more than two days' cost of the war effort. Subsequently, the priority assigned to the B-36 program was raised, although still not to a level equal to the B-29, or even the B-32.[18]

During detailed design, Convair engineers replaced the original twin tails with a single 47-foot-high vertical stabilizer that decreased weight by 3,850 pounds, provided additional directional stability, and lowered base drag. It

The mostly complete XB-36 being rolled out of the Experimental Building. Note the massive 110-inch single main landing gear originally used for the undercarriage. The YB-36 and XC-99 would also use this arrangement. The main landing gear doors have not yet been installed, and would not be for the first few test flights. Although the XB-36 had the fairings for the tail radar and tail turret, neither was actually installed. (Peter M. Bowers Collection)

was also in keeping with the general direction of the aircraft industry at the time. Some of the initial designs for the B-29 had twin tails, but Boeing had ultimately selected a taller single unit. Even Consolidated had begun with twin verticals on the XB-32, but production airplanes used a single vertical surface. The PB4Y-2 variant of the B-24 was also produced with a single vertical, as were a few late-model B-24s. The change to the XB-36 was approved on 10 October 1943, along with a 120-day delay in delivery.[19]

By mid-1944 the military situation in the Pacific had improved significantly. The Marianas campaign was near its end, and preparations were being made to deploy B-29s to attack the Japanese Home Islands. The Army no longer believed that a very-long-range bomber was urgently needed, but nevertheless signed a $160 million contract for 100 production aircraft on 19 August 1944. The schedule for the XB-36 was unchanged, and the first production B-36 was to be delivered in August 1945, with the last arriving in October 1946. Only now, the contract did not carry any priority at all, essentially ensuring that no materiel could be procured as long as the war lasted; the schedule would obviously not be met.[20]

Following the surrender of Germany and the end of the war in Europe, American aircraft production was cut by 30 percent, amounting to a reduction of 17,000 aircraft over an 18-month period. However, memories of the bloody Pacific island-hopping battles were fresh, and the contract for the very-long-range B-36 was untouched.[21]

Nevertheless, the pending production of the B-36 caused other concerns. For instance, on 14 May 1944, the Air Materiel Command began investigating which airfields could accommodate very large bombers. The primary concern was the massive stress exerted on the runways and taxiways by an aircraft as large as the B-36. Initially, the Army suggested the use of dual wheels on each main landing gear strut, similar – but larger – to those used on the B-29. However, in order to fit the main gear into the wing when it was retracted, Convair decided

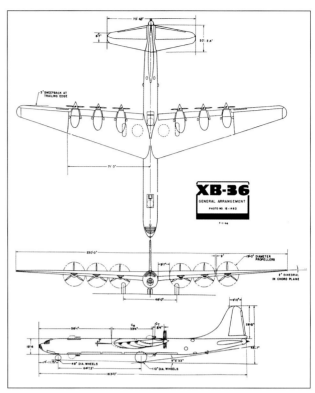

This July 1944 drawing shows the location of the four gun turrets. The lower forward turret would be deleted in production models to provide room for the search radar antenna, while the two aft turret locations would be moved rearward in back of bomb bay No. 4. (San Diego Air & Space Museum Collection)

to use a single 110-inch-diameter wheel per side. It really made little difference since the runway load was significant in either case.[22]

The result of the airfield survey was not encouraging since it discovered only three runways capable of supporting the B-36.[23] In July 1945, the Army Air Forces directed that a new landing gear be devised to distribute

Later in its career, the XB-36 received the same four-wheel bogie main landing gear as production airplanes. Note the buzz number on the fuselage; "BM" was the code for B-36, used with the last three digits of the serial number. (Convair)

Just before it was retired, the XB-36 was used to test a tracked landing-gear system. There was no specific intent to equip production airplanes with the system, but the XB-36 provided a convenient very heavy airplane for tests. (Lockheed Martin)

At left, Grace Purcelly poses with the wrench used to loosen the single lug on the 110-inch wheels. In the center, three women sit inside one of the Goodyear tires, showing how large it really was. The XB-36 was not the first airplane to use large main landing gear. Years earlier, the Beardmore Inflexible (at right) used 87-inch-diameter main wheels when it made its maiden flight at Martlesham Heath Airfield, England, on 5 March 1928. The Inflexible was a large airplane for its time, with a span of 157.5 feet and a maximum weight of 37,000 pounds. The single example was scrapped in 1930. (Right: Don Pyeatt Collection; Others: Convair)

the aircraft weight more evenly, thus reducing the need for specially built runways. One of the major roadblocks encountered with designing a multi-wheel undercarriage for the B-36 had been developing adequate brakes. These became available in early 1948, and the production dual-tandem (four-wheel) bogie-type undercarriage used 56-inch wheels and allowed the B-36 to use any airfield suitable for the B-29. Ultimately, only the XB-36, YB-36, and XC-99 would use the 110-inch landing gear.[24]

Revised performance estimates for the XB-36 were still proving discouraging, mostly because the gross weight had increased from 265,000 to 278,000 pounds. Top speed had gone from an estimated 369 to 323 mph, while the service ceiling had dropped from 40,000 to 38,200 feet. The estimated range had gone from 10,000 miles to 9,360 miles. Although the B-36 might not be any faster than the B-29, it was still vastly superior in terms of range and payload. In comparison, the B-36 was 1.85 times as heavy as the B-29, but it could carry ten times the bomb load to 5,500 miles.[25]

On 8 September 1945, one month after the Japanese surrender and almost six years after the original contract had been signed, the XB-36 (42-13570) was rolled out in

The 110-inch gear (above) was originally used on the XB-36, YB-36, and XC-99. Beryl Erickson (at right) remembered, "The [tube] thickness was not very uniform, and balancing the tires was difficult. Nonetheless, the tires never gave us any operational trouble, and I think we flew 75 total flights with those tires on the two airplanes [XB-36 and YB-36]. But it required a specialized crew several days' work to mount one tire." (National Museum of the United States Air Force Collection)

Cold War Peacemaker

Curtiss Aircraft test pilot Herb Fisher with his son, Herb Fisher, Jr., inspecting the first model of 19-foot-diameter, 3-blade Curtiss-Wright propeller for the XB-36 (right). Essentially identical propellers would be used for most of the production run but vibrated at some speeds and new, square-tipped propellers were fitted to the entire fleet in 1952. (Curtiss photo via Herb Fisher, Jr.)

Fort Worth. At the time, it was expected that final outfitting and taxi tests would consume the next six months. In May 1946, Secretary of War Robert P. Patterson told a House subcommittee that the aircraft was "due to fly next month," a prediction that would be repeated several times during the summer. The aircraft finally made its maiden flight on 8 August 1946 piloted by Beryl A. Erickson and G. S. "Gus" Green, along with John D. "JD" McEachern, William P. "Bill" Easley, A. W. Gecman, Joe M. Hefley, R. E. Hewes, and W. H. Vobbe.[26] It was the largest and heaviest aircraft ever flown, and the 37-minute flight was generally uneventful.[27]

Early test flights confirmed that the aircraft's top speed was only about 320 mph, and two major problems soon surfaced – a lack of proper engine cooling and propeller vibrations – although both of these had been extensively investigated during wind-tunnel testing and using a ground test rig. A two-speed cooling fan was developed that largely eliminated the cooling problem, but nothing could be done to ease the vibration other than strengthening the affected structures (primarily the flaps), which added yet more weight. Late in the production run, a new propeller was finally developed that minimized the vibration. The XB-36 was used for aerodynamic and systems testing but lacked any military equipment and did not represent the production configuration.

The last flight of the XB-36 was on 13 January 1948 and lasted 5 hours 10 minutes. Even before the first flight, it had been discovered that, like many wartime prototypes, the XB-36 suffered from substandard materiel and workmanship. Coupled with several major configuration changes, this made it prohibitively expensive to bring the XB-36 up to production standards. The aircraft was officially retired on 30 January 1952, although it had last moved under its own power in October 1951. In the interim, the airplane was used primarily for ground training, to evaluate various proposed changes to the interior configuration, and as a surrogate for the early NB-36H development. In May 1957, the airframe was turned over to Carswell AFB as a fire-fighting aid and was eventually destroyed.[28]

The XB-36 was sufficiently different structurally that Convair and the Air Force elected not to bring it up to production standards. The airplane was used for various tests for several years, but was ultimately used to train crash crews in the Carswell AFB fire pit (above) and was destroyed. (Convair)

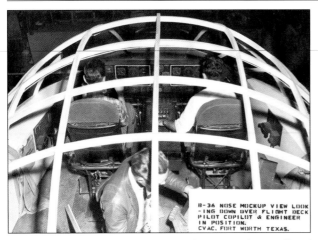

The bubble-type canopy used on production airplanes offered significantly improved visibility over the original airliner-style canopy of the XB-36. This is the mockup on 15 September 1945. Note the more-complete instrument panel. (Convair)

The wooden mockup was built in Fort Worth, and originally used a somewhat more streamlined canopy than was eventually fitted. Note the antenna immediately ahead of the windscreen and the nose turret. (San Diego Air & Space Museum Collection)

YB-36

As the first XB-36 was being built, it became obvious that numerous changes would be necessary based on new requirements and wartime experience. As early as June 1944, the Army had directed Convair to build a new nose-section mockup that included a nose turret with two 20mm cannon and a revised forward crew compartment with a raised flight deck and expansive canopy. This mockup was inspected on 9–10 November 1944 and subsequently approved for production. On 7 April 1945, the Army ordered Convair to complete the second XB-36 (42-13571) closer to the expected production standard with the new nose and bomb bay Nos. 3 and 4 moved together instead of being separated by the aft turret bays. The aircraft was redesignated YB-36 (not YB-36A as sometimes reported).[29]

The entire issue of defensive armament for the new bomber had been in constant flux. When the original XB-36 mockup had been inspected in July 1942, it included upper and lower forward turrets equipped with two 37mm cannon, each controlled by a gunner in the turret. This explains why the XB-36 did not have forward sighting blisters. In the aft fuselage, an upper turret housed two .50-cal. machine guns, while a lower turret had four .50-cal. guns. These turrets were controlled by two upper and two lower sighting blisters (one each per side), forcing the fire control system to deal with issues of alternate control and double parallax computations. A pair of 37mm tail guns was controlled from a remote position in the aft crew compartment.[30]

By April 1944, the defensive armament had changed considerably. General Electric proposed installing eight retractable turrets – four on the upper fuselage, four on

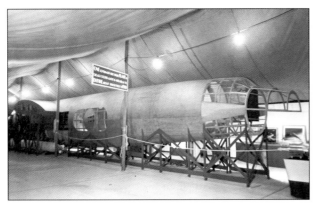

For reasons unknown, the XB-36 mockup was moved to Wright Field, shown here at the October 1945 Air Forces Fair. The sign is interesting, saying that "One government-built engine plant in Chicago occupies almost as much area as the entire aircraft industry in 1939." (National Museum of the United States Air Force Collection)

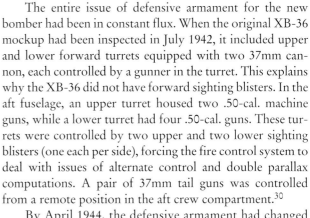

Convair engaged Henry Dreyfuss Designs, of New York, to design an ergonomically correct flight deck for the YB-36. This is the mockup of the forward panel, showing the simplistic instrumentation that Dreyfuss expected the bomber to use. In reality, the instrument panel became much more complicated than depicted here. (San Diego Air & Space Museum Collection)

the lower fuselage – plus a non-retractable tail turret, each equipped with two 20mm cannon. The new system was based heavily on the computers and sighting stations originally developed for the B-29 and Northrop P-61 Black Widow. In June 1944 a nose turret was added, and on 15 July 1945, the APG-3 radar being developed for the B-29 was included for the tail turret. Soon afterward, a decision was made to delete the two lower forward turrets to make room for the new APQ-24 search radar that replaced the original APG-7 that used antennas in the leading edge of the wing. This was essentially the defensive system used on production aircraft, although Convair and General Electric had a long, hard road ahead to get it all to work as expected.[31]

The YB-36 flew for the first time on 4 December 1947, making a 1-hour, 50-minute circuit around Fort Worth. At this point the YB-36 still had the 110-inch single-wheel undercarriage, and lacked armament and most production equipment. On 19 December 1947, during its third flight, the YB-36 reached an altitude of more than 40,000 feet, an outstanding achievement for the time. Beginning on 27 May 1948, after 89 hours of flight-testing, the single-wheel landing gear was replaced by the production dual-tandem undercarriage and 3,500-hp R-4360-41 engines were fitted in place of the original 3,000-hp R-4360-25s. The YB-36 first flew in this configuration in June 1948, and Convair made 36 test flights that accumulated 97.5 hours. Parts of the defensive armament system were fitted at various times during these flights to test the hardware General Electric was developing.[32]

The YB-36 was turned over to the Air Force on 31 May 1949 where it was used as another B-36A. Subsequently, the YB-36 was returned to Fort Worth in October 1950 to be remanufactured into an RB-36E in lieu of the first B-36A (YB-36A) that had been tested to destruction at Wright Field.[33]

The 110-inch main landing gear used on the XB-36, YB-36, and XC-99 was a great deal taller than the average person. This is actually the XC-99 with its flight crew prior to its maiden flight. (San Diego Air & Space Museum Collection)

The Air Force would add 1,952.5 flight hours to the airframe before it was retired in early 1957. The aircraft was turned over to the Air Force Museum at Wright-Patterson AFB, but it was declared surplus and scrapped when the new museum facility was built. Ralph Huffman acquired parts of the airplane and subsequently sold the remains to Walter Soplata; these still exist on his farm in Newbury, Ohio.[34]

The YB-36 (42-13571) shows the new nose profile, complete with a trials nose turret, but the airplane still has the original 110-inch main landing gear. This too would soon be replaced by production units. Note that the large search radar radome is installed in what was originally the lower forward turret bay. (Lockheed Martin)

From the beginning, the engineers were worried about cooling the R-4360s buried in the wings. This ground test stand, shown on 7 March 1945, was built outside the Experimental Building in Fort Worth to study airflow, cooling techniques, and vibration characteristics. The stand was used throughout most of the early development program. (Roger Cripliver Collection)

The XB-36 meets the partially completed first B-36A (44-92004) during the 15 June 1947 Family Day at the Convair plant. This particular B-36A is frequently called the YB-36A and only made two flights: once around the pattern at Fort Worth, and then a ferry flight to Wright Field, Ohio, where it was purposely destroyed during structural testing. (Convair)

B-36A

The B-36A was essentially similar to the YB-36, including the use of 3,000-hp R-4360-25 engines. The four bomb bays could accommodate 72,000 pounds of conventional bombs, but no provisions existed for carrying atomic weapons. The defensive armament system was not ready, so the B-36As were unarmed except for tail turrets on some airplanes. The maximum takeoff weight was 310,380 pounds, due mainly to structural limitations of the landing gear. With 24,121 gallons of fuel and a 10,000-pound bomb load, the B-36A had a combat radius of 3,880 miles. The reduction in fuel required to carry the maximum 72,000 pounds of bombs resulted in a radius of only 2,100 miles. With full fuel and no weapons, the aircraft could be ferried 9,136 miles. Performance was optimistically listed as 345 mph at 31,600 feet with 10,000 pounds of bombs, and a service ceiling of 29,100 feet.[35]

Each of the four cavernous bomb bays on the B-36A was covered with sliding doors – reminiscent of the B-24 – that were mounted on rollers and moved in tracks around the fuselage contour. The doors on bomb bay Nos. 1 and 4 were single-piece units that slid up the left side of the fuselage. The two middle bomb bays had doors split down the centerline that slid up both sides of the fuselage since the wing prevented the use of a single-piece design. The doors were slow to operate, tended to stick in the extremely cold temperatures at high altitudes, and significantly increased drag when open. A better solution would need to be found, but all A- and B-models used these doors.[36]

The crew complement of the B-36A was listed as 15, but this included eight gunners who had no weapons and functioned mainly as spotters. The other seven crewmembers were pilot, copilot, radar-bombardier, navigator, flight engineer, and two radiomen.

On 3 August 1947, two months after the photo at the top of this page was taken, the first B-36A was displayed during Army Air Forces Day at Carswell. This time the airplane had "City of Fort Worth" painted on the nose, the first of three B-36As and a single B-36J that would wear the name. (Don Pyeatt Collection)

Another shot from the 15 June 1947 Family Day showing the XB-36 and the partially completed first B-36A. The wing leading edges had not been installed yet, probably indicating that work inside the wings, especially inspecting the fuel tanks, had not been completed. (Convair)

The YB-36A (44-92004) was rolled out of the factory in early June and made its maiden flight on 28 August 1947, actually beating the YB-36 into the air by almost four months. Between the rollout and first flight, the aircraft was displayed at several public events at the factory and nearby Carswell AFB. This aircraft was fitted with only enough equipment for a ferry flight to Wright Field where it was used as a structural loads airframe and tested to destruction. The aircraft made two flights totaling 7 hours 36 minutes, one around the pattern at Fort Worth to prove everything worked, and the final flight to Wright Field with Col. Thomas P. Gerrity and Beryl Erickson at the controls. The YB-36A was formally accepted by the Air Force on 30 August 1947, only two days after its first flight. The Air Materiel Command accepted the first "operational" B-36A (44-92005) in May 1948 and the aircraft was delivered to the Air Proving Ground Command at Eglin AFB for climatic testing on 18 June 1948.[37]

On Monday, 22 March 1948, Convair officials announced that the 7th Bombardment Wing (Heavy) at Carswell AFB – on the other side of the runway from the Convair plant would become the first operational unit for the B-36 when the first of 100 aircraft was delivered "sometime this week."[38] The 7th Bomb Wing responded by sending four flight engineers and five crew chiefs to Convair for training.[39] However, the announcement proved premature as on-going modifications to the aircraft delayed its delivery more than three months.

The B-36A suffered from the types of problems normally encountered by complex, new aircraft. The fuel tanks leaked, the new alternating-current electrical system was troublesome, engine cooling was still not adequate, and the propellers continued to vibrate. None of these problems were insurmountable, and Convair engineers continued to work on solutions. Nevertheless, a great deal of negative press was generated, largely attributable to the U.S. Navy and its supporters in Congress and elsewhere.

The first B-36A only made two flights: one around the pattern at Fort Worth (shown here over Plant 4 on 28 August 1947) to ver-ify everything was working as intended, and one to Wright Field whee it would be used as the structural test airframe. By the time of its maiden flight, all traces of its City of Fort Worth *name had disappeared.* (Jay Miller Collection)

Finally, in April 1948, the tide began to turn and the B-36 was able to demonstrate its potential. On 8–9 April, a B-36A (44-92013) made a 33-hour, 10-minute flight covering 6,922 miles, shuttling between Fort Worth and San Diego. Beryl Erickson and Arthur S. "Doc" Witchell, Jr., had fuel remaining for another 206 miles if it had been necessary. The aircraft was flown with sufficient ballast to compensate for the lack of defensive armament, and carried 10,000 pounds of dummy 500-pound bombs that were dropped from 25,000 feet over the Air Force Bombing Range at Wilcox, Arizona, 15 hours into the flight. Unfortunately, problems with two engines limited the average cruising speed to a disappointing 214 mph.

The first B-36A was slowly tested to destruction to determine its ultimate structural strength. At one point, the airframe had to be turned upside down so that loads could be applied to the bottom of the wings – these photos show it being flipped inside the hangar at Wright Field. (Ed Calvert Collection)

The airplane most remembered as the City of Fort Worth *was actually the third to carry the name: B-36A 44-92015. This airplane carried the name on both sides of the nose, and is shown here with the "Triangle J" tail markings used by the 7th Bomb Wing during the late 1940s. Note the lack of a nose turret and gunsights in the forward blisters.* (John Wegg)

A month later, on 13–14 May 1948, Erickson and Witchell used the same B-36A (44-92013) to conduct a second long-range simulated tactical mission. The aircraft had a gross weight of 299,619 pounds, including 10,000 pounds of dummy bombs, 5,796 pounds of simulated 20mm ammunition, and ballast to compensate for the lack of turrets and other equipment not fitted to the B-36As. The 36-hour, 8-minute flight covered 8,062 miles at an average 223 mph. The aircraft landed with 986 gallons of fuel remaining, which could have extended the mission by 508 miles. This was a typical B-36 mission, with the first 369 miles flown at 5,000 feet, followed by a power climb to 10,000 feet. This altitude was maintained until 30 minutes before the target when the aircraft climbed to 25,000 feet and commenced a maximum speed bomb run that included 17 minutes of evasive maneuvers. The flight home was made at 25,000 feet.[40]

Four days later, another B-36A dropped twenty-five 2,000-pound bombs from 31,000 feet over the Naval Range at Corpus Christi, Texas, during a 7,000-mile

flight. This was followed on 30 June 1948 by a B-36A dropping 72,000 pounds, the heaviest bomb load yet carried by any aircraft. The B-36 had just demonstrated that it was a true intercontinental bomber.[41]

On 26 June 1948, the first B-36A (44-92015) to be delivered to the Strategic Air Command (SAC) was taxied under its own power from Consolidated-Vultee to the 7th Bomb Wing at Carswell. The airplane was named *City of FORT WORTH*, and was assigned to the 492nd Bomb Squadron.[42] This was the third B-36 to be named for the city in which it was built; the YB-36A used the name when it was publicly displayed before its flight to Wright-Patterson, and the third B-36A (44-92006) also used the name, largely because it was the only B-36 in Fort Worth for a while.

The twenty-second and last B-36A was accepted in February 1949, and all but two of them were assigned to the 7th Bomb Wing at Carswell. Since the aircraft lacked defensive armament, they were used primarily for training and

The third B-36A (44-92006) became the second City of Fort Worth, *using a more pleasing script logo than the original airplane. The name was apparently only applied to the left side of the nose, and it is not certain how long it remained.* (Convair)

This plaque was affixed to the third City of Fort Worth *(44-92015) when it was delivered.* (Courtesy, Fort Worth Star-Telegram Collection, The University of Texas at Arlington Library)

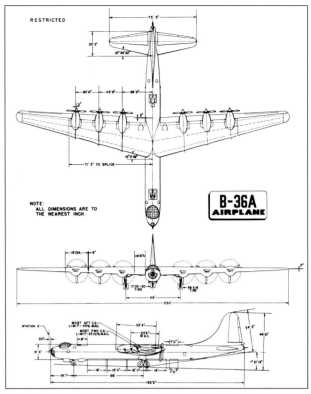

The B-36A was generally similar (excepting the jet engines) to all production aircraft to come after it. Compare the location of the gun emplacements, particularly aft, to those on the XB-36 shown on page 53. Also note the revised forward fuselage and canopy contours. (San Diego Air & Space Museum Collection)

further flight-testing. In reality, they were down for maintenance as often as not as Convair and the Air Force worked through various problems. Fortunately, the service life of the B-36A was extremely short, the last one (44-92017) being remanufactured into an RB-36E by July 1951.[43]

B-36B

The B-36B was the first potentially operational version and used 3,500-hp R-4360-41s with water injection in place of the earlier –25 engines. This required a major structural change to the wing, but all earlier aircraft were eventually modified to accept the more powerful engines. In addition, the sixteen 20mm cannon were installed in six retractable remotely operated turrets each equipped with a pair of cannon, plus two more pairs in nose and tail turrets. The guns were aimed using computing gunsights situated at two blisters on the forward fuselage and four blisters on the aft fuselage. The tail turret was directed by an AN/APG-3 gun-laying radar, and the nose turret used a periscopic gunsight mounted in the bombardier's compartment. Bolt-in armor panels were provided to protect all but the inboard fuel tanks (these would be empty and purged by the time the aircraft was under threat) and all of the engine oil tanks.[44]

Convair intended to equip the B-36B with the new Farrand Y-1 retractable periscopic bombsight, but development problems resulted in the tried-and-true M-9 Norden being used instead. Aircraft equipped with the Norden are easily identifiable by the flat, glazed panel in the nose. The bomb bay arrangement was similar to the B-36A, but structural changes allowed the B-36B to carry up to 86,000 pounds of bombs, a rather significant 14,000-pound increase. This meant the airplane could carry two 43,000-pound bombs, but the same sliding-type bomb bay doors

used on the B-36As were retained. Eighteen of the aircraft (44-92045/92062) were equipped with guidance equipment for two 13,000-pound VB-13 Tarzon guided-bombs. This early precision-guided weapon was controlled via radio link by an operator in the B-36 viewing a television picture

Squadron personnel line up for inspection prior to the flight crew boarding City of Fort Worth *for its maiden flight by an all-military crew on 28 June 1948.* (Courtesy, Fort Worth Star-Telegram Collection, The University of Texas at Arlington Library)

Scenes inside Air Force Plant 4 during the production of 384 B-36 intercontinental bombers. Production was ongoing from late 1946 through 10 August 1954 when the last B-36J was delivered. Twenty-two of the airplanes went through the production line twice, when the single YB-36 and 21 B-36As were remanufactured into RB-36Es. (Convair and Lockheed Martin)

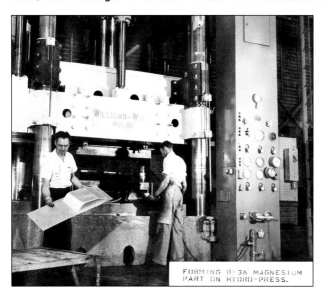

B-36 WING CENTER FIXTURE

MAJOR COMPONENTS

MAJOR COMPONENTS

B-36 A
MAJOR COMPONENTS
TAIL SECTIONS, TAIL CONES, VERTICAL STABILIZER, BOMB BAYS & NOSE SECTION

B-36 A
DIE CASTING

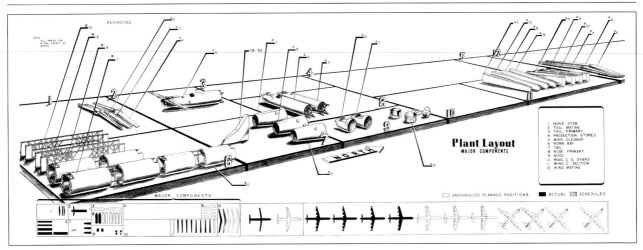

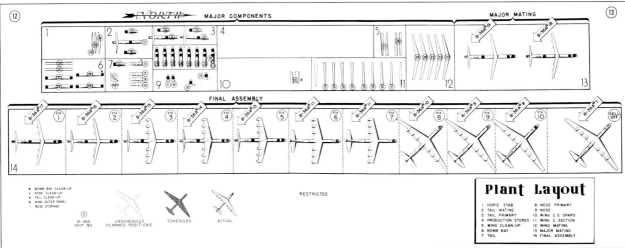

The general layout of the Plant 4 assembly line changed somewhat as the program progressed. The top drawing is from the B-36A era, while the other dates from the production of B-36Hs. Noteworthy is that the main hall, that comfortably held two side-by-side B-24 and B-32 lines, could barely hold a single B-36 line – in fact, the B-36s had to be turned 45 degrees to fit. (Convair)

from the nose of the weapon. The last 47 aircraft (44-92045/087 and 095/098) were equipped from the factory to carry a Mk III "Fat Man" atomic bomb in bomb bay No. 1. It appears that at least the first few B-36Bs were also equipped with provisions to carry the McDonnell F-85 Goblin parasite fighter in the forward bomb bay, although it is unlikely any equipment was actually installed.[45]

Like the B-36A, the crew of the B-36B was normally fifteen: pilot, copilot, radar-bombardier, navigator, flight engineer, two radiomen, three forward gunners, and five rear gunners. In this case, the gunners actually had something to do, although continuing problems with the defensive armament did not allow them to do it well.

The first B-36B (44-920026) made its maiden flight on 8 July 1948 with Beryl Erickson at the controls, and subsequent testing indicated its performance was generally better than expected. The top speed was up to 381 mph, and the service ceiling increased to 42,500 feet. An average cruising speed of 300 mph could be maintained at 40,000 feet. The Air Force accepted its first B-36B (44-920026) on 25 November 1948 and assigned it to the 7th Bomb

Wing at Carswell, which already operated the B-36As in a training role. The 11th Bomb Wing would also be activated at Carswell with the B-36B, receiving its first aircraft (44-92050) on 18 March 1949.

In 1947, construction had begun on a new base at Limestone, Maine, to accommodate the B-36 while plans were being made for additional B-36 groups to be based at Rapid City, South Dakota, and Fairfield-Suisun, California. Even given the long-range capability of the B-36, the airplane could not attack all of its targets directly from the normal bases in the United States. In response, the Air Force selected a series of pre-strike staging bases in the far north, with flight paths that took them near (or over) the North Pole – a route that caused new problems. The magnetic compasses that were still being used as the primary navigation tool at the time did not function well at extreme latitudes. As a result, Project GEM (global electronics modification) was initiated to provide equipment for worldwide navigation as well as various cold-weather modifications. (B-29s and B-50s also received air-to-air refueling capabilities as part of GEM.) After suitable polar navigation

A late-production B-36B (44-92078) taking off from Carswell, with Plant 4 in the background. Note the small "United States Air Force" on the forward fuselage, the wing badge on the nose, and the 8th Air Force badge on the tail. By this time the first batch of B-36As, visible on the ramp, were already being disassembled for conversion into RB-36Es. (via Frank F. Kleinwechter)

Most people think of the B-36 as a nuclear bomber, but it was conceived and manufactured as a conventional bomber, albeit one capable of carrying a dizzying array of iron bombs. These are 1,000-pounders. (Left: Jay Miller Collection; Right: Frank Kleinwechter)

equipment was installed, the 7th Bomb Wing began deploying B-36Bs to bases in Goose Bay, Labrador, Limestone, and Eielson Field near Fairbanks, Alaska. These aircraft had their wingtips and empennages painted bright red in case they were forced down in rough terrain or snow.[46]

In a maximum range demonstration, a B-36B from the 7th Bomb Wing/436th Bomb Squadron flew a 35-hour round-trip simulated bombing mission from Carswell to Hawaii on 7–8 December 1948 piloted by Maj. John D. Bartlett and 1st Lt. William H. Grabowski. A 10,000-pound load of dummy bombs was dropped in the ocean a short distance from Hawaii. The flight covered more than 8,100 miles, although the average cruising speed was only 236 mph. Nevertheless, this proved the B-36, given the right circumstance, could attack almost any target in the world. Interestingly, the B-36 penetrated Hawaiian airspace without being detected by the defensive forces on

the islands, an embarrassment they did not appreciate since it came 7 years to the day after Pearl Harbor.[47]

More demonstrations followed. On 29 January 1949, a B-36B established a bomb-lift record by carrying a pair of dummy 43,000-pound bombs at Muroc AFB (now Edwards AFB). The first was released at an altitude of 35,000 feet, the second from 41,000 feet, both at a speed of 350 mph. The entire flight averaged 250 mph and covered 2,900 miles. The bombs were 26.85 feet long and 4.5 feet in diameter and had to be released in a specific sequence – the forward bomb was dropped first, and the sudden release of weight jolted the nose upward. If the rear bomb had been released first, the resultant nose-down moment might have been too severe to recover. Maj. Stephen P. Dillon and Doc Witchell piloted the aircraft.[48]

On 12 March 1949, a B-36B from the 7th BW/492nd BS established a distance record of 9,600 miles flown in

If the B-36 seemed gigantic by most definitions, its bomb bays were even more so. Designed before the advent of nuclear weapons, the four B-36 bomb bays were designed to carry every weapon in the inventory, from 100-pound flash bombs to 43,000-pound T-12 bunker-busters. Eventually, the B-36 would be the only aircraft capable of carrying the Mk 17 thermonuclear weapon, a device it fortunately never had to deploy in anger. (National Archives College Park Collection)

The last B-36A (44-92025) flies formation with a Boeing B-29A (44-62074), both from the 7th Bomb Wing based at Carswell. This particular B-29 was later transferred to the Royal Air Force as a Washington B.1. (Frank F. Kleinwechter Collection)

This B-36B (44-92056) has a nose turret, but no cannon. It is also missing the nose turret gunsight (the small hole to the left of the center glazed panel) and has a Norden bombsight behind the oval glazed panel. (Lockheed Martin)

43 hours 37 minutes, with enough fuel remaining for 2 more hours of flying – proving the B-36 could remain aloft for 2 days, totally self sufficient. Leaving Carswell on 10 March at 12:20 p.m., the bomber flew north to Minneapolis, west to Great Falls, and then to Key West where it flew over President Truman at his vacation home. Leaving Florida, it dropped 10,000 pounds of bombs into the Gulf of Mexico. It then turned northwestward and flew over Fort Worth and Denver, back to Great Falls, and then to Spokane before changing course again for Fort Worth. The airplane was ordered to land after two engines failed and because severe weather was approaching the airfield. A 10,000-mile mission was undoubtedly possible under ideal conditions.[49]

Although confidence building, these missions were not truly representative of the state of the B-36 fleet. During 1949, SAC rarely had more than 40 B-36s on hand, and only 5 to 8 of these were considered operationally capable. The 7th Bomb Wing was, in essence, a service test unit. Similar to the B-36A, many of the B-36B's initial problems resembled those of any other new and complex aircraft. Parts shortages were acute, and it was often necessary to cannibalize some B-36Bs to keep others flying.[50]

In addition, the APQ-24 was neither as reliable nor as accurate in service as it had been during testing. The problem was eventually traced to faulty vacuum tubes and inadequate crew training. The complex General Electric

The B-36Bs were subjected to many cold-weather tests since it appeared the most likely way to get to the Soviet Union was over the North Pole. Here 44-92044 sits on a snow-covered ramp waiting for its crew to arrive for a mission. The red markings would allow searchers to find an airplane forced down in the snow-covered Arctic. (Air Force Historical Research Agency Collection)

defensive armament was prone to frequent failures. Although conceptually similar to the system on the B-29, it was vastly more complex; a necessity to ensure it was capable of handling the ever-increasing speeds of the fighters it was designed to shoot down. The APG-3 gun-laying tail radar also proved to be remarkably troublesome. As late as February 1950, the commander of the 8th Air Force was complaining, "… there was little point in driving a B-36 around carrying a lot of guns that didn't work."

By the end of 1950, three accidents involving Carswell-based B-36Bs had claimed the lives of twelve airmen with each accident being the result of equipment failure. The first accident on 16 September 1949 was a result of propeller pitch reversal that caused a B-36B to crash into Lake Worth at the end of the Carswell runway. The second crash, on 14 February 1950 in Canada, was determined to be a result of engine icing.[51] The third crash was a result of multiple equipment failures that exemplified the many problems plaguing the new bomber.

In the third crash, a B-36B (44-92035) departed Carswell at 5:05 a.m. on 22 November 1950 en route to practice at the Matagorda Island aerial gunnery range. Three minutes into the flight, an alternator failed and was taken off-line, to be followed a minute later by flames trailing behind the number-one engine. The engine was shut down, its propeller feathered, and a bromide fire bottle activated. The aircraft proceeded on its mission with five engines running normally, not an unusual occurrence for the B-36.

Arriving at the gunnery range at 7:00 a.m., the aircraft's gunners began firing their 20mm cannon. Moments later, the aircraft commander was informed that the APQ-24 radar "blew up and was smoking." The radar operator determined that vibration from the aircraft's guns was causing internal short circuits in the radar. Almost simultaneously with the radar failure, the liaison transmitter failed, followed by total failures of two of the starboard gun turrets. Attempts to manually retract the turrets also failed. Suddenly, number-three engine failed and was shut down. With only one engine operating on the left wing, the aircraft commander aborted the mission and turned the aircraft toward Kelly AFB at San Antonio.

En route to Kelly, the flight engineer discovered he had no mixture or turbo controls for the remaining engines. (Vibrations from the cannon firing had also disabled all electrical engine controls.) Attempts to salvo 1,500 pounds of practice bombs failed when the bomb bay doors failed to open. Worsening weather conditions precluded a landing attempt at San Antonio and then at Bergstrom AFB in Austin, only 80 miles distant. The aircraft commander was forced to return to Carswell, an additional 155 miles from Austin. With only 21 miles remaining to Carswell, number-five engine seized. A bailout order was given. One crewmember died when his head struck the feathered number-three propeller; another died after his parachute failed to deploy. The remaining

The B-36 (44-92007 shown here) was a frequent participant in fire power demonstrations at Eglin AFB, and often conducted its missions at very low level so the watching dignitaries could get a good view. (Air Force Historical Research Agency Collection)

crew survived, albeit with several serious injuries. The bomber crashed and burned near Cleburne, only 20 miles south of Carswell. A subsequent investigation determined the crash could have been prevented by the presence of a conventional mechanical engine mixture control system.[52]

The problems seemed larger than normal, but the B-36 was a larger-than-normal aircraft and firmly entrenched in the public view. Unfortunately, the "super-duper" bomber was not living up to its hype and the Soviets would surely learn of its many deficiencies. The aircraft were constantly being reconfigured or awaiting modification and, in reality, a fully operational capability was not achieved until 1952.[53]

Nice bottom view of a red-tail B-36B (44-92033) showing the buzz number painted on the underside of the left wing and the original location of the national insignia. (Lockheed Martin)

One of the more interesting concepts investigated for the early B-36s was the ability to carry spare engines with each airplane when they deployed to forward operating bases. Special pods were developed that could each carry two complete R-4360s. The pods were bolted onto the racks in bomb bay No. 1 – note the open sliding-type bomb bay doors. Unfortunately, the carriers would not work with the newer snap-action doors used on the B-36D and subsequent models. (San Diego Air & Space Museum Collection)

Nevertheless, the B-36B was proving to be capable, if somewhat slow. The Air Force and Convair were looking for ways to improve the speed of the B-36, and everybody concerned was working on improving the reliability of the aircraft and its systems. It was now obvious that B-36 production would exceed the original 100-aircraft order, and that the airplane would be the Air Force's primary nuclear deterrent until development of the jet-powered B-52, and all of its supporting infrastructure (tankers, etc.), was completed, something not expected until 1955 at the earliest.

There were numerous proposals to equip the B-36 with turboprop engines, usually 5,500-shp Wright T-35s or 10,000-shp Northrop T-37 Turbodynes. Some of the proposals were for tractor configurations; others retained the normal pushers with the engines buried in the wing. Neither of these engines materialized, and the B-36 proposals never advanced past paper studies.

While the B-36Bs were being manufactured, Convair attempted to develop the B-36C, equipped with Variable Discharge Turbine (VDT) engines, to increase performance.

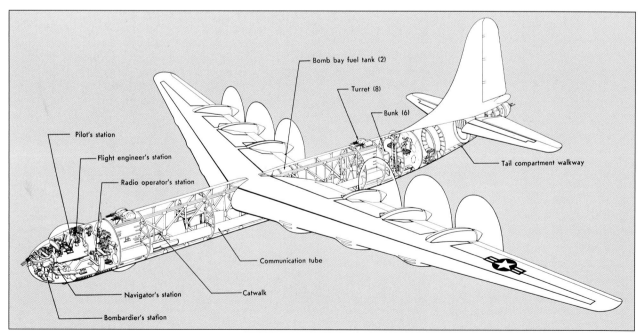

There was not much difference between the B-36A and B-36B, other than the latter had most of the operational equipment that had been deferred from the earlier airplanes. The basic configuration of the airframe did not change substantially throughout its production, other than adding the jet pods and several attempts to reconfigure the interior for more comfort and efficiency. (U.S. Air Force)

This B-36A (44-92010) was part of a display at Andrews AFB near Washington, DC, in February 1949 that included a North American B-45, Boeing XB-47, and a Northrop YB-49 flying wing, as well as numerous fighters. (AFFTC History Office Collection)

A red-tail B-36B (44-92040) on display in September 1950. The center bomb bays are open, meaning they have probably not yet been equipped for nuclear weapons since their configuration became classified afterward. (Peter M. Bowers Collection)

When this did not pan out, the Air Force approved a more modest upgrade that added General Electric J47-GE-19 turbojet engines to the basic B-36B configuration, creating the B-36D. This change was approved while the B-36Bs were being manufactured. Convair was contracted to build 73 B-36Bs,[54] but the Air Force directed 11 of them to be modified with jet engines on the production line; four were completed as B-36Ds and seven as RB-36Ds. The Air Force also ordered all B-36Bs be converted into D-models.

By the time the last B-36B was accepted, some had already been returned to Convair to be converted into B-36Ds, with many of the conversions being performed in an Diego because Fort Worth was fully engaged building new bombers. The B-36B phase-out from service was almost as quick as that of the B-36A. Twenty-five B-36Bs were already undergoing conversion during the first half of 1951, and the last of the 60 converted B-36Bs was redelivered during February 1952. Two of the bombers had crashed before they could be converted.

The development of workable multi-disc brakes and high-pressure tires made it possible to replace the 110-inch main gear used on the first three airplanes with a four-wheel bogie that used 56-inch-diameter tires for all production airplanes. The revised main gear distributed weight more evenly, making it possible for the B-36 to use any runway that had accommodated B-29s. (National Archives College Park Collection)

B-36C

Given that none of the large turboprop engines were panning out, in March 1947, Convair proposed that 34 of the original 100 aircraft be completed as B-36Cs powered by 4,360-hp R-4360-51 Variable Discharge Turbine (VDT) engines.[55] The VDT engine was also going to be used on the B-50C (B-54) and Republic F-12 (production XR-12) Rainbow. (See Appendix E for further information.)

Unfortunately, the use of the VDT engines on the B-36 dictated a change from a pusher to a tractor configuration, requiring a significant redesign. Although the engine remained in the normal position behind the main wing spar, its orientation changed to face forward, and each engine drove a tractor propeller through a 10-foot shaft that extended through the entire wing chord. This necessitated changes to the training edge flaps, the internal cooling systems, and the forward fuselage (to withstand the propeller vibrations).[56]

Initially, Convair estimated the VDT engines would provide a top speed of 410 mph, a 45,000-foot service ceiling, and a 10,000-mile range with a 10,000-pound bomb load. To offset the cost of adapting the VDT engine to the B-36, Convair suggested financing the airframe modification for one prototype by deleting three B-36s from the original procurement contract. This was approved by the Air Force in July 1947.

During the late 1940s, several aircraft were envisioned that would use Pratt & Whitney's R-4360 Variable Discharge Turbine (VDT) engines, including the Boeing B-54 version of the B-50 bomber. (Air Force Historical Research Agency Collection)

Unfortunately, by mid-1948 revised performance estimates showed a cruising speed over a range of 7,250 miles was only 262 mph – 23 mph slower than a standard B-36B over the same range. It had become apparent that the B-36C was not going to materialize, and the Air Force considered cancelling the entire B-36 program. By this time, some in Strategic Air Command had lost faith in the

The Republic XR-12 Rainbow was the most promising of the VDT-powered airplanes. Two prototypes, powered by normal turbo-supercharged R-4360s, demonstrated a top speed in excess of 450 mph; the VDT engines would have increased this and allowed even higher altitudes than the 45,000 feet of the prototypes. Unfortunately, the Rainbow, and a proposed airliner variant, never flew with the VDT engines and did not enter production. (Cradle of Aviation Museum Archives)

B-36 as a long-range strategic bomber, and believed this relatively slow aircraft would be useful only for such tasks as sea-search or reconnaissance.[57]

Much of this was based on emotion and misinformation. In August 1949, Maj. Gen. Frederic H. Smith, Jr., testified before the House Armed Services Committee regarding a series of evaluations conducted in late 1948. These had shown that the standard B-36B surpassed the B-50 in cruising speed at very long range, had a higher service and cruise ceiling, a larger payload capacity, and a much greater combat radius (assuming no refueling of the B-50). The speed tests had been conducted to the B-50's maximum range – if the tests had been conducted to the B-36's maximum range, then the results would have favored the B-36 even more since the B-50 would have had to slow down to refuel. An evaluation at the same time showed that the B-36B was superior to the proposed B-54 in all regards except speed over the target, and the addition of jet engines on the B-36D would cure this deficiency.[58]

However, it was the Soviets – and Air Force Plant 4 itself – thatwere ultimately responsible for saving the B-36 program. On 18 June 1948, the blockade of Berlin began. One week later, Secretary of the Air Force William Stuart Symington decided to continue the B-36 program in its entirety since it was the only truly intercontinental bomber available at the time, and to "not lose the industrial potential of the government-owned Fort Worth plant just when new production miracles might be demanded – as they were after Pearl Harbor."[59] With many World War II defense plants closed and their engineers and production workers dispersed into the general workforce, keeping Air Force Plant 4 in operation became a national defense priority.

However, five aircraft (44-92099 through 44-92103) still had to be cut from the original 100-aircraft order to compensate for inflation and to pay for the ill-fated B-36C project. The VDT-equipped B-36Cs that had been ordered would be completed as jet-augmented B-36Ds.[60]

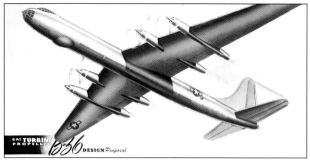

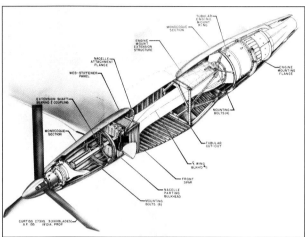

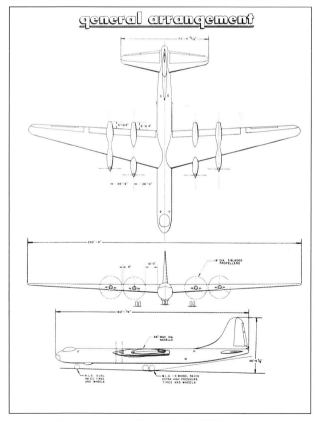

The B-36C was not the only tractor configuration Convair investigated and this proposal used four Wright T35 Typhoon turboprop engines rated at 5,500-shp each driving 19-foot-diameter Wright propellers. The T35 was the first large U.S. turboprop and was also used in several early Boeing B-52 and Convair YB-60 designs before those airplanes switched to all-jet power. Ultimately, the T35 never entered production. (Left: Air Force Historical Research Agency Collection; Others: San Diego Air & Space Museum Collection)

The J35 installation differed from the production J47 installation. The bottom of the nacelles were not sculptured, and the later sway brace was not used. This nacelle also did not have the retractable doors over the engine faces. (Lockheed Martin)

The jet demonstrator was not a true prototype D-model since it did not have any of the other improvements planned for the production airplane, such as the snap-action bomb bay doors or improved engines and systems. (Lockheed Martin)

B-36D

Fortunately, the VDT-powered B-36C was not the only way Convair had devised to increase the speed of the B-36. On 5 October 1948, Convair proposed installing a pair of turbojet engines under each outer wing panel. These engines could be used during takeoff and for short bursts of speed at critical times, and would have only a minimal effect on range, more because of the additional drag than the relatively small amount of fuel they used.

Unlike the extensive changes needed to install the VDT engines on the C-model, or any number of the turboprop concepts, only minor modifications were required to mount the jet nacelles. In fact, Convair was confident that a prototype B-36 with jet engines would be ready to fly less than 4 months after Air Force approval. This, however, was delayed because of defense budget restrictions in December 1948 and the decision a month before to convert the B-36As into RB-36E reconnaissance aircraft. It should be noted that as originally

To increase the speed of the B-36 over its target, the Air Force authorized the modification of a single B-36B (44-92057) jet demonstrator on 4 January 1949, and the aircraft made its first flight on 26 March 1949. The intended engine was the General Electric J47, but these were unavailable, forcing the demonstrator to use General Electric J35s. (National Archives College Park Collection)

Remarkably few changes were needed to the B-36 to accommodate the new engines beyond the required instrumentation and controls. The engines themselves were modified to run on avgas instead of jet fuel and had their own oil supply. (Lockheed Martin)

The production J47-equipped pods were externally identical to those used on the Boeing B-47. Collapsible aerodynamic covers were installed (open at left, closed above) to minimize drag when the engines were not operating. (Lockheed Martin)

planned, the RB-36Es did not include jet engines – they were simply B-36As modified with photo and radio-intercept reconnaissance capabilities.

The modification of a single B-36B (44-92057) jet demonstrator was authorized on 4 January 1949, and the aircraft made its first flight on 26 March 1949. Due to the unavailability of J47 engines, the demonstrator used four Allison J35 engines in pods manufactured by Convair. The only external differences from production pods were that this installation did not include a sway-brace that was used to correct a slight vibration problem and that the undersides of the nacelles were not "sculpted" like the B-47. This aircraft was not a prototype D-model as is often reported – it incorporated none of the other features of the new aircraft such as the snap-action bomb bay doors. A second B-36B (44-92046) equipped with modified B-47 pods was also used during the J47 test program.

As usual for a maiden B-36 flight, Beryl Erickson and Doc Witchell were at the controls when 44-92057 made its 3-hour 15-minute flight with the jet pods. Although the first flight took place at 5:50 p.m. on a Saturday, several thousand Convair employees turned out to watch it.[61]

The most obvious change for the B-36D was two pair of 5,200-lbf General Electric J47-GE-19 turbojets in pods underneath the outer wing panels (although some early aircraft apparently used -11 engines initially). To save time and money, the pods were generally similar to those developed for the inboard nacelles on the Boeing B-47 Stratojet medium bomber. The outrigger landing gear and some of the supporting structure was deleted, although the aerodynamic fairing and taxi light on the bottom of the pods were retained. Initially, the struts and pods were even manufactured by Bell Aircraft Company on the same Buffalo, New York, production line used to make B-47 pods.[62]

Beginning in May 1951, the pods were manufactured in a new Bell facility located 12 miles from the Convair Fort Worth plant. Special collapsible aerodynamic covers were installed over the engine inlets to minimize drag when the engines were not operating. The engines themselves were modified to burn standard aviation gas instead of jet fuel so that the B-36 could feed them from the existing fuel supply. Controls for the jet engines were mounted on a separate panel above the pilots' heads, while instrumentation was provided on two subpanels mounted below the main instrument panel. Surprisingly, the flight engineer was not provided with any jet instrumentation or controls other than some fire warning lights.[63]

Initially, the intake cowlings were painted a distinctive bright red. This change was effected, not to enhance the

After retirement, one set of J47s and their pod were installed, upside down, on top of a New York Central Budd car. Tests on a perfectly straight 24-mile section of track showed the car could reach a top speed of 183.7 mph. (John E. Parnell Collection)

aircraft's appearance or to designate Air Force unit assignments, but rather for operational reasons. Red, a traditional warning color, reminded ground crews to use caution when working around jet intakes. While taxiing, the brightly contrasting color also enhanced a pilot's perception of wingtip clearance from other objects on the ground. In flight, the bright red was visible through the collapsible aerodynamic covers when they were open – a valuable piece of information since there was no instrument panel indication of their position. The cowlings were painted during manufacturing immediately before the aircraft entered flight test.[64] As time went on and jet engines became more common, the initial rationale became less important and the cowlings began to be painted a variety of colors to indicate unit assignments.

The D-model used the same 3,500-hp R-4360-41 engines that powered the B-36B, although they would be updated to -41A models with the same horsepower sometime during the service life of the aircraft. The maximum gross weight increased to 357,500 pounds, a figure that would remain constant across all models until the advent of the B-36J. Another major improvement was that most of the flying surfaces were now covered with magnesium skin instead of doped fabric. The retractable tail "bumper" that had been installed on the A/B-models was deleted on new-builds, but was retained on the B-36Bs that were completed as D-models.

The Farrand Y-1 retractable periscopic bombsight had run into apparently insurmountable development problems, so a non-retractable version called the Y-3 was installed in most B-36Ds. Since the Y-3 bombsight used a small periscope protruding from the right side of the for-

The snap-action, folding bomb bay doors operated quicker and produced less drag and the original sliding doors. The device on the ground is the bomb hoist that was placed on top of the fuselage and used to load bombs into the airplane. (Marvin Hilliard)

ward fuselage bottom, the flat glazed panel in the nose was covered over with aluminum. Of course, on aircraft still equipped with the Norden bombsight (and all RB-36s), this panel was glass, complete with its own windshield wiper.[65]

The B-36D was fitted with "snap-action" bomb bay doors instead of the sliding doors fitted to the preceding B-36A/Bs. These could open and close in only 2 seconds, minimizing the drag penalty usually associated with getting ready to drop bombs over the target. Only two sets of doors were provided, one covering the forward bomb bays

This B-36D (44-92036) shows the two most prominent upgrades – the jet pods and the snap-action bomb bay doors. This airplane had begun life as the eleventh B-36B and was converted into a D-model in San Diego. (National Archives College Park Collection)

B-36s were frequently staged at the Convair seaplane base while in San Diego undergoing modification. Most B-to-D-model conversions took place in San Diego due to lack of capacity in Fort Worth. (San Diego Air & Space Museum Collection)

(Nos. 1 and 2), and the other covering the aft bays (Nos. 3 and 4). All B-36Ds were delivered with the ability to carry a Mk III "Fat Man" atomic bomb in bomb bay No. 1, chosen primarily because the bombs still had to be armed in flight and the forward bomb bay was the most accessible. Conventional bomb capacity was generally similar to the B-model. An improved APG-32 tail radar replaced the APG-3 used in the B-36B.

The nomenclature for the 15 crewmembers changed slightly: aircraft commander, two pilots, two engineers, navigator, bombardier, two radio operators, an observer forward, and five gunners aft. In reality, one of the radiomen operated the electronic countermeasures (ECM) equipment, the other operated the nose turret, while one of the pilots and the observer operated the forward upper gun turrets.

The last 11 B-36Bs were equipped with jet engines on the assembly line, becoming seven RB-36Ds and four B-36Ds prior to delivery. The first new-build B-36D made its maiden flight on 11 July 1949, was accepted by the Air Force in August 1950, and was promptly sent to Eglin AFB for testing. By June 1951, 26 B-36Ds had been delivered, and the last of 76 B-36Ds was accepted in August 1951.[66]

Given the large boost to performance, the Air Force decided to retrofit the jet engines to all existing B-36Bs (which became B-36Ds)[67] as well as the B-36As being remanufactured into RB-36Es. The Fort Worth plant was already consumed with building new B-36s and remanufacturing the B-36As, so after the first four B-36Bs (44-92026, 034, 053, and 054) were converted, the modification effort was transferred to San Diego. At either location, each aircraft was completely overhauled and new control surfaces, jet engines, and the snap-action bomb bay doors were added. The first B-36B (44-92043) arrived at San Diego on 6 April 1950, and made its initial flight as a B-36D on 5 December 1950. The last modified aircraft (44-92081) was redelivered to the Air Force on 14 February 1952.[68]

The third B-36D (44-92090) was used for an accelerated service test program. The airplane flew more than 500 hours during the first 73 days and underwent a thorough 7-day inspection every 120 flight hours. Each flight was a simulated tactical mission that was accomplished as close

Another view of the seaplane base showing a variety of B-36s – some with jet engines and some without – during the B-to-D-model conversion effort. Note the Convair R3Y Tradewind flying boat at the end of the ramp. (San Diego Air & Space Museum Collection)

The extensive use of magnesium shows up well here – the dull areas are magnesium skin; the shiny areas are aluminum. Aluminum was used primarily in pressurized areas since magnesium is too brittle to withstand frequent pressurization cycles. (Convair)

The original propellers had round tips, but caused a severe vibration that irritated the crew and contributed to metal fatigue in the wing and aft fuselage. (Convair)

Two crewmembers who conducted much of the Convair flight test work on the B-36. Beryl A. Erickson (right) and John D. "JD" McEachern (left), looking at a drawing on 4 August 1954. (Convair)

A B-36D (44-92037) from the 42nd BW in July 1955. Note that the cannon are missing from the tail turret. As can be seen, it was possible to walk under most of the fuselage without slouching. (Dave Menard Collection)

The first new-build B-36D (44-92095) was originally ordered as a B-model, but was completed on the assembly line with the jet engines, snap-action bomb bay doors, and other improvements. These were the typical markings that most D-models were delivered in. (San Diego Air & Space Museum Collection)

This B-36D (44-92065) was assigned to the 326th BS/92nd BW at Fairchild AFB, Washington, in May 1955. The unit insignia on the nose (insert), based on characters from Alley Oop cartoons, and the squadron stripes on the vertical stabilizer, serve to identify the aircraft's assignment. Caricatures of Alley Oop, a pterodactyl, "T-Rex," and other prehistoric creatures that adorned aircraft of the 92nd Bomb Wing, were created by cartoonist V. T. Hamlin, who started the Alley Oop cartoon strip while he was a reporter with the Fort Worth Star-Telegram. Alley Oop was seen riding his pet brontosaurus "Dinny" on aircraft of the 326th Bomb Squadron, and on a saber-tooth tiger on aircraft of the 325th. The 325th continues the tradition today with Oop and the saber-tooth proudly emblazoned on Northrop-Grumman B-2A Spirits along with its original motto "Fame's Favored Few." (W. Balogn via Richard Freeman)

The first B-36B (44-92043) arrived at San Diego on 6 April 1950, and made its initial flight as a B-36D on 5 December 1950. In addition to the modifications, the airplanes received depot-level maintenance; note the new skin on the vertical stabilizer. (San Diego Air & Space Museum Collection)

This airplane (44-92096) had been ordered as a B-model but was completed as a B-36D on the assembly line, along with three other bombers and seven reconnaissance airplanes. The B-36D was arguably the first combat-ready version of the giant bomber, and was equipped to carry atomic weapons. (Lockheed Martin)

as practical to how a normal Air Force unit would fly the airplane. The missions attacked "targets" that ranged from the Dakotas to Florida and from the Pacific to the Atlantic. Most of the simulated bombing runs were conducted at 40,000 feet. Flights averaged approximately 25 hours each, although one lasted more than 39 hours.

Although the Air Force originally claimed the new engines boosted the top speed to 439 mph at 32,120 feet and increased the service ceiling to 45,020 feet, this was later revised to 406 mph at 36,200 feet and a service ceiling of 43,800 feet. Whether this discrepancy was due to miscalculation, some overzealous public relations (the Congressional hearings were underway at the time), or changes in the aircraft themselves is not certain.

RB-36D

As with many things surrounding the B-36, Curtis LeMay strongly influenced the decision to procure a reconnaissance version. LeMay had commanded B-29 strikes against Japan in World War II and was disturbed by the lack of a reconnaissance capability to photograph the same targets the bombers could attack. One of his first actions upon taking command of SAC was to insist on an up-to-date supply of strategic reconnaissance aircraft. The B-36 was chosen as a reconnaissance aircraft for much the same reasons as it was for a strategic bomber – altitude and range. In fact, all of the original SAC bombers – B-29, B-36, B-45, B-47, and B-50 – had reconnaissance variants at LeMay's

The first San Diego B-to-D conversion nears completion on 16 November 1950; the airplane would make its first flight in this configuration less than two weeks later. Note the lack of a serial number (it was 44-92043) on the tail because of the new skins that were applied during maintenance. (San Diego Air & Space Museum Collection)

urging. Initially, there was even a reconnaissance variant of the B-52, although very few were produced before SAC decided it would rather have more bombers and rely on the Lockheed U-2 and other assets for intelligence gathering.

In the case of the B-36, just over one-third (142) of the production aircraft were configured for reconnaissance. These were assigned to the 5th Strategic Reconnaissance Wing (SRW) at Travis AFB, 28th SRW at Rapid City (later Ellsworth) AFB, the 72nd SRW at Ramey AFB, Puerto Rico, and the 99th SRW at Fairfield-Suisun (later Travis) AFB, California. Although new RB-36 deliveries continued until late 1953, by 1954 all of them were being reconfigured for a primary nuclear strike capability, with reconnaissance left to the much faster, but shorter-ranged, RB-47s.

The B-36 reconnaissance program was approved during early 1948, and a mock-up of the camera installation was completed at Fort Worth on 17 March 1949. The RB-36D and RB-36E programs progressed almost simultaneously, with the largest difference being all RB-36Ds would be new-builds while the 22 RB-36Es were remanufactured from the YB-36 and 21 B-36As. In actuality, there was little difference between the aircraft other than their production heritage, and the two types proceeded down the production line interspersed.

The RB-36 carried a crew of 22; the additional crewmembers were needed to operate and maintain the photographic and electronic reconnaissance equipment. The area that normally housed bomb bay No. 1 became a 16-foot-long pressurized compartment that contained up to 14 cameras, as well as a small darkroom that allowed film cartridges to be reloaded in flight (but contrary to many reports, did not develop or print the film). Adding this compartment involved changing the forward and aft

Gen. Curtis Emerson LeMay (15 November 1906 – 1 October 1990) was the commander of the Strategic Air Command and believed his reconnaissance aircraft should equal his heavy bomber's capability. (U.S. Air Force)

bomb bay bulkheads into pressure domes, eliminating the bomb bay doors, and changing the exterior skin to aluminum since magnesium could not tolerate the pressure cycles. The shiny aluminum in this area provides easy

This B-36B (44-92026), used as an aerodynamic testbed for the RB-36D's radomes, has caused much confusion over the years. Many reports indicate the airplane is an RB-36D that first flew without jet pods; this is not the case. The airplane simply was used to evaluate the four large FECM radomes on the nose and bottom of the fuselage. (San Diego Air & Space Museum Collection)

As built, all RB-36s carried large ferret ECM antennas in streamlined radomes located under where bomb bay No. 4 was located on the bomber versions. The short doors for bomb bay No. 3 may be seen to the right of the radomes. The radomes were moved farther aft when bomb bay No. 4 was modified to carry nuclear weapons. (Lockheed Martin)

An unusual photograph showing all of the ECM-receiving antennas mounted on the side of an RB-36. All aircraft could carry these, but normally they were kept inside the airplane unless they were needed on a particular mission. Bomb bay No. 4 has been activated on this airplane, evidenced by the long bomb bay No. 3/4 door behind the short No. 2 door. (Lockheed Martin)

identification of the reconnaissance aircraft. Several camera windows were installed on the sides and the bottom of the compartment, each covered by a sliding door.[69]

As initially configured, the RB-36 was not equipped to carry bombs. Bomb bay No. 1 had been converted into the pressurized camera compartment. Bomb bay No. 2 was modified to carry eighty 100-pound T86 (or M46) flash bombs, and bomb bay No. 3 generally contained a 3,000-gallon auxiliary fuel tank, but could carry flash bombs instead. Bomb bay No. 4 was deleted and the area used for a special pallet that held ferret ECM (FECM) equipment. Three large radomes were mounted on the bottom of the fuselage (where the aft bomb bay doors were normally located) and a single similar radome under

the nose. Using the ferret equipment, operators on board the RB-36 could record and analyze radar and communications signals while the aircraft flew close to Soviet territory.[70] Convair took the opportunity to lighten the aircraft by installing new bulkheads on either end of what had been bomb bay No. 4 since it no longer carried the stress of a heavy bomb load.

A single set of 33.66-foot doors covered the two middle bomb bays. Since the aircraft were not equipped as bombers, the K-system (K-1 or K-3A, as appropriate for the model) was not installed, although the aircraft continued to carry the APQ-24 search radar. Given that they carried no bombs, the reconnaissance models were not equipped with Norden or periscopic bombsights. The

A single ferret ECM radome was located under the nose of each RB-36. All reconnaissance airplanes used Norden bombsights, meaning they kept the glazed panel in the nose instead of the periscopic bombsight used by the dedicated bombers. (San Diego Air & Space Museum Collection)

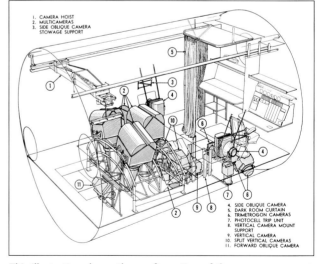

This illustration shows the configuration of the camera compartment that was installed where bomb bay No. 1 was located on the bomber versions. The dark room was provided to load film into the canisters and could not process film in flight as is often reported. (U.S. Air Force)

normal defensive armament of sixteen 20mm cannon was retained on all production RB-36s.

The first RB-36D (44-92088) made its maiden flight on 14 December 1949, only 6 months after the jet demonstrator had flown, and less than a month after the Air Force approved the aircraft for production. This flight, piloted by George Davis and Francis Keen, lasted 7 hours 1 minute. Numerous reports have suggested that the first flight of the RB-36D was conducted without the jet pods. Most likely, researchers are confusing this with photos of the single B-36B (44-92026) that had been used to evaluate the aerodynamic effect of the RB-36 radomes.[71]

The RB-36D preceded the B-36D into service with SAC by a couple of months, and the first seven RB-36Ds came off the production line before any jet-augmented bombers. All of the 24 RB-36Ds were "new-builds," although the first 7 had originally been ordered as B-36Bs, they were completed on the production line and delivered as RB-36Ds. None of the B-36Bs that had been delivered without jet pods were converted into RB-36Ds.

All RB-36Ds were delivered to the 28th Strategic Reconnaissance Wing at Rapid City AFB between June 1950 and May 1951. Due to various materiel shortages, the RB-36Ds did not become operationally ready until June 1951, although several "peripheral" reconnaissance missions had apparently been flown as early as July 1950.

The performance of the RB-36D was similar to its bomber counterparts with a few subtle differences. Since the reconnaissance version generally took off with less payload but more fuel, it tended to be a little faster and fly a little higher early in the mission. However, because it did not drop its major payload (the reconnaissance gear), the RB-36 was a little heavier on the return flight than the bombers, so it was a little slower.[72]

A Convair test crew made the longest known B-36 flight flying an RB-36D (44-92090). The flight took off at 9:05 a.m. on 14 January 1951, and landed at 12:35 p.m. on 16 January – 51.5 hours in the air. Although this flight was unusual, most B-36 flights lasted more than 10 hours, and it was not unusual for missions to last 30 hours. The average training mission was scheduled for 24 hours.[73]

In early 1954, the first RB-36D (44-92088) was modified to carry a Boston Camera with a 240-inch-focal-length lens. Even the B-36 could not actually carry

The front flight deck of an RB-36D (49-2696) looked pretty much like the bomber version. The jet throttles were located on the overhead, and the jet instruments were on the sub-panels underneath the main instrument panel. (Lockheed Martin)

A pair of RB-36Ds from the 28th Bomb Wing at Ellsworth AFB, South Dakota. The nearest airplane (49-2688) appears to have a lightning bolt insignia on its jet pod. (National Museum of the United States Air Force Collection)

a camera more than 20 feet long, so the lens used a set of mirrors to achieve the 240-inch effective length. Each negative measured 18x36 inches and the camera was reportedly able to photograph a golf ball from 45,000 feet. A large circular opening was cut into the left side of the fuselage and the camera was installed in the normal camera compartment with the film magazines protruding below the fuselage in an angular bulge. The camera was tested for about a year prior to being removed from the RB-36D in 1955 and installed in a Boeing C-97 Stratocruiser. This RB-36D was never used operationally, and the camera was donated to the Air Force Museum in 1964.

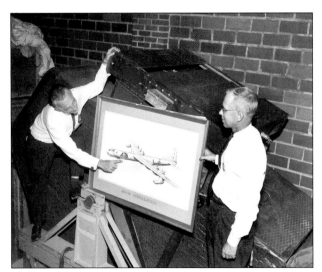

In a posed photograph, W. D. Halsey and N. B. Robbins inspect a drawing of the Boston Camera. Halsey is holding onto the camera, which is behind the poster. (Lockheed Martin)

On 16 June 1954, the four RB-36-equipped heavy strategic reconnaissance wings were assigned a primary strategic bombardment role, with reconnaissance becoming a secondary capability. By this time, SAC had shifted most reconnaissance to the RB-47, and the RB-36s were more useful as nuclear deterrents, although they retained a comprehensive latent reconnaissance capability. On 1 October 1955, the RB-36 reconnaissance wings were redesignated heavy-bombardment wings, although little changed but the name. Ironically, the airplanes were still incapable of carrying bombs.

To cure this shortcoming, all of the RB-36s rotated back through the Convair plant for major modifications to allow nuclear weapons to be carried. The FECM equipment carried in the bomb bay No. 4 location was moved into the aft fuselage between bulkheads 10.0 and 12.0, and the three large radomes were relocated directly under the new location. Bulkheads[74] 7.0, 8.0, and 9.0 were replaced or modified to accept the load required to carry bombs; this essentially meant that bulkheads 8.0 and 9.0 were replaced with units similar to the normal B-36 bulkheads since the RB-36 units had been redesigned to save weight. The bomb bay doors were also changed to more closely match the bomber models – Nos. 3 and 4 were covered by a single set of new 32.375-foot-long doors, while bomb bay No. 2 was covered by a set of 16-foot doors. An M-9 Norden bombsight was installed, similar to the B-36B; no RB-36s carried the Y-3 periscopic sight. While they were at Convair, most RB-36s also received a "weather reconnaissance" modification that allowed them to collect rudimentary meteorological data during flight. Despite the modifications, the entire reconnaissance capability was retained.[75]

RB-36E

In an effort to quickly gain an intercontinental reconnaissance capability, Gen. LeMay ordered the mostly useless B-36A fleet converted into RB-36Es. Like the RB-36D, the RB-36E was designed for all-purpose strategic reconnaissance, day-and-night mapping and charting, as well as bomb damage assessment missions.

Since the YB-36A (really the first B-36A) had been purposely destroyed during structural testing, the original YB-36 (42-13571) was also modified to RB-36E standard to provide 22 aircraft. As originally envisioned, these were really RB-36Bs in that the 22 aircraft would be brought up to B-36B standard and equipped with cameras for reconnaissance. As the detailed design evolved, the changes grew, including the need for a new pressurized compartment in the forward fuselage to contain the cameras and the crew needed to operate them. The addition of the FECM equipment in the aft bomb bay meant the bulkheads on either side of bomb bay No. 4 could be lightened. These changes required that much of the fuselage would need to be disassembled and replaced. When the Air Force opted to install jet engines and snap-action bomb bay doors on the last few B-36B production aircraft (and call them B-36Ds), the same changes were extended to the RB-36E configuration.

The remanufacturing effort was much more involved than is normally reported. After the aircraft arrived back at Convair, they were stripped of all equipment, which was returned to the vendor or depot for maintenance and upgrading. The airframes were then stored on the flight line for a few months while special jigs were built. Eventually, each airframe was broken down into its major components – forward fuselage, mid-fuselage, wings, etc. These components were refurbished, brought up to the B/RB-36D standard, and reintroduced onto the production line interspersed with D-models. On the production line, the RB-36Es were treated just like any other new-

The RB-36E was more complicated than is generally reported. The aircraft were not, in truth, "modified" but were instead "remanufactured." This involved breaking them into their major structural components and reintroducing them onto the assembly line for a second time. Here are four B-36A forward fuselages awaiting their turn. (Lockheed Martin)

build B-36. For unexplained reasons, there was a single exception – one aircraft (44-92008) went through the remanufacturing process in the open air on the ramp next to Building 4. (The aircraft was neither the first nor the last to be remanufactured, so there appears to be no rationale.)

As part of the remanufacturing effort, the R-4360-25 engines were replaced by R-4360-41s, and the aircraft were equipped with the four J47 jet engines. The same cameras and electronic systems scheduled for the RB-36D were used. The aircraft were also fitted with the 20mm defensive armament that had not been ready when they were initially built. For all intents, the aircraft were identical to RB-36Ds except for their production heritage, and the last aircraft was completed in July 1951.

B-36A aft fuselages, main wing boxes, and empennages stored between the Hangar Building (left) and Building 4 (right) on 15 September 1950. For unexplained reasons, one RB-36E was assembled in this outdoor area. (Lockheed Martin)

Most of the airframe components would be used again except the forward fuselage aft of the gun bay; this housed bomb bay No. 1 on the bombers, but received a new camera compartment for the recce versions. (Lockheed Martin)

This is the YB-36-cum-RB-36E (42-13571) late in its career. Note the nose turret has been replaced by a fiberglass cover and the forward sighting blisters have been faired-over, part of the Featherweight III program. Like all recce versions, this airplane retained the glazed Norden bombsight panel, complete with its windshield wiper, throughout its career. Note that the white "high altitude camouflage" was not masked, but instead was free-hand sprayed. (Convair)

Earlier in its career, the "YB" as it was called by Convair, had been the first airplane through the SAM-SAC maintenance program; this is its delivery ceremony when it was returned to the Air Force. Note the nose turret and blister. (Lockheed Martin)

The last B-36A (44-92017) to be converted to an RB-36E was redelivered to the Air Force on 27 April 1951. Note that the nose turret has not been installed. The shiny aluminum camera compartment shows up well here. (Lockheed Martin)

This RB-36E (44-92020) was assigned to the 5th SRW at Travis AFB. This photo was taken near Travis AFB in August 1952. Note the location of two serial numbers on the vertical stabilizer (one is under the Circle X). (Warren Bodie via Richard Freeman)

This RB-36E (44-92023) was also assigned to the 5th SRW at Travis AFB, and was photographed in August 1952. Note the location of the serial number compared to the airplane from the same unit in the top photograph. (Warren Bodie via Richard Freeman)

Most RB-36s also received a "weather reconnaissance" modification that allowed them to collect rudimentary meteorological data. A weather observer's station was added in the lower part of the nose compartment and included a humidity indicator, clock, altimeter, and radio altimeter. A barometric pressure, temperature, and humidity probe was added to the right side of the extreme nose just behind the glazed panels. A radiosonde equipment rack was added at the intermediate frequency ECM operator's station in the aft compartment. The dispenser was installed in the floor on the centerline of the rear compartment where the strike camera was carried in the bombers. Controls for the dispenser were installed at the high-frequency ECM station on the right side of the aft compartment, and also at the right lower gunner's blister. The photo at right shows the MA-1 dispenser station looking outboard toward the right-hand side. (Lockheed Martin)

B-36F

On 13 April 1949, the Air Force ordered 17 B-36Fs and 19 RB-36Fs, although an additional 19 bombers and 5 reconnaissance versions would be ordered the following year. The B-36F differed from the B-36D primarily in having improved R-4360-53 engines rated at 3,500 hp (dry) or 3,800 hp with water-alcohol injection. Late-production aircraft (beginning with 50-1064) also had two A-7 dispensers capable of dropping 1,400 pounds of chaff to confuse enemy radar, although some aircraft used one A-6 and one A-7 dispenser instead. The maiden flight of the first B-36F (49-2669) took place on 18 November 1950.[76]

Among 25 major improvements in the new engine – already tested on a modified B-36D (44-92054) – were the use of fuel injection and a new ignition system that increased reliability during high-altitude operations. The more powerful engines boosted the top speed to 417 mph and the service ceiling to 44,000 feet. However, at first, the R-4360-53 engines were not entirely satisfactory because of excessive torque pressure, ground cooling issues, and combustion problems. These were resolved fairly quickly, and the new engines proved quite reliable in service. The fuel injection, in particular, eased many of the maintenance burdens and operational constraints from the engine.[77]

In June 1951, three crews from the 7th Bomb Wing were assigned to Convair to participate in the B-36F Accelerated Service Test Program. Six B-36Fs (49-2703, 49-2704, 49-2705, 49-2670, 49-2671, and 49-2672) were used during the accelerated service tests, and Convair conducted detailed inspections of the aircraft every 100 flight-hours. The aircraft were flown by Air Force personnel, but maintained jointly by Convair and Air Force personnel. The purpose of the tests was to provide infor-

Many of the improved systems for the F-model were first tested on a modified B-36D (44-92054). This testbed would be used to verify almost all major modifications to the B-36 fleet, with particular emphasis on fire-control system improvements. Note the radar units protruding from the nose and that all six retractable turrets are deployed. (Clarence Edward Calvert Collection)

mation for the development of systems and assemblies, and to provide operational and maintenance data on the airplane and the new -53 engine. By operating the aircraft at Convair's facilities, the service life of parts or assemblies could be carefully evaluated and at the same time, the factory maintenance facilities and methods could be used as examples to improve Air Force procedures. Under these conditions, the Air Force pilots, engineers, and crewmen were exposed to "the optimum in training by 'living with' the developments and operational problems evolved on the B-36F and RB-36F airplanes almost from the time of their operational inception."[78]

The flying phase of the test series ended on 11 July 1951, followed by some paperwork before the first

These photos show some of the fire-control system modifications to the B-36D testbed. At left, a large radome protrudes from the normal Norden bombsight location, but the normal nose turret is in place. At right, the airplane has two chin radomes – undoubtedly liberated from the recce parts bin – and a very un-aerodynamic-looking protrusion from the nose turret location. This airplane was also used to test certain B-58 Hustler systems, and probably other unknown classified work. (Lockheed Martin)

The second crash of an F-model in three months occurred on 28 May 1952 when 50-1066 landed short at Carswell and burned, killing seven crewmembers. (Clarence Edward Calvert Collection)

F-model (49-2671) was delivered to the 7th BW/9th BS on 18 August 1951. All 34 B-36Fs were delivered to the 7th Bomb Wing at Carswell.[79]

On 6 March 1952, a new B-36F (50-1067) burned at Carswell after its left main landing gear collapsed as the airplane touched down on the runway. Fortunately, the crew sustained only minor injuries. This prompted concern over the integrity of the landing gear, and after a fleet-wide inspection, the Air Force decided that all B-36 models required landing gear modifications. Aircraft were cycled through San Antonio, San Diego, and Fort Worth to receive the upgraded landing gear. The bad luck surrounding the F-model's introduction to service continued on 28 May 1952 when an airplane (50-1066) landed

short at Carswell, killing seven crewmembers. On 4 August 1952, gasoline overflowed from the No. 3 fuel tank vent on a B-36F (49-2679) while it was parked on the ramp at Carswell, and the exhaust from a B-10 power unit ignited the spilled fuel. Three crewmembers sustained minor injuries, and the aircraft from the 7th BW/436th BS was a complete loss.[80]

RB-36F

The 24 RB-36Fs mated the improvements of the B-36F with reconnaissance equipment generally similar to the RB-36D. The first RB-36F made its maiden flight on 30 April 1951 and the last was delivered in December 1951.[81]

Continuing the seemingly bad luck surrounding the F-model, during early 1952, an RB-36F suffered a pressure bulkhead failure while flying at 33,000 feet. The airplane landed without incident and there were no injuries. The accident was traced to a defective bulkhead, and all B-36s were restricted to altitudes below 25,000 feet until the entire fleet could be inspected and defective bulkheads replaced. While the accident investigation was ongoing, the Air Force declined to accept any new aircraft from Convair. Eventually Convair traced the problem to a comparatively minor manufacturing flaw and instituted a fix for all affected aircraft.

B-36G

The B-36G was a swept-wing, jet-powered version of the B-36F. Two B-36Fs (49-2676 and 49-2684) were ordered converted to B-36Gs, but the designation was changed to YB-60 before they were completed. (See Appendix B for further details.)

The crew of the first B-36F (49-2669) poses in their David Clark Company S-2 partial-pressure suits. The S-2 was identical to the more popular T-1 suit, but did not include a built-in anti-g suit; a garment hardly required in a B-36. (Lockheed Martin)

The flight engineer station on the first B-36F (49-2670) delivered to the Air Force. The F-model featured fuel-injected engines and a new ignition system, necessitating major changes to the instrumentation. (Lockheed Martin)

B-36H

First announced on 5 November 1950, the B-36H was the major production version of the B-36, with 83 being built. The B-36H was substantially similar to the B-36F, but relocated the K-system electronic components into the pressurized forward compartment to facilitate in-flight maintenance, and featured a rearranged flight deck with a second flight engineer station, an improved instrument panel for the pilots, and revised night lighting at all crew stations.[82]

An improved defensive armament system was also introduced, and a new AN/APG-41 gun-laying tail radar was introduced on 51-5742. This unit used twin tail radomes, and was essentially two APG-32s that were coupled, allowing one radar to track an immediate threat while the second continued to scan for others. A new propeller was fitted that used square-tip blades instead of the original round tips. This propeller was more efficient at high altitude and cured, at least mostly, the vibration issue that had long plagued the B-36. The propeller was subsequently retrofitted to all earlier aircraft, including XC-99. Slightly improved ECM equipment was included, as were two A-6 or A-7 dispensers that carried 1,400 pounds of chaff to confuse enemy radars (something introduced on late B-36Fs). The engines were the same as on the B-36F.[83]

The B-36H made its maiden flight on 5 April 1952, although deliveries to operational units did not begin until December 1952 due to the hiatus on accepting new aircraft because of the B-36F pressure bulkhead failure.

The crew of the first B-36H (50-1083) assembles for its maiden flight. Note missing squadron logo on the nose and the covered-over panel where the Norden bombsight was located on aircraft not equipped with the Y-3 periscopic sight. (Convair)

RB-36H

The Air Force bought 73 reconnaissance versions of the B-36H. The cameras and FECM equipment were generally similar to the earlier RB-36s, while all other systems were identical to the B-36H.[84]

This B-36H (50-1085) was used in Operation IVY and was designated as the third RASCAL carrier, although it was apparently never used by that program. The airplane still has a nose turret, but does not have any cannon installed in it. (U.S. Air Force)

In addition to the B-36's iconic sound, its contrails were said to be an unforgettable sight as the aircraft flew overhead at high altitude. (Frank F. Kleinwechter, Jr.)

A B-36H (52-1350) with its landing gear mid-way through its retraction sequence. The airplane was taking off from Eglin AFB, Florida on 13 May 1956. (National Archives)

Although it appears this RB-36H (51-13741) has received the full Featherweight III modification (no nose turret), records indicate it was only a Featherweight II. Note the open upper turret bay doors and the white anti-flash paint. (Fred Johnsen Collection)

A typical B-36H (51-5704) near the end of its career. The airplane has been modified as a Featherweight III, and has the high-altitude camouflage white paint on the bottom of the fuselage and wings. (Museum of Flight Collection)

An RB-36H on the maintenance line at Plant 4. All B-36s would come home to Fort Worth several times during their careers for maintenance and modifications. SAM-SAC was among the first programs in the Air Force where the original manufacturer was largely responsible for the depot-level maintenance of a weapons system. Note the tail radar on the RB-36H is exposed as the ground crew works on it and the shelters over the cockpit area to reduce the heat inside the airplane. (Lockheed Martin)

A line of factory-fresh airplanes at Plant 4. The nearest airplane is an RB-36H (52-1388) that shows the square-tip propellers introduced on the H-model, although they were quickly retrofitted to the rest of the B-36 fleet. (Lockheed Martin)

A vision of the future. A Featherweight III B-36J leads a formation that includes its all-jet replacement, the Boeing B-52 Stratofortress, and its younger stablemate, the supersonic Convair B-58 Hustler. The B-58 would have a short and troubled career, while the B-52 is still in service. (Lockheed Martin)

The classic takeoff photo of the last B-36J departing the Fort Worth plant with its first Air Force crew enroute to Fairchild AFB. The final 14 J-models were completed as Featherweight III airplanes, the only Featherweights built as such; all others were modified after they were delivered. (Lockheed Martin)

B-36J

The B-36J was the final production version and represented the last propeller-driven heavy bombers delivered to the Strategic Air Command. It had two additional fuel tanks, one in each outer wing panel, which increased the fuel load by 2,770 gallons. The B-36J also had a stronger landing gear that permitted a gross takeoff weight of 410,000 pounds, a rather substantial increase of 52,500 pounds. The only external change was a single elongated radome to cover the twin antennas of the APG-41A gun-laying radar in the tail, a change that had been introduced during B-36H production.

The first B-36J made its maiden flight in July 1953, and the last B-36J (52-2827) was rolled out on 10 August 1954 and delivered to the Air Force four days later. Later B-36Js were delivered with new "high-altitude camouflage" white paint protecting sensitive areas of the lower wing and fuselage. The same "anti-flash" paint scheme, meant to protect from the heat flash of a nearby atomic weapon detonation, was subsequently applied to most (perhaps all) other B-36s. The last 14 of the 33 B-36Js were completed as Featherweight III aircraft, with the last being delivered to the Air Force on 14 August 1954. These were the only Featherweight aircraft to be completed as such on the production line (others were modified after production).[85]

J. D. Lee signing the nose of the last B-36J (52-2827) as it makes its way down the Convair production line on 18 December 1953. The page he is signing reads, "Dear John Oh! How I hate to see you go" and has 11 columns of signatures. The B-36 had been in production for just over five years. (Lockheed Martin)

The aft fuselage of the last B-36J. Even during these waning days of production, the censor has scratched out the Convair production number (the white blotch at the extreme right). Note the man on top of the radome fairing, and the location for the two tail-gun radar antennas. (Lockheed Martin)

A rare public open house was held at Government Aircraft Plant 4 on 14 August 1954 to ceremonially present the last B-36 to the Air Force. All of the gathered dignitaries stand for the National Anthem (left), played by an Air Force band while a formation of 7th Bomb Wing B-36s flew over the ceremony (right). After the formal ceromony, Convair employees and their families were allowed to tour the last B-36 and the XC-99 that was also present. (Lockheed Martin)

The last B-36. Interestingly, although the airplane has received its high-altitude camouflage, it is missing the star-and-bar national insignia on the aft fuselage. The airplane would be retired less than 5 years after it was delivered. (Lockheed Martin)

    Cold War Peacemaker

Featherweights

Even given the great range of the B-36, there were compromises between the weapons that could be carried and the distance at which targets could be attacked. In the early 1950s, it was not yet evident that high-yield thermonuclear weapons ("H-bombs") would eventually become fairly small and lightweight, so devising a means to extend the range of the bombers was paramount. Interestingly, although in-flight refueling would become standard on almost all Air Force aircraft – including some ancient B-29s and most B-50s – it seems to have never been seriously considered for the B-36 fleet.

As an alternative, on 28 January 1954 the Air Force approved the first phase of Project FEATHERWEIGHT[86] to increase the operational range and altitude of the B-36. Featherweight defined three configurations. Configuration I involved the tactical unit (i.e., Bomb Wing) removing all of the retractable turrets, auxiliary bomb racks (i.e., for conventional bombs), and crew comfort items immediately before a retaliatory strike. This idea was ultimately rejected because of the potential delay (possibly several days) in the unit being able to undertake missions.[87]

Configuration II ("Tactically Stripped Featherweight" or "Partial Featherweight") removed all extraneous equipment from each aircraft, except the guns, ECM equipment, auxiliary bomb racks, and crew comfort items. The turrets were slightly reconfigured to allow their rapid removal when required, and as many external protuberances as possible were removed to decrease drag. Periscopic sextants and high-altitude operating equipment were added, and flush plexiglass covers for all six sighting blisters were procured but not normally installed. These

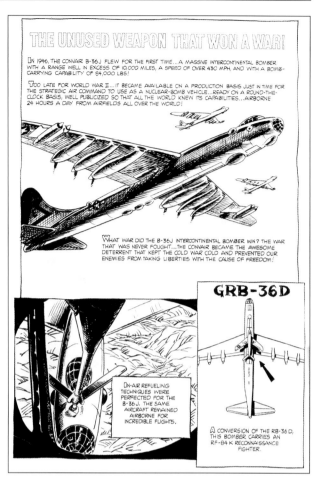

Its difficult to determine if the Air Force ever seriously investigated aerial refueling for the B-36, but at least one magazine believed they had perfected it. This is the 7 May 1966 issue of *Air War Stories*. (Don Pyeatt Collection)

The Air Force family of aircraft, circa the mid 1950s. The centerpiece B-36 was in the process of being replaced by the B-52 (upper left corner), and the all-jet tankers (KC-135, on the left) were replacing the KB-50 and KC-97 on the right. (U.S. Air Force)

modifications were accomplished at the depot level (either Convair or San Antonio) and resulted in a weight reduction of 4,800 pounds. If needed, the turrets could be removed in less than a day, and the flush blister covers installed to eliminate several thousand additional pounds. Surprisingly, these seemingly small modifications resulted in an increase in range of between 25 percent with guns and 39 percent without guns. This configuration was applied across all types of B/RB-36s, and the aircraft had a "-II" appended to their designation, sometimes written as "(II)" – B-36D-II or B-36D(II) – being equivalent.[88]

The ultimate Featherweight was Configuration III ("Full Featherweight") also conducted at the depot level. All defensive armament except the tail turret and its radar was permanently deleted, as were the forward and upper aft sighting blisters. The lower aft blisters were retained on most aircraft since they provided a convenient location for crewmembers to observe the engines for oil leaks. On some aircraft, flush plexiglass covers, providing another small decrease in drag, replaced these blisters. The chaff dispensers and ECM equipment were retained, and in some cases brought up to a later standard. Most of the remaining crew comfort equipment (bunks, galley, sound deadening, carpet, etc.) was also deleted, along with the astrodome on top of the cockpit.[89]

Flight test engineers A. S. "Doc" Witchell and J. D. McEachern, wearing high-altitude suits during test flights at Fort Worth. The David Clark Company S-2 partial-pressure suits were identical to the more popular T-1 suits except for lacking an anti-g capability. (Convair)

An Air Force technician climbs into an engine air intake on 24 April 1949. The B-36, like any mechanically complex device, required a gret deal of maintenance. The sheer size of the airplane made this, at the same time, easier, and much harder. (National Archives College Park Collection)

Without guns, the crew could be reduced, usually by two of the aft gunners (the forward gunners generally had other duties). Since most of the insulation had been removed from the pressurized compartments, the temperature at high altitude would be unbearable so provisions were added for heated flying suits. The new flying suits contained integral communications equipment, so the fixed intercom system and speakers were removed. These modifications removed 15,000 pounds from each airplane, and resulted in a range increase of between 25 and 40 percent (depending on the B-36 model) over the Featherweight II configuration. These modifications resulted in a true, unrefueled intercontinental capability, especially for the B-36J-III aircraft with their additional fuel tanks and higher gross takeoff weight.[90]

The weight and drag reduction increased the top speed of the modified B-36Ds to 418 mph and modified B-36Hs to 423 mph. Perhaps more importantly, the reduction in weight allowed a significant increase in operating altitude – up to 47,000 feet officially, and well over 50,000 feet according to many former crewmembers.[91]

The entire operational B-36 and RB-36 fleet underwent Featherweight modifications, with all B-36 modifications completed by December 1954 and all RB-36s following by March 1955. The last 14 B-36Js were manufactured to the Featherweight III configuration.[92]

Modification Programs

The B-36 probably spent more time in maintenance and modification programs than any other operational aircraft of the era. Much of this had to do with the pace of technical change during the early 1950s; new weapons and electronics were constantly being added to the airplane. Fixing latent defects – sometimes caused by the Air

Maintenance docks were installed at Fort Worth, San Diego, and the depot at San Antonio that allowed the engines and wings to be serviced in the shade. Each wing was covered by two sections, each 36 feet deep and 60 feet long. Curtains covered the open side during rain. (San Diego Air & Space Museum Collection)

Several different tail codes may be seen on these airplanes at San Diego on 16 October 1952. The nearest is a B-36F (49-2680) from the 7th Bomb Wing, followed by several airplanes from the 92nd Bomb Wing at Fairchild AFB, Washington. The Cold War drove around-the-clock work at most locations. (Lockheed Martin)

Force's desire to take delivery of the aircraft early before Convair had finished fixing it – caused other problems. In particular, the first 95 airplanes spent a majority of their early careers being modified.

Project WORTHMORE processed 53 airplanes between 2 June 1952 and 6 August 1953 through a general maintenance effort that included IRAN (inspect and repair as necessary) work and the incorporation of various modifications. Project FIXIT ran in parallel with WORTH-MORE and was responsible for fixing damage caused by the 1952 tornado that hit Carswell AFB. The decontamination program processed six B-36s and four RB-36s that had been used to monitor atomic testing. Various phases of

Project ON TOP and the ECM Follow-On program kept the nuclear weapons and ECM capabilities of the fleet up-to-date. The FECM-DECM program processed 64 RB-36s between 20 July 1954 and 13 July 1956 to increase the effectiveness of their electronic systems. There were a variety of other programs.[93]

Between 1953 and 1957, Convair and the Air Force jointly ran SAN-SAN (for San Diego and San Antonio, the two locations where it was performed) where the B-36 fleet was cycled through for inspection, repair, and modernization as required. Project CREW COMFORT installed refrigerators, bunks, improved lavatories, and other items beginning in 1950, although all of this equipment was

Convair workmen apply the "high-altitude camouflage" paint to the bottom of a B-36 fuselage. Very little was masked off, and most of the line was "fuzzy" as a result. The first few airplanes were painted in the Experimental Building, but most were sprayed in the open air on the ramp. (Lockheed Martin)

Project SAN-SAN performed major maintenance and modifications on the B-36 fleet. Here a B-36D (49-2657) is shown at San Diego – the project was also active at the depot in San Antonio. As with most B-36 activities, work continued well into the night. (San Diego Air & Space Museum Collection)

subsequently removed during Project FEATHER-WEIGHT. Project RELIABLE relocated most of the K-system components in early aircraft into the pressurized area of the forward fuselage to keep the components at a more constant temperature and allow in-flight access for monitoring and repair. The H-model introduced the K-system changes onto the production line.[94]

The sheer amount of maintenance, coupled with a lack of qualified military personnel, forced the Air Force to subcontract with Convair for many organizational and depot functions. In June 1953, Convair announced that it would be initiating "an unprecedented program of prime importance to the entire aircraft industry." The hyperbole referred to Project SAM-SAC (Specialized Aircraft Maintenance-Strategic Air Command), "a continuing maintenance and modernization program which eventually will encompass all B-36 aircraft." The goal of SAM-SAC was to standardize the B-36 fleet around a set number of configurations, allowing parts to be interchanged more easily and for maintenance procedures to be standardized. The program meant that roughly 25 B-36s would be undergoing heavy maintenance at Fort Worth constantly through 1957.[95]

Another view of Plant 4, with the compass rose in the foreground. Some of the servicing positions around the plant had maintenance docks; others did not – it depended on the type of work being performed at each locations. The large hangar at the right is the Experimental Building. (Lockheed Martin)

Air Force Plant 4 toward the end of the B-36 era. The Nuclear Area for the NB-36H program is at center in the foreground. The two YB-60s may be seen up the ramp from the Nuclear Area; note the second YB-60 is missing its rudder, removed to support the first aircraft. The XB-36 is at lower right in the open field. At least 40 B-36s are parked around the factory. (Lockheed Martin)

Wright Field Concept

As usual, the Army did not rely completely on industry to develop new concepts. Engineers at the Engineering Division of the Aircraft laboratory at Wright Field routinely designed aircraft that would never be produced, mainly as exercises to keep their skills sharp and to compare against what the industry was developing.[96]

The MCD-392 design that was compared against the Boeing, Consolidated, and Douglas proposals was certainly innovative. The 280-foot wing provided 7,140 square feet of area – more than double the B-29 and 2,368 square feet more area than the eventual B-36. The single vertical stabilizer towered 48.5 feet above the tail wheel. The design gross weight was 500,000 pounds, and the 283,390-pound useful load included up to 120,000 pounds of bombs and 23,500 gallons of fuel. Maximum speed was estimated at 388 mph with a service ceiling of 36,250 feet. With the entire 120,000 pounds of bombs, range was estimated at 6,100 miles, increasing to 9,100 miles with half the bomb load. Ferry range was 12,000 miles.

At first glance, the MCD-392 looked much like an overgrown B-19. However, closer examination revealed that the engine configuration was vastly different: a pusher propeller inboard on each wing with a tractor propeller outboard. A pair of unspecified 3,600-hp liquid-cooled engines drove each counter-rotating propeller. Each nacelle contained a gun turret at one end, engines in the middle, and a propeller at the other end.

The wing was very thick, and much like the Northrop XB-35 flying wing, the bomb load was spread span-wise instead of being concentrated completely in the fuselage. This provided a relief in the bending moment of

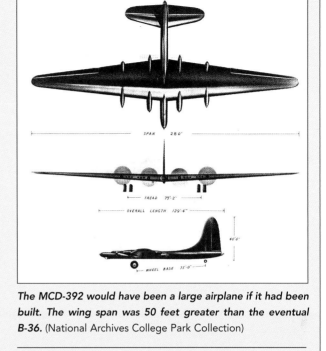

The MCD-392 would have been a large airplane if it had been built. The wing span was 50 feet greater than the eventual B-36. (National Archives College Park Collection)

the wing, allowing a lighter structure. Each of the nacelle turrets housed four .50-cal. machine guns, and the nose and tail had turrets with four 20mm cannon. Unlike the single main wheels selected by Consolidated, engineers at Wright field elected to use two wheels, in an unusual configuration, for each main landing gear.

The Army never intended to build the MCD-392, but it was a useful design exercise for the Wright Field engineers and provides an interesting comparison for the B-36 designs.

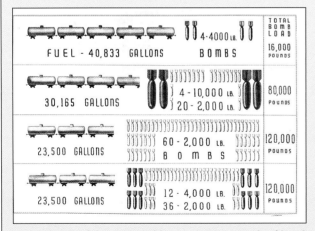

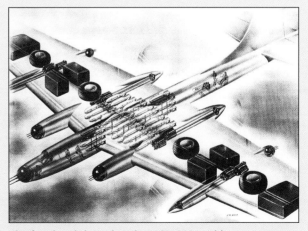

Later models of the B-36 could carry 84,000 pounds of bombs in the four bomb bays, but the MCD-392 could carry a staggering 120,000 pounds of bombs, plus an additional 150,000 pounds of fuel. Unlike the B-36 where the bomb bays were located along the length of the fuselage, the bomb load in the MCD-392 was spread span-wise between the two inboard engine nacelles. Each main landing gear had two struts, with one retracting inboard and one outboard of the outer engine nacelle. This would have placed a lot of landing stress far out on the wing structure. (National Archives College Park Collection)

Strategic Deterrent: B-36 Vulnerability

Fifty years after it was retired, the question remains of just how vulnerable the B-36 was. Despite claims the B-36 was too slow to perform its mission, in reality it was one of the fastest piston-engine bombers built. Nevertheless, as the jet age dawned, the bomber appeared slow in comparison to what came next. Regardless of its actual speed capabilities, the Air Force claimed the B-36 could fly at altitudes that contemporary fighters could not easily or routinely achieve. The Air Force contended that when a fighter did manage to get to 45,000 feet, it was as slow or slower than the bomber, and often unable to maneuver except on essentially ballistic trajectories. The B-36's large wing area allowed it to be fairly maneuverable at high altitudes, and the standard defense against a fighter attack was to make a sharp turn, something the fighter could not follow.

The Navy disagreed with the conclusions from these evaluations, but at the time presented little evidence to support its claims. In reality, both Navy and British – and possibly Soviet – fighters would have stood a better chance than Air Force fighters at high altitudes. The U.S. Air Force had adopted a doctrine that emphasized a fighter's speed over most other attributes, resulting in a generally higher wing loading than aircraft from other countries or the Navy. This greatly diminished the Air Force fighters' high-altitude maneuverability.

The popular vision of a strategic bombing mission is that the airplane takes off, climbs to its maximum altitude and speed, and flies to its target. Even with an all-jet aircraft such as the B-52, this is not necessarily true, since long-range and high-speed are usually mutually exclusive. Although the B-52 quickly climbs to its service ceiling where its jet engines are the most efficient, it settles in at an economical cruising speed for most of the mission, reaching its maximum speed only as it approaches enemy airspace.

Air Force jet fighters, such as this North American F-86F Sabre (52-4355) had a difficult time operating at the altitudes the B-36 would attack their targets from, perhaps lulling the Air Force into a false sense of security. Other nations designed their fighters to different criteria. (National Archives College Park Collection)

Piston-powered airplanes, however, used different mission profiles since their engines and propellers were not particularly efficient at high speeds or extreme altitudes. In the case of the B-36, the oft-quoted 400-mph speed and 40,000-foot altitudes were only applicable for short periods over the target.

A typical long-range bombing mission for a Featherweight III B-36J assumed a target 4,150 miles distant, for a total mission of 8,300 miles, plus reserves. With 10,000 pounds of bombs and full defensive armament and chaff, the airplane would take off weighing 330,000 pounds, well below its maximum weight. The outbound cruise portion of the mission would be flown at only 5,000 feet, an altitude where the R-4360s and big propellers were operating at maximum efficiency; the airplane could climb to 5,000 feet in 14 miles. The cruise speed during this portion of the mission was only 279 mph.[97]

The development of workable air-to-air missiles greatly increased the vulnerability of the B-36, and all other bombers. Not a truly workable example, this is a prototype Ryan AAM-A-1 Firebird (MX-799) missile under a North American F-82 Twin Mustang (44-65179) in 1946. (National Archives College Park Collection)

Early British jet fighters generally sacrificed top speed for a larger wing, allowing them to operate more efficiently at high altitude than U.S. Air Force fighters. This is a Gloster Meteor F.4 (VW784:M) under the wing of a B-36 at RAF Lakenheath on 17 January 1951. (National Archives College Park Collection)

Under ideal conditions, any jet fighter could fly with a B-36, although this photo shows a Northrop F-89D Scorpion (54-207) at a fairly low altitude (note the terrain in the background). Given the serial number of the F-89, this photo was likely taken in 1955 or 1956. (National Archives College Park Collection)

After flying for approximately 3,000 miles, the B-36 would begin climbing to its 45,000-foot combat altitude. It would take almost 2 hours and a little more than 550 miles to climb from 5,000 feet to 45,000 feet, and the airplane would reach its combat altitude approximately 500 miles from the target. Fuel was budgeted to fly at maximum continuous power[98] for 15 minutes before reaching the target and 10 minutes after weapons release; this equated to 425 mph and covered just over 150 miles.

The airplane would remain at 45,000 feet for approximately 500 miles after dropping its bombs, and then start a slow descent to 20,000 feet for the rest of the flight home. With total time in the air of 44.2 hours, the mission would consume 136,209 pounds of fuel.

Obviously, the B-36 would be extremely vulnerable during its low-level fly-out to the target area. And it is debatable how realistic the assumption was that the enemy

would only defend a 500-mile radius around a strategic target. Ignoring these possible breaches in logic, however, let's take a look at how vulnerable the B-36 was during its 45,000-foot, high-speed attack. Since we do not have good, unbiased data for the Soviet fighters of the era, we will use U.S. Navy fighters as surrogates.

The McDonnell F2H Banshee was used by the U.S. Navy from 1948 to 1959 and by the Royal Canadian Navy from 1955 until 1962. The Banshee was a development of the FH Phantom – it had straight wings, a single seat, and a pair of 3,150-lbf Westinghouse J34 turbojets buried in the wing roots. Armament consisted of four 20mm cannon in the nose with 150 rounds per gun. The empty weight was 9,865 pounds with a combat gross weight of 14,447 pounds. The airplane made its maiden flight on 11 January 1947 and the first operational aircraft were delivered in August 1948. Interestingly, a proposal to pit a series of F2H-1 intercepts against B-36s was made in August 1949, but this exercise apparently never took place. There was some concern on both sides at the senior level that rules of engagement, cheating, and bad luck might well result in an unwanted outcome. From a national perspective, the failure of the B-36 to get through would also have diminished the appearance of strength important to relations with the Soviet Union at that time. That said, Navy fighter squadron VF-51, flying Grumman F9F Panthers, was reportedly ordered to get gun camera photos of attacks on B-36s flying practice missions on the West Coast.[99]

The Navy Board of Inspection and Survey (BIS) report issued on 31 July 1951 provides the performance of the Banshee. Maximum speed at sea level was 577 mph, decreasing to 561 mph at 15,000 feet. The rate of climb at sea level was 7,000 feet per minute, diminishing to 1,690 feet per minute at 40,000 feet. The service ceiling was 47,800 feet and it took 22 minutes from brake release to reach that altitude at an average speed (mil power) of 259 mph. Maximum

Early U.S. Navy jet fighters also traded top speed for a larger wing that enabled them to operate more efficiently from aircraft carriers. Nevertheless, the McDonnell FH-1 Phantom (BuNo 111788), which entered service in August 1947, could not fly much above 40,000 feet. (Tommy Thomason Collection)

Each generation became more capable, and the McDonnell F2H-3 Banshee (BuNo 126344), a slightly later version of the airplane the Navy proposed using to intercept B-36s during tests, could exceed 47,000 feet altitude, although it took 22 minutes to do so. (Jim Hawkins Collection)

speed at the service ceiling was 506 mph, only 81 mph faster than the B-36 at the same altitude. The airplane had a maximum combat radius of 570 miles, but that was assuming a climb to only 25,000 feet; climbing to 45,000 feet reduced this to somewhat less than 400 miles with a maximum endurance of 90 minutes from takeoff to landing.[100]

The Navy found that the airplane had unsatisfactory stability and control characteristics while maneuvering above 30,000 feet, and the rate-of-roll was unsatisfactory above 460 mph (these deficiencies were mostly corrected on the subsequent F2H-2). The highest Mach number at which the airplane was tactically useful was found to be 0.80, mostly due to buffeting, neutral longitudinal stability, and high maneuvering control forces found at higher speeds. The tests noted, however, that the "F2H-1 has excellent climb and dive characteristics and is capable of sustained flight above 50,000 feet altitude," seemingly negating the Air Force's claim that the B-36 could fly higher than contemporary jet fighters.[101]

The mission profile of the B-36 assumed it would meet little or no opposition until it was within 500 miles of its target, when the bomber finally reached 45,000 feet. This logic, in retrospect, appears flawed, but may not have been. Moscow is approximately 500 miles inside the Soviet border when approaching from friendly (or at least neutral) territory to the north, the direction the bombers would be approaching from their Arctic routes. Approaching directly from the sea, without overflying other countries, Moscow is about 850 miles from the northern coast.

The Mikoyan-Gurevich MiG-15 (NATO reporting name Fagot) was specifically designed to intercept the Boeing B-29 Superfortress, and was evaluated in mock air-to-air combat trials against an interned ex-U.S. B-29 and a Soviet-built Tu-4 (Bull) copy of the bomber. The MiG-15 carried two 23mm cannon with 80 rounds per gun and a single 37mm cannon with 40 rounds. These weapons provided tremendous punch in the interceptor role, but the two

The pace of change was phenomenal during the B-36 era. By the time the bomber was retired, this McDonnell F-101A Voodoo (53-2426) had been used by Maj. Adrian E. Drew to set a new absolute world speed record of 1207.6 mph on 12 December 1957. (National Archives College Park Collection)

weapons had radically different ballistics, and some United Nations pilots in Korea reported the unnerving experience of 23mm shells passing over them while the 37mm shells flew under. Perhaps the MiG-15's greatest inadequacy as an interceptor was a lack of radar; the pilot relied on ground-controlled intercept directions to get him into the proximity of the bombers and his optical gunsight to aim.[102]

Assuming the MiG-15 roughly approximated the performance of the F2H-1, Soviet radar (or observers) needed to provide approximately 30 minutes notice to allow the fighters to climb to 45,000 feet, and that assumes the bomber was passing nearly over the fighter base. This means the radar would need to detect the bomber 175 to 225 miles from the base. This was likely possible, even given the primitive radar of the era, despite repeated Air Force claims that radar could not detect an aircraft flying at 40,000 feet.[103] However, at the time radar was useful

Kuybyshev-built MiG-15bis 235 Red (c/n 122035) during manufacturer's tests. The introduction of the MiG-15 was confirmation that the Soviets would soon be able to counter the American bomber force. (Yefim Gordon Archive)

The MiG-17 began arriving at operational units in October 1952 and provided the defense against bombers. Effective Soviet air-to-air missiles did not arrive until after the B-36 was retired. (National Museum of the United States Air Force Collection)

The replacement for the B-36 was the Boeing B-52 Stratofortress which was a good deal faster and flew just as high. Unfortunately, combat in Southeast Asia would prove the B-52 was vulnerable to the same fighter and ground-to-air missile threats that forced the retirement of the B-36. (U.S. Air Force)

primarily for establishing azimuth, not necessarily height. If the fighters were waiting at the wrong altitude, it might not be possible for them to correct (especially if the bombers were higher) while the bomber was still within range and before the fighters ran out of fuel. Even during the F2H-1 tests, the high-power climb to 45,000 feet severely limited the range available for interception if the initial vector proved deficient or the B-36 turned to evade the fighters.

Unsurprisingly, the evidence seems to support the contention that both sides (the bomber advocates and the fighter advocates) highlighted their strengths and downplayed their weaknesses. By 1952, jet fighters were undoubtedly capable of climbing to the operating altitudes used by the B-36, although their endurance and maneuverability at those altitudes are more in question. However, the fighter advocates usually ignored the limited endurance of the fighters along with the fact that success-

fully engaging the bombers required precise timing to ensure the fighters were in the right place, at the right altitude, at the right time; 50 miles, 5,000 feet, or 5 minutes were probably all deal breakers.

Then there is the question of exactly what the fighters could do once they found the bombers. In the beginning, the B-36 was a particularly well-armed aircraft, capable of unleashing an incredible amount of firepower against any fighter attacking it. In the days before air-to-air missiles – the American AIM-9 Sidewinder did not enter service until 1956 and the Soviet K-13/R-3S (AA-2 Atoll) until 1958 – the fighter would need to get close enough to use its single 37mm and dual 23mm cannon. The 37mm cannon had a greater range than the 20mm cannon on the B-36, although the 23mm cannon roughly approximated its American counterpart. The B-36 had a more sophisticated targeting system (although still not radar-directed except the tail turret) and much more ammunition (between 400 and 600 rounds per gun, depending on the location). Of course, all of that changed with the Featherweight airplanes since they lacked anything other than tail guns.

Although the B-36 was a large target, it was also a difficult target, being fairly maneuverable at altitude, well armored, and able to withstand substantial battle damage (two or three engines could be disabled and the airplane could continue to fly). Still, there is little doubt that a well-placed swarm of MiG-15s could take down at least some of the bombers. And by the mid-1950s, the improved MiG-17 (Fresco) was beginning to enter service equipped with radar and, within a couple of years, air-to-air missiles; this combination would certainly be able to defeat the B-36 in any reasonable scenario.

So the question of the vulnerability of the B-36 remains indeterminate and probably would have depended on the same factors that decide most combat: skill, determination, and more than a little luck. Fortunately for both sides, the matter never had to be put to a test.

The 1957 introduction of the Lavochkin S-75 (SA-2 Guideline) surface-to-air missile forever changed the way Americans looked at Soviet airspace. Given its ability against the B-52, there is little doubt the SA-2 could have killed a B-36. (U.S. Air Force)

The MiG-21 was introduced as the last B-36 was retired, and along with its Vympel K-13 Atoll air-to-air missiles, the MiG proved deadly to B-52s over Southeast Asia. (National Museum of the United States Air Force Collection)

Serial Numbers

Designation	Serial Number(s)	Qty	Contract No.	Notes
XB-36-CF	42-13570	1	W535-ac-22352	
YB-36-CF	42-13571	1	W535-ac-22352	To RB-36E. Originally reserved for Air Force Museum. Remains still exist on Walter Soplata's farm in Newbury, Ohio
XC-99-1-CO	43-52436	1	W535-ac-34454	In the collection of the National Museum of the United States Air Force
B-36A-1-CF	44-92004 – 44-92006	3	AF33-038-AC7	To RB-36E (except 44-92004, Static Test Article)
B-36A-5-CF	44-92007 – 44-92011	5	AF33-038-AC7	To RB-36E
B-36A-10-CF	44-92012 – 44-92017	6	AF33-038-AC7	To RB-36E
B-36A-15-CF	44-92018 – 44-92025	8	AF33-038-AC7	To RB-36E
B-36B-1-CF	44-92026 – 44-92037	12	AF33-038-AC7	To B-36D
B-36B-5-CF	44-92038 – 44-92049	12	AF33-038-AC7	To B-36D
B-36B-10-CF	44-92050 – 44-92064	15	AF33-038-AC7	To B-36D (92057 was jet prototype). Remains of 44-92051 at Socorro, New Mexico (formerly at Sandia Labs)
B-36B-15-CF	44-92065 – 44-92079	15	AF33-038-AC7	To B-36D (except 92075 and 92079, both crashed)
B-36B-20-CF	44-92080 – 44-92087	8	AF33-038-AC7	To B-36D
B-36D-1-CF	44-92095 – 44-92098	4	AF33-038-AC7	Ordered as B-36B; built as D-model
B-36	44-92099 – 44-92103	5	AF33-038-AC7	Cancelled to pay for abortive B-36C
B-36D-5-CF	49-2647 – 49-2654	8	AF33-039-2182	
B-36D-35-CF	49-2655	1	AF33-039-2182	Last B-36D delivered
B-36D-15-CF	49-2656 – 49-2657	2	AF33-039-2182	
B-36D-25-CF	49-2658 – 49-2663	6	AF33-039-2182	
B-36D-35-CF	49-2664 – 49-2668	5	AF33-039-2182	
RB-36D-1-CF	44-92088 – 44-92094	7	AF33-038-AC7	Ordered as B-36B; built as D-model
RB-36D-5-CF	49-2686	1	AF33-039-2182	
RB-36D-10-CF	49-2687 – 49-2693	7	AF33-039-2182	
RB-36D-15-CF	49-2694 – 49-2697	4	AF33-039-2182	
RB-36D-20-CF	49-2698 – 49-2702	5	AF33-039-2182	
B-36F-1-CF	49-2669 – 49-2675	7	AF33-039-2182	
B-36F-1-CF	49-2677	1	AF33-039-2182	
B-36F-5-CF	49-2678 – 49-2683	6	AF33-039-2182	
B-36F-5-CF	49-2685	1	AF33-039-2182	
B-36F-10-CF	50-1064 – 50-1073	10	AF33-039-2182	
B-36F-15-CF	50-1074 – 50-1082	9	AF33-039-2182	
RB-36F-1-CF	49-2703 – 49-2711	9	AF33-039-2182	
RB-36F-5-CF	49-2712 – 49-2721	10	AF33-039-2182	
RB-36F-10-CF	50-1098 – 50-1099	2	AF33-039-2182	
RB-36F-15-CF	50-1100 – 50-1102	3	AF33-039-2182	
YB-60-1-CF	49-2676	1	AF33-039-2182	Ordered as B-36F-1-CF
YB-60-2-CF	49-2684	1	AF33-039-2182	Ordered as B-36F-5-CF
B-36H-1-CF	50-1083 – 50-1091	9	AF33-039-2182	
B-36H-5-CF	50-1092 – 50-1097	6	AF33-039-2182	
B-36H-10-CF	51-5699 – 51-5705	7	AF33-039-2182	
B-36H-15-CF	51-5706 – 51-5711	6	AF33-039-2182	
B-36H-20-CF	51-5712 – 51-5717	6	AF33-039-2182	
B-36H-25-CF	51-5718 – 51-5723	6	AF33-039-2182	
B-36H-30-CF	51-5724 – 51-5729	6	AF33-039-2182	
B-36H-35-CF	51-5730 – 51-5735	6	AF33-039-2182	

Designation	Serial Number(s)	Qty	Contract No.	Notes
B-36H-40-CF	51-5736 – 51-5742	7	AF33-039-2182	
B-36H-45-CF	52-1343 – 51-1347	5	AF33-038-5793	
B-36H-50-CF	52-1348 – 51-1353	6	AF33-038-5793	
B-36H-55-CF	52-1354 – 51-1359	6	AF33-038-5793	
B-36H-60-CF	52-1360 – 51-1366	7	AF33-038-5793	
RB-36H-1-CF	50-1103 – 50-1105	3	AF33-039-2182	
RB-36H-5-CF	50-1106 – 50-1110	5	AF33-039-2182	
RB-36H-10-CF	51-5743 – 51-5747	5	AF33-039-2182	
RB-36H-15-CF	51-5748 – 51-5753	6	AF33-039-2182	
RB-36H-20-CF	51-5754 – 51-5756	3	AF33-039-2182	
RB-36H-20-CF	51-13717 – 51-13719	3	AF33-039-2182	
RB-36H-25-CF	51-13720 – 51-13725	6	AF33-039-2182	
RB-36H-30-CF	51-13726 – 51-13731	6	AF33-039-2182	51-13730 on display at Castle Air Museum, CA
RB-36H-35-CF	51-13732 – 51-13737	6	AF33-039-2182	
RB-36H-40-CF	51-13738 – 51-13741	4	AF33-039-2182	
RB-36H-45-CF	52-1367 – 52-1373	7	AF33-038-5793	
RB-36H-50-CF	52-1374 – 52-1380	7	AF33-038-5793	
RB-36H-55-CF	52-1381 – 52-1386	6	AF33-038-5793	
RB-36H-60-CF	52-1387 – 52-1392	6	AF33-038-5793	
B-36J-1-CF	52-2210 – 52-2221	12	AF33-038-5793	52-2217 on display at Strategic Air and Space Museum, Nebraska; 52-2220 on display at the National Museum of the United States Air Force
B-36J-5-CF	52-2222 – 52-2226	5	AF33-038-5793	
B-36J-5-CF	52-2812 – 52-2818	7	AF33-038-5793	
B-36J-10-CF	52-2819 – 52-2827	9	AF33-038-5793	52-2827 long displayed in Fort Worth; now displayed at the Pima Air & Space Museum, Arizona

Significant Modifications

Designation	Serial Number(s)			Notes
RB-36D-1-CF	44-92090			GRB-36D-III – FICON Carrier Aircraft
RB-36D-1-CF	44-92092			GRB-36D-III – FICON Carrier Aircraft
RB-36D-1-CF	44-92094			GRB-36D-III – FICON Carrier Aircraft
RB-36D-10-CF	49-2687			GRB-36D-III – FICON Carrier Aircraft
RB-36D-10-CF	49-2692			GRB-36D-III – FICON Carrier Aircraft
RB-36D-15-CF	49-2694			GRB-36D-III – FICON Carrier Aircraft
RB-36D-15-CF	49-2695			GRB-36D-III – FICON Carrier Aircraft
RB-36D-15-CF	49-2696			GRB-36D-III – FICON Carrier Aircraft
RB-36D-20-CF	49-2701			GRB-36D-III – FICON Carrier Aircraft
RB-36D-20-CF	49-2702			GRB-36D-III – FICON Carrier Aircraft
RB-36F-1-CF	49-2707			JRB-36F – FICON and Tom-Tom Test Aircraft (sometimes, incorrectly, called GRB-36F)
NB-36H-20-CF	51-5712			Nuclear Test Aircraft. Originally B-36H. Damaged in Carswell tornado. XB-36H on 11 March 1955. NB-36H on 6 June 1955.
DB-36H-1-CF	50-1085			Rascal Missile Launch Aircraft. Originally B-36H. DB-36H in July 1955.
DB-36H-15-CF	51-5706			RASCAL Missile Launch Aircraft. Also TANBO XIV Refueling Evaluation. Originally B-36H. DB-36H in January 1955. JDB-36H in February 1955. EDB-36H in August 1955. JDB-36H (again) in November 1955.
DB-36H-15-CF	51-5710			RASCAL Missile Launch Aircraft. Originally B-36H. EDB-36H in September 1952. JDB-36H in November 1955.

CHAPTER 3

THE BLEEDING EDGE
1940'S HIGH-TECHNOLOGY

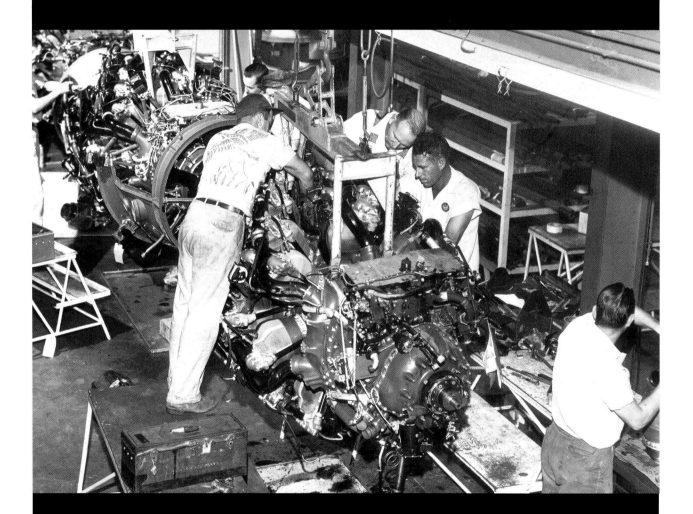

The Pratt & Whitney R-4360 Wasp Major was the most technically advanced and complex reciprocating aircraft engine produced in the United States in large numbers. Later versions of the turbo-supercharged engine developed 3,800 hp and an almost unbelievable 7,506 pound-feet of torque. (Lockheed Martin)

The B-36 certainly represented a crossroads. It was the last new piston-powered bomber developed by the Air Force (yes, the B-50 came later but was largely a derivative of the B-29); it was also one of the first operational bombers to use jet engines. Initial versions of the airplane used the tried-and-true Norden bombsight, while later versions fielded one of the first modern bombing-navigation systems. The B-36, along with the contemporary Northrop XB-35 Flying Wing, pioneered the 3,000-psi hydraulic system that would become an aviation standard until the Bell V-22 Osprey and Boeing 787 Dreamliner introduced 5,000-psi systems half a century later. The B-36, and XB-35, also pioneered the use of alternating-current instead of direct current.

As a weapon, the B-36 was the last operational bomber that had been designed without regard for nuclear weapons, and – after suitable modifications – was among the first bombers assigned to the nuclear deterrent role. It was the last bomber to have an extensive defensive armament system, and the first to have a self-defense decoy designed for it (although never used). The B-36 paved the way for air-launched missiles, and was the only operational heavier-than-air vehicle to carry parasite fighters.

Defensive Armament

The defensive armament installed on the B-36 represented the ultimate expression of the self-defense concepts that came into being during World War II. Although most later bombers (through the Douglas B-66 Destroyer) would continue to include tail armament, the B-36 was the last that made extensive use of turrets to provide complete hemispheric coverage.

After investigating several different concepts, Convair and the Air Force decided to use a variation of the General Electric remote control turret (RCT) that had found its first extensive use on the B-29, A-26, and P-61 during World War II. The basic B-36 defensive armament consisted of eight remotely controlled turrets, each equipped with two 20mm cannon. The nose and tail turret were non-retractable and provided limited coverage directly ahead and behind the aircraft. Six other turrets were located in pairs on the upper forward fuselage, upper rear fuselage, and lower rear fuselage. Another pair of turrets was originally intended in the lower forward fuselage, but were replaced by the APQ-24 radar antenna on production aircraft. Flush doors covered the retractable turrets when they were not in use. The turrets were designed to operate at altitudes up to 50,000 feet in temperatures between –50 degrees F and 122 degrees F.[1]

Each turret was operated electrically from a gunner's sighting position located apart from the turret it controlled. Unlike the sights in the B-29, which could be switched to control different turrets, each sight in the B-36 was dedicated to the turret closest to it. Four different types of sights were used on the B-36: yoke, pedestal, hemisphere, and tail.

The B-36 defensive armament was tested in the air and on the ground. Here, MSgt Ernest W. O'Brien (left) and SSgt John J. Mauldin inspect a B-36 turret and firing chamber designed and constructed by personnel of Weapons and Demonstration Branch at Eglin AFB, Florida, for the otherwise unidentified Project 6492. (Air Force Historical Research Agency Collection)

The yoke sights were located in the four upper sighting blisters and controlled the upper turrets. They could be rotated in elevation from 90 degrees above to 45 degrees below horizontal, and in azimuth from 110 degrees forward to 110 degrees aft of broadside. The gunner tracked the target by manipulating the entire sight.

The pedestal sights were located in the lower blisters and controlled the lower turrets. They could be rotated in elevation from 45 degrees above to 90 degrees below horizontal, and in azimuth from 105 degrees forward to 105 degrees aft of broadside. Again, the entire sight was manipulated to follow a target.

The yoke and pedestal sights had a small clear glass plate through which the gunner looked while aiming. When the sight was powered on, a view through the plate showed a center-aiming dot surrounded by a circle of dots. By setting the attacking fighter's wingspan with the target dimension knob and framing the target correctly, the gunner supplied the range of the attacking fighter to the computer. At the same time, the gunner was expected to track the fighter accurately and smoothly, providing azimuth, elevation, and relative speed (relative angular velocity) to the computer.

The B-36D (44-92054) armament test ship was used to test changes to the standard defensive system. Later in its career, the airplane was used to test systems for the B-58 and possibly other aircraft. (National Archives College Park Collection)

1.	UPPER FWD TURRETS (TWO 20 MM)	5.	NOSE TURRET (TWO 20 MM)	10.	UPPER AFT SIGHTING STATIONS
2.	UPPER FWD TURRET FIRE CONTROL	6.	UPPER FWD SIGHTING STATIONS	11.	TAIL TURRET (TWO 20 MM)
3.	NOSE TURRET FIRE CONTROL	7.	LOWER AFT TURRETS (TWO 20 MM EACH)	12.	AN/APG-3 UNIT
4.	NOSE SIGHTING STATION	8.	TAIL TURRET FIRE CONTROLS	13.	TAIL GUNNER STATION (AN/APG-3 CONTROLS)
		9.	LOWER AFT SIGHTING STATIONS	14.	UPPER AFT TURRETS (TWO 20 MM EACH)
				15.	AFT TURRET FIRE CONTROLS

RESTRICTED
AN O1-5EUC-2

Figure 4-299. Armament General Arrangement

The remote-controlled turret system fitted to the B-36 was the most extensive defensive armament ever to equip an operational aircraft. This is a B-36B, but all models except the Featherweight IIIs were generally similar. (U.S. Air Force)

A hemispheric sight offset to the right side of the nose controlled the nose turret. This was a horizontally mounted, double prism periscopic sight designed to give the gunner a full hemisphere of vision. The gunner, without changing his position, could see 90 degrees to the right or left of straight-ahead, as well as 90 degrees up or down from horizontal. The eyepiece of the sight was fixed, and the gunner controlled the turret by manipulating control handles immediately below the sight. The hemisphere sight operated on much the same principle as the yoke and pedestal sights, except the gunner sighted through a single eyepiece with one eye. A dummy eyepiece blocked the unused eye, and could be rotated to accommodate either right or left eye-dominant gunners.

The tail turret was aimed by a radar set that was controlled by a gunner facing rearward in the aft compartment (some RB-36s shifted the gunner facing the side of the aft cabin). The *SAC B-36 Gunnery Manual* boasted, "The gun-laying radar is highly developed and unbelievably accurate." Three different gun-laying radars were used; the APG-3 in the B-36B was quickly replaced by the APG-32 in the B-36D, while the APG-41 was used in the H- and J-models. The early sets used a single antenna, while the APG-41 used two antennas above the tail turret, although in some later aircraft these were covered by a single elongated radome.

Each of the turrets was equipped with two M24E2 or M24A1 20mm automatic cannon with a selectable rate of fire between 550 and 820 rounds per minute. Late in their

A nose turret was added to the B-36 based on wartime experience, forcing an early redesign of the entire nose section between the XB-36 and the A-model. Unlike the fuselage turrets, the nose turret was not retractable, although it was rather streamlined. (San Diego Air & Space Museum Collection)

Detailed photos of a B-36B were taken by Paramount Studios while preparing for the making of movie Strategic Air Command. This is the gun sight for the nose turret, which was located on the right side of the nose compartment. (Walt Jeffries Collection via Mike Machat Collection)

Details of the M24A1 20-mm cannon in the aft upper turrets with the covers removed. At 600 rounds per minute, these provided considerable firepower. The cannon were heated, but early airplanes still suffered from cold-related problems. (U.S. Air Force)

The upper forward turrets of an RB-36 are loaded at Rapid City AFB. Note that several panels are removed from each turret; these will be replaced after the turrets are readied for flight. (Ed Griemsmann via the Fred Johnsen Collection)

careers, the rate of fire was fixed at 700 rounds per minute for the tail guns and 600 for all others. Each gun weighed 100 pounds, was 77.7 inches long (52.5 inches of this was the barrel), and had a muzzle velocity of 2,730 feet per second. The nose turret had 800 rounds (400 per box), while all other turrets had 1,200 rounds (600 per box).

Four different types of 20mm ammunition were approved for use on the B-36: M97 high-explosive incendiary, M96 incendiary, AP1 armor-piercing incendiary, and AP-T armor piercing with tracer. An M95 target practice round was also available, as was a "drill" round which was used to practice loading and handling.

The upper and lower fuselage turrets were electrically retractable to reduce drag, but could also be extended or retracted manually by means of a handcrank. A flush panel that slid down the outside of the fuselage when opened covered each turret. The turrets were stowed in unpressurized compartments that could be entered in flight if required, and also served as a means of emergency escape during ground accidents (explaining why many photos show the turret doors open during taxi). The retractable turrets were equipped with fire interrupters to prevent self-inflicted damage to the propellers, wings, or tail, and were also equipped with contour followers to prevent the guns from striking the aircraft, or pointing at parts of the aircraft housing personnel.

The Strategic Air Command determined that a three-ship "V" formation provided the maximum defensive

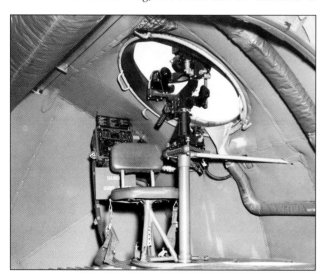

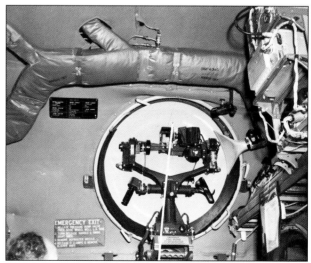

Paramount photos of the left upper aft sight (left) and left lower aft sight. Each sight controlled a single turret, and there was a matching set of sights for the right turrets; this was different than the B-29 and P-61 where a sight could control multiple turrets. In addition to the sight, the system used a thyratron controller, a signal system, an input resolver, and an analog computer. The operation of all the sights was essentially the same. The system was very advanced for its time, and initially experienced a considerable number of problems. Eventually, General Electric got the sophisticated system to work well. (Walt Jeffries Collection via Mike Machat Collection)

The B-36H introduced a dual APG-41 radar system that had two radomes; earlier aircraft with the APG-3 and APG-32 had only a single radome. Very late airplanes still had two antennas but used a single enlongated radome. Like the other turrets, the tail turret used two 20-m cannon. (U.S. Air Force)

The tail turret from inside the fuselage looking aft. The dual ammunition boxes were on each side of the fuselage just forward of bulkhead 17.0 (upper left corner) and had a long feed back to the cannon in the tail turret. This was the only turret that remained on the Featherweight III airplanes. (U.S. Air Force)

firepower. In this formation, the aircraft in the lead trained all of its turrets forward (the lower and upper aft turrets swiveled completely forward to provide upward and downward coverage). The aircraft on each side trained all of its turrets to that particular side. The exception, of course, was the tail turret that always faced aft. This plan left no area covered by less than two turrets (four cannon), and simplified coordination between the gunners. This formation was called HOME TOWN, and was the standard attack formation at altitudes under 35,000 feet.

Above 35,000 feet, the importance of beam attacks was lessened since few contemporary fighters could keep up with the B-36 at high altitudes. Consequently, the HOME TOWN areas of search and fire were modified to provide more protection to the rear. This TAIL HEAVY formation

primarily involved training the lower aft turrets of all aircraft to the rear (and downward). At these altitudes, it was expected that most attacks would come from below and rearward, although there was a chance of a fighter climbing to altitude and waiting for the bombers directly ahead.

Despite the tremendous effort expended on its development, the defensive armament system was never truly satisfactory and was ultimately removed from the Featherweight III airplanes.[2]

Decoys

The use of the McDonnell ADM-20B (formerly GAM-72) Quail decoy missile aboard the B-52 during the 1960s was not a new idea. On 16 August 1954 the Air Force

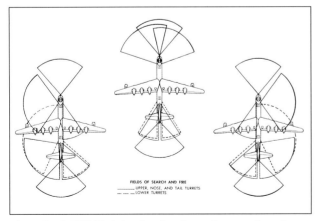

The HOME TOWN defensive fire formation was based on a three-ship formation with each aircraft covering a specific quadrant. The tactic was intended to provide additional firepower to the rear where attacks were expected. (U.S. Air Force)

The GAM-71 Buck Duck decoy was initially developed using Convair funds, but the Air Force subsequently funded the development program. This is a test unit that will be dropped from a B-29. Note the folding wings. (Lockheed Martin)

Cold War Peacemaker

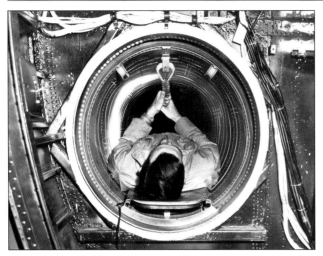

Like the B-29 before it, the B-36 had a "communications tube" that allowed crewmembers to transit between the forward and aft pressurized compartments. The pressurized tool ran along the lower left side of all four bomb bays and included a movable cart to make the transit easier. A crewmember laid on his back and pulled himself through the tube using a rope attached to the ceiling. These photos show JD McEachern climbing from the opening in the aft compartment. Handles were provided on the bulkhead above the opening to assist crewmembers climbing into and out of the tube. (National Archives College Park Collection)

awarded Convair a contract to develop the GAM-71 Buck Duck decoy for the B-36. Convair had been investigating the concept using company funds for several years prior to the contract, going so far as to manufacture a production-representative prototype. The decoy was conceptually identical to the later Quail – a small missile carried in the bomb bay and launched during the final target penetration. The Buck Duck was designed to accurately simulate the radar return of a B-36, and it was initially expected that one aircraft per formation would carry seven decoys, while the other aircraft carried bombs. There was, however, no reason that each bomber could not carry a couple of decoys in one bomb bay and still carry bombs in the others.[3]

Although not terribly challenging from a technical perspective, the Buck Duck program ran into delays due

to funding constraints and other priorities at Convair. The first production decoy was completed on 24 November 1954 and an engineering inspection was held on 2–3 December 1954. Although a dozen serial numbers (55-3490/3501) had been allocated, only three additional decoys were manufactured. A couple of months later than expected, the Buck Duck program began captive-carry flights under the wing of a B-29 on 14 February 1955, and the first of at least seven glide flights from the same B-29 were conducted a month later. For reasons that could not be ascertained – but probably relating to the imminent B-36 phase-out – the Buck Duck program was cancelled in January 1956. No record could be found indicating that the vehicle had ever flown a powered flight, or been carried by a B-36.[4]

A photo deep in the tube (above) shows it was not lit, although it did have a couple of small windows that allowed a view into the bomb bays. At right is the opening into the forward compartment. (National Archives College Park Collection)

Access to the R-4360s was available from several areas, including panels in the air intakes (shown above), and a catwalk that ran through the wing and allowed minor maintenance while the airplane was in flight. Given the amount of attention the massive piston engines required, all of this was probably a good thing. (National Archives College Park Collection)

The B-36 was a popular attraction at air shows, such as the one at Idlewild Airport that this young boy is attending. The airport officially opened on 31 July 1948 on the first day of a nine-day International Air Exposition that included this B-36A (44-92015). The opening ceremonies of the "New York International Airport" were presided over by President Harry S. Truman and included a flyover of 1,400 military aircraft including an impressive three-ship formation of B-36s. The airport, known colloquially as "Idlewild," was renamed the John F. Kennedy International Airport in December 1963. The sign contains some interesting facts about the bomber, and highlights that Gen. George C. Kenny was the commander of the Strategic Air Command. (National Archives College Park Collection)

Naturally, Buck Duck was a small vehicle, with an overall length of 13 feet and a wingspan of 14 feet. The wings folded to produce a package only 5 feet wide. The launch weight was just 1,550 pounds. Most records indicate that a single XLR85 rocket engine produced 900-lbf and could propel the decoy to Mach .55 and a range of 230 miles. There are reports, however, that the decoy used a small turbojet engine instead. Radar reflectors were fitted around the Buck Duck in order to approximate the radar return of the big bomber. Two Buck Ducks could be carried in each bomb bay except No. 3, which could only carry a single decoy due to the wing spar.[5]

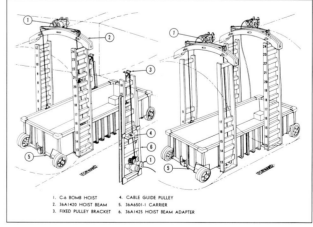

When deploying overseas, the B-36 could carry many of its own tools and supplies in these cargo carriers. A total of seven carriers could be carried in the bomb bays (two in each except No. 2). Many of the early demonstration flights flown by the B-36As used the cargo carriers to load zinc bars that were used to simulate the armament and other systems that were not installed on the A-models. Although used extensively on the early models, the carriers found less use once heavy airlift became available. (Lockheed Martin)

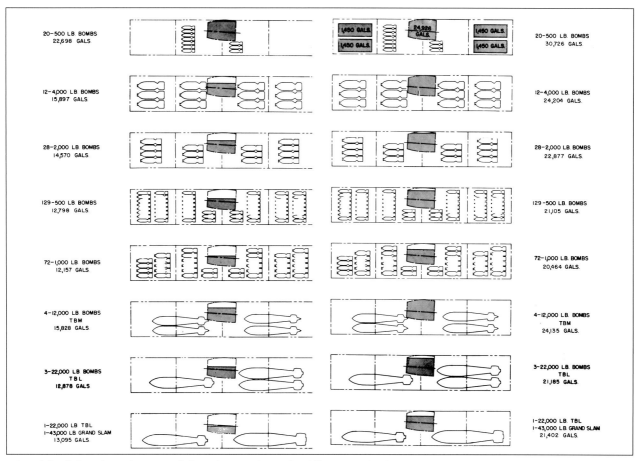

A bomb load chart from the B-36B (left) and B-36J shows the difference in load-carrying ability between the two models. The main difference is in fuel load, which is illustrated by the shaded area of the wing fuel tank shown between bomb bay Nos. 2 and 3, although the words to the side of the chart are easier to read. Many other combinations were possible. (U.S. Air Force

Conventional Bombs

Interestingly, the *SAC B-36 Gunnery Manual* contained a fairly large chapter on bombs and bombing equipment. This was because "as a gunner, you have duties and responsibilities not directly concerned with gunnery … you will assist [the bombardier] in the loading, fuzing, and arming of all bombs."[6]

Bomber versions of the B-36 were equipped with four large bomb bays. On the XB-36, the aft bomb bay (No. 4) was separated from the three forward bays by the aft gun turrets. Beginning with the YB-36, the four bomb bays were together. This arrangement allowed bomb bays 1–2 and 3–4 to be combined to carry large bombs.

The B-36A and B-36B used electrically controlled, cable-operated doors that slid in tracks up the side of the lower fuselage. The doors on bomb bay Nos. 1 and 4 were single-piece units that slid up the left side of the fuselage. The two middle bomb bays had doors split down the centerline and slid up both sides of the fuselage – the location of the wing prevented using a single-piece design. Each door was 16.1 feet long. The doors were slow to operate,

tended to stick in the extremely cold temperatures at 40,000 feet, and created undesirable drag at a time when speed was of the essence. Beginning with the B-36D, the aircraft were equipped with hydraulically actuated "snap-action" doors that opened in approximately 2 seconds. There were two sets of 32.375-foot-long doors, one set covering the combined bomb bay Nos. 1 and 2, and the other set covering Nos. 3 and 4. The B-36B models were retrofitted with the new doors as they became B-36Ds.

Initially, the RB-36s were not configured to carry bombs, only photo flash bombs in bomb bay No. 2 and an auxiliary fuel tank in bomb bay No. 3. Reconnaissance versions installed a pressurized compartment in the space previously used by bomb bay No. 1 that housed up to 14 cameras, a darkroom that allowed film cartridges to be reloaded, and the crew to operate and maintain the equipment. A special pallet that contained various ferret ECM equipment was carried in the area that was normally used by bomb bay No. 4, and was easily identified by the three large radomes protruding below the same area. Later this equipment was moved into the aft fuselage and the radomes were placed under the lower aft fuselage, allowing bomb bay No. 4 to be configured to carry a nuclear weapon. The bomb bay doors were also changed to more closely match the bomber models – Nos. 3 and 4 were covered by a single set of new 32.375-foot long doors, while bomb bay No. 2 was covered by a set of 16-foot doors that were modified from the original set of doors. Previously, bomb bays Nos. 2 and 3 had been covered by a single set of doors that were 33.66 feet long.

Thirty-six removable bomb racks of 15 different types were furnished with each bomber. The racks and associated equipment were designed to accommodate conventional bombs weighing 500, 1,000, 1,600, 2,000, 4,000, 12,000, 22,000, or 43,000 pounds. In addition, bombs weighing 100, 115, 125, 250, 325, or 350 pounds could be carried at the 500-pound stations. When the three largest bomb sizes were carried, it was necessary to combine two adjacent bomb bays. The lower portion of the bomb bay No. 1 aft bulkhead and the bomb bay No. 2 forward bulkhead (called bulkhead 6.0) could be swung to the side of the fuselage when the 12,000-, 22,000-, or 43,000-pound bombs were being loaded and released. The same was true for the bulkhead (8.0) between bomb bay Nos. 3 and 4, although

due to the 72,000-pound load limitation, only a single 43,000-pound bomb could be carried by the A-model.

The B-36 was capable of carrying 67 different types of conventional, incendiary, cluster, and chemical bombs, as well as several types of mines. Because of electrical fuzing constraints, only a single type of bomb could be carried in each bomb bay, although each bay could carry different types if necessary. The end bomb bays (Nos. 1 and 4) could carry a maximum of thirty-eight 500-pound bombs, nineteen 1,000-pound bombs, eight 2,000-pound bombs, or three 4,000-pound bombs. The two middle bomb bays (Nos. 2 and 3) were not as tall as the other two due to the wing carry-through structure, and could carry twenty-eight 500-pound bombs, sixteen 1,000-pound bombs, six 2,000-pound bombs, or three 4,000-pound bombs. Alternately, two 12,000-pound bombs, or a single 22,000-pound or 43,000-pound bomb could be carried in the combined bay 1–2 and bay 3–4. Bombs weighing up to 4,000 pounds each were carried on fifteen different types of removable bomb racks mounted vertically along the sides of the bomb bay in the traditional style. Larger bombs used special slings instead of conventional suspension lugs and shackles.[7]

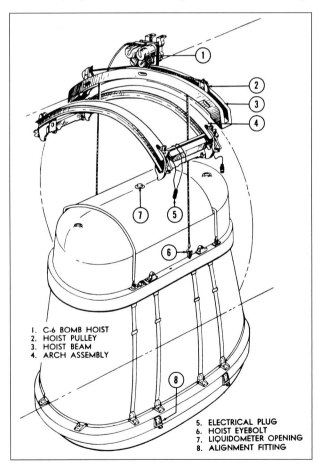

1. C-6 BOMB HOIST
2. HOIST PULLEY
3. HOIST BEAM
4. ARCH ASSEMBLY
5. ELECTRICAL PLUG
6. HOIST EYEBOLT
7. LIQUIDOMETER OPENING
8. ALIGNMENT FITTING

Bomb bay No. 3 could carry a 3,000-gallon auxiliary fuel tank in all aircraft, and bomb bay No. 2 could carry one in some aircraft. The tank was little more than a shell with a rubber fuel cell inside. It could be jettisoned in flight. (U.S. Air Force)

The Bell VB-13 Tarzon was an early attempt at a guided bomb. The first 18 B-36Bs were equipped to carry two Tarzons each, with a special guidance position in the aft compartment and another at the normal bombardier's station. (Jay Miller Collection)

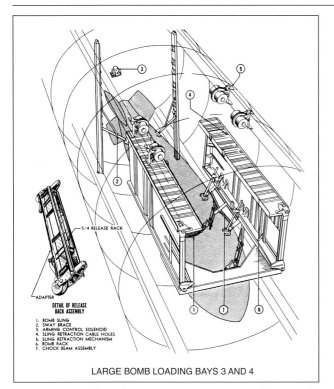

DETAIL OF RELEASE
RACK ASSEMBLY
1. BOMB SLING
2. SWAY BRACE
3. ARMING CONTROL SOLENOID
4. SLING RETRACTION CABLE HOLES
5. SLING RETRACTION MECHANISM
6. BOMB RACK
7. CHOCK BEAM ASSEMBLY

LARGE BOMB LOADING BAYS 3 AND 4

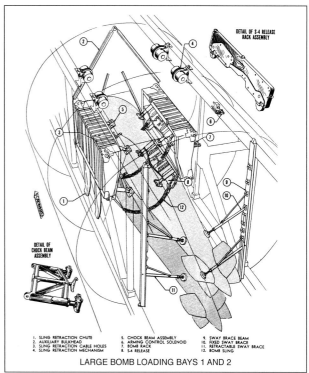

1. SLING RETRACTION CHUTE
2. AUXILIARY BULKHEAD
3. SLING RETRACTION CABLE HOLES
4. SLING RETRACTION MECHANISM
5. CHOCK BEAM ASSEMBLY
6. ARMING CONTROL SOLENOID
7. BOMB RACK
8. S-4 RELEASE
9. SWAY BRACE BEAM
10. FIXED SWAY BRACE
11. RETRACTABLE SWAY BRACE
12. BOMB SLING

LARGE BOMB LOADING BAYS 1 AND 2

Two illustrations from the SAC B-36 Gunnery Manual showing how a single 43,000-pound T-12 bomb (left) or two 22,000-pound T-14 Grand Slam bombs were loaded in the bomb bays. In either case, a portion of the bulkhead that separated bomb bays 1-2 or 3-4 had to be removed to provide clearance for the large weapon. The 43,000-pound bomb was 26.85 feet long and 4.5 feet in diameter. If two were carried, the forward bomb had to be released first to prevent a radical nose-down pitching moment. (U.S. Air Force)

An early attempt at a precision-guided weapon was the Bell VB-13 Tarzon. This was essentially a British 12,000-pound "Tall Boy" bomb fitted with forward and rear shrouds with control surfaces that allowed the bomb to be guided to its target. The 21-foot-long, 54-inch-diameter, free-falling weapon was tracked visually by means of a colored flare in its tail and guided to its target via an ARW-38 radio link with the aircraft that dropped it. Development of the bomb had begun during World War II, but had been halted after V-J Day. The program was resurrected briefly in 1950, and 18 early B-36Bs (44-92045/92062) were equipped to carry two Tarzons each, although it is unclear how often the weapon was actually dropped from the aircraft. Interestingly, the provisions for carrying and controlling the bombs were retained when the aircraft were converted to B-36Ds. Although the bombs did not see action with the B-36, approximately 30 Tarzons were dropped from B-29s during the Korean conflict, with eight of them destroying or damaging the bridges they were aimed at.

The maximum 86,000-pound bomb load carried by later B-36s is the heaviest ever carried by an American bomber. Even the "big belly" B-52Ds used during Vietnam could only carry 60,000 pounds (twenty-four 750-pound and eighty-four 500-pound), while the B-1B only carries 42,000 pounds (eighty-four 500-pound) of bombs (although its theoretical load limit is 75,000 pounds). As a point of reference, one of the most respected interdiction aircraft in the current Air Force inventory is the F-15E Strike Eagle. Fully loaded, with a maximum fuel and weapon load, the F-15E weighs 86,000 pounds – the B-36 could carry that amount of bombs.

Instead of weapons, bomb bay No. 3 could carry a 3,000-gallon auxiliary fuel tank in all aircraft, and bomb bay No. 2 could carry one in selected aircraft.[8] Several sources report that all four bomb bays in some aircraft could carry these fuel tanks, but this could not be confirmed through official sources.[9] Early auxiliary tanks were interesting in that they were basically metal frames with a suspended fuel-proof "rubberized" canvas bag that contained the fuel.[10] The Firestone Tire and Rubber Company manufactured the fuel cell. A later version of the fuel cell, manufactured by Goodyear, consisted of a rubber bladder inside a metal shell.

In a rather unique concept to assist the B-36 in deployments, both the ground power carts and a special cargo carrier were designed to be loaded into the bomb bays. Two cargo carriers were supplied by Convair with each aircraft, complete with wheels and tow bars to facilitate ground handling. Each cargo carrier could carry up to 14,000 pounds of loose items. Bomb bay Nos. 1 and 4 could each carry two of the cargo carriers (stacked on top of each other), while the middle two bomb bays could each carry a single carrier.[11]

At the end of World War II, the only aircraft capable of carrying atomic weapons were a handful of Silverplate B-29s and 32 SADDLE TREE airplanes. All could carry the 10-foot-long Mark III "Fat Man" or its Mk 4 replacement. (Jim Hawkins Collection)

The Boeing B-50, and the stillborn B-54, were derivatives of the B-29 and were too small to carry the first generation of thermonuclear weapons, although all were capable of deploying atomic weapons. (U.S. Air Force)

Atomic Bombs

Interestingly, the B-36 was not designed to carry atomic bombs, and the first 41 aircraft were not capable of doing so as delivered from the factory. But then, at the time no other bomber had been so designed either, and in 1946 only a few specially modified Silverplate B-29s were capable of carrying the new atomic devices. By the end of 1947, the Air Force had only 32 B-29s modified under Project SADDLE TREE available to carry atomic weapons. Many of these were described as "quite weary" after their wartime service, and all were assigned to the 509th Bombardment Group. Even more frustrating was a lack of training, mainly due to tight security requirements from the organizations that controlled the bombs.[12] At the beginning of 1948, only six crews were fully qualified to drop the atomic bomb, although sufficient partially trained personnel existed to assemble another 14 crews if necessary. Other complications included the fact that no air base in the world had all the equipment on hand necessary to assemble and load an atomic bomb, and there were only two qualified bomb assembly teams in the country.[13]

Part of the reason the Northrop flying wings did not garner more support within the Air Force was that the XB-35 had bomb bays too shallow to accommodate the 5-foot diameter, 10-foot-long Mk III "Fat Man" or its Mk 4 replacement.[14] The bombs had to be carried semi-submerged, resulting in a 6-percent loss in top speed and a 10-percent loss in combat range. The B-29 (and the B-50) had bomb bays that could only accommodate weapons

A good balancing act, considering the T-12 bomb weighed 43,000 pounds. Each of the ten B-2 "Hydraulic Bomb Lift, Mobile" had a nominal 50,000-pound capacity, although at least two were modified to handle 55,000-pound hydrogen bombs. (Air Force Historical Research Agency)

A 43,000-pound T-12 bomb on display at the Carswell open house in May 1950. This demolition bomb had an extremely thick nose section designed to penetrate hardened targets. Only a handful of these weapons were manufactured, and the B-36 was their only delivery vehicle. (Jack Kerr)

Whether the Northrop B-35 Flying Wing was truly a competitor to the B-36 has always been the subject of debate. The available documentation shows the Air Force considered having Convair produce the B-35 (the service felt Northrop's production capabilities were lacking for such a large program), but in any event, only a handful of the flying wings were built before the program was unceremoniously ended and the airframes destroyed. Perhaps the most serious shortcoming of the B-35, and its all-jet B-49 derivative, was that the bomb bays were too small to carry the first generation of thermonuclear weapons; a fact that guaranteed that B-36 production would continue. (Garry R. Pape Collection via the Gerald H. Balzer Collection)

shorter than 12 feet long, eliminating carriage of bombs such as the 15-foot-long Mk 7. The B-36 had no such limitations.

Part of the problem during the late 1940s was that weapons developers would not tell the Air Force the physical characteristics of their weapons until they were in production, and even then the data was highly classified. The designers provided "preliminary data" that was often substantially different from the weapon that finally emerged. This had been most evident on the North American B-45 program where the final weapon would not fit in the bomb bay of the light bomber. Modifications to aircraft bomb bays to accommodate atomic weapons were also considered "restricted" under the Atomic Energy Act of 1946. This was reiterated in May 1947 when the Atomic Energy Commission (AEC) stated "…any aircraft modification which would allow a reasonably accurate estimate of size, weight, or shape of the bomb … must continue to be Restricted Data." This meant that you had to be cleared in order to simply look

inside an empty bomb bay (many officials tried to enforce this restriction years after it had been lifted). The Air Force finally convinced the AEC that an empty bomb bay should be unclassified until the suspension lugs and sway braces were installed, since little information could be gained from the geometric shape of most bomb bays.[15]

Given this situation, it is unsurprising that early nuclear weapons were designed without much regard to the aircraft that might carry them. Each bomb had a different center of gravity, sometimes radically different shapes, and required different suspension equipment and sway braces. This greatly complicated the design of aircraft bomb bays. The problem is exemplified by the situation surrounding the Mk 6 weapon. As early as August 1949 the Air Force had requested that Sandia Laboratory supply drawings of the weapon to allow the Air Force to begin planning for its introduction to the inventory. Sandia refused, indicating they would turn over the data after the bomb design had been frozen for production (something

The B-Reactor at Hanford, Washington, was the first large-scale plutonium production facility. Commissioned by the Manhattan Engineering District during World War II, the reactor was designed and built by DuPont based on experimental designs tested by Enrico Fermi at the University of Chicago. The graphite-moderated and water-cooled reactor generated the equivalent of 230 megawatts. The B-Reactor was one of three reactors – along with the D and F reactors – built about six miles apart on the south bank of the Columbia River. The B-Reactor started production in September 1944, the D-Reactor in December 1944, and the F-Reactor in February, 1945. The plutonium for the Trinity device, tested at Los Alamos in New Mexico, and the Mk III "Fat Man" bomb dropped on Nagasaki was created in the B, D, and F reactors. The B-Reactor was decommissioned in February 1968, and it was designated a National Historic Landmark on 25 August 2008. (National Archives College park Collection)

The Mk III "Fat Man" atomic bomb dropped on Nagasaki was 10.6 feet long, 5 feet in diameter, and weighed 10,200 pounds. The plutonium device produced the explosive equivalent of 21,000 pounds of TNT (21 kilotons). The first "stockpiled" weapon was the very similar Mk 4 that could be configured to yield 1, 3.5, 8, 14, 21, 22, or 31 kilotons. (U.S. Air Force)

The Mk 17 was the first mass-produced thermonuclear weapon deployed by the United States. It was 25 feet long, 5 feet in diameter, weighed 42,000 pounds, and had a yield of 15 megatons. Total production was 200 Mk 17s and 105 similar Mk 24s. To put this in perspective, it would take a train 180 miles long to carry one million tons (a megaton) of TNT! (U.S. Air Force)

that did not occur until mid-1951). The Air Force commented that Sandia "consistently ignored our requirements and had used dimensions which required redesigning of handling, loading, and carrying equipment."

The B-36 was impacted less by these problems than most aircraft simply because it was essentially a large tube – a very large tube. In the end it could be modified relatively easily to carry almost any size or shape bomb the designers could dream up. It was the only aircraft capable of carrying the monstrous 25-foot-long, 42,000-pound Mk 17 thermonuclear weapon.[16]

Despite a great deal of rhetoric, the components required to enable a bomber to carry early atomic weapons were relatively simple. A special bomb suspension system was installed, along with the appropriate sway braces and suspension lugs. Electronic "T-boxes" controlled, tested, and monitored the bomb during flight, while arming controls and a method to insert the "capsule" that allowed the bomb to go critical were also required.

Concurrently with the weapons programs, Project GEM (global electronics modernization) provided worldwide navigation equipment and cold weather modifications

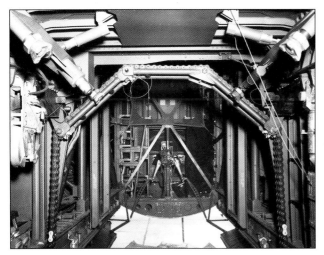

A nuclear-equipped bomb bay showing the universal bomb suspension (UBS) system. This was one of the B-36Hs based at Kirtland AFB in 1955. The UBS could accommodate weapons 15-60 inches in diameter and 128 inches long. (National Archives College Park Collection)

The same B-36H shows its "Special Bomb Rack Panel" that controlled the release of nuclear weapons. This airplane was configured to carry nuclear weapons in bomb bays No. 1 and No. 4 – other airplanes could carry them in all four bomb bays. (National Archives College Park Collection)

R-4360

The Pratt & Whitney R-4360 Wasp Major engine was used to power the B-36, B/KB-50, C/KC-97, C-119, and C-124 aircraft, among others. It represents the most powerful and complex reciprocating aircraft engine produced in large numbers in the United States. The passing of the KC-97 from the Air Force inventory in the late 1970s marked the closing of the era of both the large piston and turbo-supercharger within the Air Force.[22]

The R-4360 was a 28-cylinder, four-row radial, air-cooled engine with a gear-driven supercharger and two exhaust-driven turbo-superchargers.[23] As the name suggests, the engine displaced 4,360 cubic inches (71.5 liters), and each cylinder had a 5.75-inch bore and 6.00-inch stroke (155.7 cubic inches per cylinder). The engine had a compression ratio of 6.7:1 in most applications. The R-4360 was 96.5 inches long, 55.0 inches in diameter, and weighed 3,670 pounds (the weight and dimensions are for the basic engine only, without the turbochargers or reduction gears). The engine used 2,500 pounds of 115/145-grade aviation fuel and 25,000 pounds of air per hour at maximum output.[24]

The engine was rated at 3,500 hp (3,000 in early -25 engines; 3,800 in late -53 units), but what is frequently overlooked is its torque rating. At 1,000 rpm, each engine provided 840-pound-feet of torque – by 3,000 rpm this had increased to a staggering 7,506 pound-feet, measured at the crankshaft. Because of the gearing selected, this was increased to more than 20,000 pound-feet at the propeller shaft.

At 20,000 feet, without the use of turbo-supercharging, the R-4360-41 would have had an output of only 1,000 hp; with its use the power output improved to 3,500 hp. The R-4360 used two different supercharging techniques. An "internal supercharger" was mounted in the airstream immediately behind the carburetor and before the cylinders. This impeller was driven by the crankshaft gear train at a fixed ratio. At takeoff, the impeller was turning at 17,000 rpm, with a tip speed of nearly 700 mph. The use of this supercharger was somewhat of a trade-off – although it doubled of the intake pressure (from 30 inches to more than 60 inches), it also added a lot of heat to the intake charge, which is generally undesirable. It was felt that the benefits outweighed the drawbacks. Interestingly, it took 435 hp to drive the supercharger. It was worth it – the supercharger increased the power output by 1,930 hp.

Each engine was also provided with two General Electric Model B-1 exhaust-driven turbo-superchargers arranged in parallel. The primary purpose of the turbos was not to increase the power rating of the engine.

Pratt & Whitney R-4360 engine assemblies ready for installation on the B-36 assembly line. The engine and cowling assembly was known as the "power egg" by factory workers. This photo makes the engine look deceptively small – at 8 feet long and almsot 5 feet in diamter, it was not. (Consolidated)

P. Elder and J. L. Goldsmith work on one of the first Ford-produced R-4360 engines for the B-36 in March 1952. In all, Ford and Pratt & Whitney produced 18,697 engines for the B-36, B-50, Boeing C-97 Stratofreighter, and Fairchild C-119 Flying Boxcar. (National Archives College Park Collection)

Instead, they allowed the sea-level power rating to be maintained up to 35,000 feet, with a gradual degradation at altitudes above that. At sea level, the turbos had the theoretical ability to provide 300 inches of manifold pressure, something that obviously could not be allowed to happen. Automatic controls kept the turbos from overcharging the system at any given altitude. Each turbocharger was equipped with an intercooler to remove waste heat from the air.[25]

Heat rejection was a major concern. The design of the cylinders and the use of forged aluminum alloy for the heads and barrel muffs permitted the machining of closely spaced deep fins that provided a 30-percent increase in exposed fin area over that previously available from cast heads. Cooling air was inducted at the leading edge of the wing and was boosted by a large engine-cooling fan before being routed by a series of baffles around the engine. Positioning an "air plug" located between the trailing edge of the nacelle and the propeller controlled the amount of cooling air admitted to the nacelle. These air plugs performed the same function as the cowl flaps on tractor installations.[26]

Even the Curtiss-Wright constant-speed, full-feathering, reversible propellers on the B-36 were unique. Their sheer size, and the fast rate-of-pitch change required, eliminated the possibility of using the traditional electric motor to control the variable pitch. Instead, the designers developed a system that used part of the power being transmitted via the propeller shaft. Pitch change was accomplished by transmitting power taken from the rotating propeller shaft through a series of gears and four clutch mechanisms. Hydraulic pressure was generated by a self-contained oil pump, and used by either the clutch or the brake on each blade, as

directed via electrical control signals from the cockpit. Engine exhaust was directed through the propeller hub to the hollow blades to prevent ice buildup.

The B-36's original propeller blades had structural limitations that resulted in flight restrictions that hampered performance. There had also been constant concerns over propeller-induced vibrations and buffeting against the fuselage sides and the horizontal stabilizer. This had been recognized even before the first flight of the XB-36, leading to investigations of using 16-foot, four-bladed propellers instead of the normal 19-foot, three-bladed units. Similar propellers had been test-fitted on the XB-36 prior to its rollout, and had been flight tested on a B-36B (44-92057) during 1950. Since the B-36 was capable of cruising with some of the engines shut down, many pilots opted to shut down the inboard engines and feather the propellers, easing the vibration on the fuselage and buffeting on the stabilizer. The evaluations of the four-bladed propeller were apparently inconclusive, and the decision was made to develop a new three-bladed unit instead.

A revised blade, made by a special flash-welding process, had a slightly broader chord and less pitch to minimize buffeting. The new propeller could be used freely except for landing and takeoff. Convair called the new unit a "high-altitude propeller." The obvious external difference was the use of square blade tips instead of the original rounded tips. This blade weighed an extra 20 pounds (1,170 pounds each), but its greater efficiency promised to compensate for the small loss in aircraft range. A batch of 1,175 new blades was ordered for installation on B-36Hs on the production line. Additional blades were subsequently ordered and retrofitted to most earlier aircraft, including the XC-99.[27]

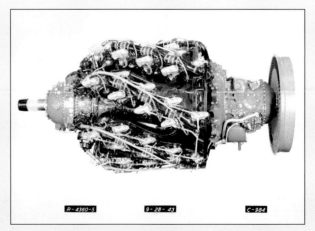

The engine was mounted at the back of the nacelle, with a long duct from the wing leading edge to the engine face. The cooling fan in front of the engine ducted air across the cylinders. Finding enough air at high altitude proved to be a problem, and many engines overheated at full power. (U.S. Air Force)

The first Pratt & Whitney R-4360-5 Wasp Major. This was a hand-tooled semi-production engine, photographed on 28 September 1943. Note the large fan (at right) that pulled cooling air across the cylinders. Although fairly reliable, the engine was maintenance intensive. (Pratt & Whitney via Roger Cripliver)

that allowed bombers to operate over and around the Arctic Circle. Project SADDLE TREE was the first effort to convert B-29s and B-36s to carry the Mk III "Fat Man" type atomic bomb, the weapon being produced immediately after the war. Primarily this involved installing the appropriate suspension equipment and the T-Boxes. Between May 1947 and June 1948, the first 18 B-36Bs were modified to the SADDLE TREE configuration while the last 54 B-models came off the production line with most of the changes already in place. By the end of 1950, the Strategic Air Command had 52 B-36s equipped with the GEM/SADDLE TREE modifications, although at any given time many of these were out of service undergoing maintenance or being modified.[17]

In late December 1950, Project ON TOP began modifying additional aircraft, this time to carry the Mk 4, Mk 5, and Mk 6 devices. At the same time, the Air Force began the development of the universal bomb suspension (UBS) system that could be easily reconfigured to accommodate atomic weapons 15–60 inches in diameter up to 128 inches long. The UBS was to be installed in B-29, B-36, B-47, B-50, and B-54 aircraft, and the development of the UBS by North American Aviation was afforded the highest national priority available – even higher than the ongoing police action in Korea. All of these modifications resulted in the B-36 being able to carry a single nuclear weapon in bomb bay No. 1 where it was most convenient for crewmembers to arm the weapon.[18]

It was not until July 1950 that SAC decided that B-36s should be able to carry more than one atomic weapon at a time. No less than three separate configurations evolved from this requirement as part of later phases of ON TOP. At least 30 aircraft (12 B-36Ds and 18 B-36Hs) were modified to carry the UBS in all four bomb bays. Other aircraft were modified to carry the UBS in bomb bay Nos. 1 and 4. Beginning in 1952, the RB-36s (all models) were modified to carry nuclear weapons in bomb bay No. 4. The fac-

tory began to equip aircraft with the UBS beginning with the B-36F, and by the time the B-36H began to roll off the production line, they could carry the UBS in two bomb bays. It was a confusing time.

By mid-1956, the configurations had stabilized somewhat. All B-36s had UBS installations in bomb bay Nos. 1 and 4 capable of carrying the Mk 6 and Mk 18 atomic weapons. After T.O. 1B-36-783 was incorporated, UBS systems were installed in bomb bay Nos. 2 and 3, again capable of carrying Mk 6 and Mk 18 weapons. Some airplanes were modified with a "large cargo system" that was capable of carrying any weapon in bomb bay No. 3, and a "medium cargo system" in bomb bay No. 4 capable of carrying anything except the Mk 14, 17, 21, and 36. Eventually, all RB-36s had a UBS in bomb bay No. 2, and some reconnaissance airplanes were equipped with the large cargo system in bomb bay No. 3 and had provisions for installing the large cargo system in bomb bay No. 4. Other RB-36s had the medium cargo system in bomb bay No. 4.

By 1951, the first thermonuclear weapon designs were being finalized. The TX-14 was 61.4 inches in diameter, 222 inches long, and weighed about 30,000 pounds; the TX-16 was 75 inches longer and weighed an additional 13,000 pounds. As a result of the Operation CASTLE atmospheric tests, the TX-16 was cancelled on 2 April 1954 and the TX-14 and TX-17 were selected for production (called "stockpiled" by the AEC) as the Mk 14 and Mk 17, respectively. A high-priority program was undertaken to modify B-36s to carry production versions of the devices. By the end of 1953 there were 20 B-36s equipped to carry thermonuclear weapons; by the middle of 1955, there were 208 aircraft. The production Mk 17 yield was estimated at 20 megatons – the most powerful weapon ever deployed by the United States, and only deliverable by the B-36. (Although the bomb would have physically fit inside the early B-52s, the Mk 17 had been retired before those aircraft were put into production.)

The original, round-tip, three-blade propellers on the XB-36 during the 20 May 1950 Armed Forces Day open house at Carswell. Each of the Wright propellers was 19 feet in diameter. Note the track gear. (Frank F. Kleinwechter, Jr.)

The effect of a propeller failure is graphically seen in this photo of No. 3 engine on a B-36D (44-92076) at Fairchild AFB in February 1954. The propellor tore away from the airplane, taking most of the rear cowling with it. (U.S. Air Force)

Electronic Countermeasures

One crucial advantage held by the B-36, and later the B-52, was that its size and load-carrying capacity gave it a great deal of room in which to incorporate new equipment. The first operational B-36s were equipped with essentially the same limited ECM equipment as contemporary B-29s. The radio operator served the additional duty of ECM operator, as in the B-29. During 1951, B-36s flew test missions at Eglin AFB to evaluate the effectiveness of the ECM and chaff systems, with results that indicated the B-36s could successfully penetrate existing radar defenses. Earlier tests against Royal Air Force night fighters equipped with airborne intercept radars had proven ineffective against B-36Bs equipped with their standard ECM suite. The B-36's best defense was a combination of high altitude and ECM.

As delivered from Convair, each aircraft contained racks and antenna mounting locations for various ECM equipment. The aircraft maintenance manuals stated, "tactical organizations will supply and install the ECM equipment." Surprisingly, although the ECM equipment was not provided with the aircraft, the numerous antennas were, although they were stowed in plywood boxes in the aft compartment and one of the cargo carriers. The antennas were installed by whatever organization supplied the ECM equipment itself.[19]

Initially, the ECM equipment for the bomber versions (the RB-36s carried a more extensive ECM suite) consisted of two configurations known as Group I and Group II, depending upon the frequency coverage desired. Group I consisted of two APT-4 transmitters that covered approximately 200 to 800 MHz (called megacycles at the time). Group II substituted an APT-1 transmitter for one of the APT-4s, extending coverage down to 90 MHz. In both cases, a pair of APR-4 receivers was installed, covering approximately 40 to 1,000 MHz. This equipment would be

significantly expanded on later bomber versions as electronic warfare became increasingly important. For instance, the APT-5A transmitter capable of covering 300 to 1,500 MHz was later added. By late 1954, a Group III had been developed that included the APR-4 and APT-4, an IP-69/ALA-2 panoramic receiver, APT-6 transmitter, APR-9 receiver, and APT-9 transmitter.[20]

The reconnaissance versions carried yet more ECM equipment, although most of it was actually "ferret" equipment designed to record and analyze enemy radio and radar transmissions. The defensive ECM systems (DECM) were located in the forward compartment and operated at an ECM station located in the same location as on the bomber versions. An additional station was added directly behind the normal ECM station to operate the low frequency (LF) ferret ECM (FECM) equipment that had its primary antenna behind the large radome just ahead of the nose gear. As built, all RB-36s had three large radomes protruding from what should have been bomb bay No. 4, and a pallet between bulkheads 8.0 and 9.0 contained most of the intermediate (IF), medium (MF), and high-frequency (HF) ferret ECM equipment. Control stations for this FECM equipment were installed in the aft compartment, with new IF and MF stations facing forward at bulkhead 10.0 at the front of the compartment. The HF operator shared the tail gunner station, which was relocated to face the right-side fuselage wall instead of toward bulkhead 12.0 at the rear of the compartment. When the Strategic Air Command directed that the RB-36 fleet should have expanded bombing capabilities, the aft FECM equipment was relocated into the aft fuselage between bulkheads 10.0 and 12.0, and the radomes were moved 20 feet aft under the rear fuselage. This freed bomb bay No. 4 to again carry bombs without compromising any of the existing ferret capability.[21]

On the GRB-36D FICON (FIghter CONveyor) aircraft (and the lone JRB-36F), a single APX-29A IFF/rendezvous set was installed. The antenna was located

One of the largest changes made by the Phase II ECM program was the installation of dual APT-16 transmitters at the intermediate and medium frequency position. Most of the electronics were mounted below the table and are not visible. (Lockheed Martin)

Technicians conduct a defensive ECM evaluation on a B-36H (51-5700) on 30 April 1955. The B-36 was the first strategic bomber with an extensive ECM suite, and techniques for using the equipment were developed in the field. (U.S. Air Force)

Late B-36Hs and all B-36Js added the APS-54 radar warning receiver to notify the crew if the airplane was being illuminated by a hostile radar. Receivers were added to the "island" between the elevator and aft fuselage and to the center of the glazed windows in the extreme nose. The photo at left shows the receiver from the inside of the airplane; the photo at right shows the external view. The small circular cover to the left of the APS-54 was where the gunsight was located prior to the airplane (a B-36H, 51-5700 in this case) being modified to the Featherweight III configuration. (U.S. Air Force)

under a large radome on top of the forward fuselage, and proved to be one of the more recognizable features of FICON carriers. The APX-29A allowed the RF-84K fighter to easily locate the waiting bomber when returning from a mission.

Late B-36Hs added an APS-54 radar-warning receiver (RWR) to tell the tail gunner or navigator if the aircraft was being illuminated by a surface or airborne radar. The APS-54 was a wide-band crystal video RWR that was effective from 2.6–11 GHz with a single forward antenna in the middle of the nose glazing and two rearward facing antennas on the trailing edge of the inboard horizontal stabilizers. The system provided limited azimuth data – basically indicating if the threat was ahead of or behind the B-36. One problem was that the APS-54 could be easily dam-

aged if the APS-23 search radar of a nearby B-36 illuminated it. This was the first "modern" RWR to enter service with the Strategic Air Command, and quickly became standard equipment on most SAC bombers.

Modernization of the ECM equipment was a large part of the Project FEATHERWEIGHT, and its $30 million price tag included several significant equipment additions, such as the APS-54 radar warning receiver, two low frequency radar jammers, and a new APT-16 S-band jammer. The alterations also included the addition of another ECM operator position, so that there were individual crew positions for crewmembers operating low, intermediate, medium, and high frequency equipment. An automatic ALE-7 chaff dispenser replaced the manual A-6 and A-7 chaff dispensers on most aircraft.

An ALT-6 transmitter antenna was located just ahead of the nose gear. The 150 Watt continuous-wave jammer was made by General Electric and transmitted in the IEEE S Band (2400–3600 MHz, NATO E and F Bands). (U.S. Air Force)

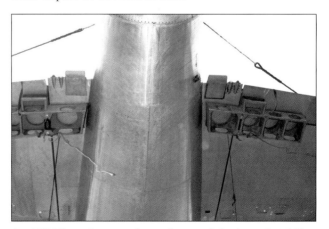

An APS-54 receiver was located on each horizontal stabilizer island. The position lights, shown outboard of each receiver, were relocated somewhat to accommodate the new system. The reflectors were part of a test setup. (U.S. Air Force)

Magnesium

One of the B-36's many nicknames was "magnesium overcast;" appropriate, considering the aircraft represented one of the few truly large-scale aviation uses of the metal. Magnesium was used as a skin material for about one-half of the fuselage, including the entire area around the bomb bays and bomb bay doors. The leading edges of the wings used 0.025- to 0.040-inch-thick magnesium skin. The trailing edge of the wing and all control surfaces (after metal replaced fabric) were also magnesium. In some of these applications, the magnesium skin needed stiffening, and "waffle" was attached to the back of the skin with a metal adhesive (Convair Metlbond or Chrysler Cycleweld). The use of an adhesive instead of more conventional fasteners (rivets, spot welding, etc.) gave a continuous attachment and avoided stress concentrations. Fatigue testing also revealed that the adhesive had a much longer service life. Originally the waffles were made from 0.016-inch aluminum alloy, but production difficulties at Convair eventually forced the subcontracting of the effort to Dow Chemical, which produced the waffles from 0.025-inch magnesium alloy, providing approximately the same weight and stiffness.[28]

One of the major external differences on the reconnaissance model was the switch from dull magnesium skin around bomb bay No. 1 to shiny aluminum skin. This was because magnesium does not respond well to pressure cycles, and when this area of the fuselage was turned into a pressurized compartment, the skin (and several bulkheads) was changed to accommodate the new requirements. Both of the other pressurized areas (forward and aft compartments) also used aluminum skin.

All of the control surfaces on the B-36A and B-36B had been covered with doped fabric, a construction technique that was tried and true. However, the increased speeds promised for the B-36D forced Convair to switch to 0.016-inch magnesium alloy to cover the elevators and rudder. The magnesium was heavier than fabric, but was necessary because the fabric tended to "balloon" at high speeds. Eventually, all models also had the fabric ailerons replaced by magnesium units.

Magnesium castings were used for the control-system drums and bellcranks, and also for numerous fittings throughout the aircraft. Magnesium was also used for many of the air ducts throughout the aircraft, although the material was difficult to seal. Most gasket materials in use at the time absorbed moisture, which corroded the flange ends on magnesium parts more so than on aluminum ones. Other materials such as silicone rubber, asbestos, or fiberglass were used in places but were not considered ideal.

Initially, magnesium was selected for the new bomber because the material was considered less "strategic" than aluminum, meaning the United States had more of it available. The metal was easier to mine and process as an ore, but it was more difficult to fabricate into usable pieces. Magnesium was also more expensive than aluminum. A variety of problems cropped up while using the metal, although it proved to be very successful on the B-36. Convair ended up developing many better techniques for using the material, including new anodizing processes that continue to be used. Ultimately, new supplies of aluminum and improved techniques to mine and process it made the widespread use of magnesium unnecessary, and the B-36 represents the ultimate large-scale aerospace use of the material.

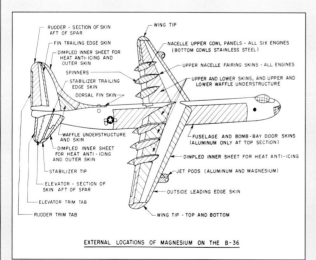

EXTERNAL LOCATIONS OF MAGNESIUM ON THE B-36

The drawing at left shows the extensive use of magnesium on the B-36. At right, a B-36D (49-2652) shows the shiny aluminum and dull magnesium used on the fuselage; aluminum was generally used in pressurized areas. The markings on this particular airplane are highly fictitious, having been applied for a Hollywood movie. (Left: Convair; Peter M. Bowers)

CHAPTER 4

CONFLICT UNFINISHED

A CHILLY PEACE AND A COLD WAR

Only a month after the Korean truce was signed, President Eisenhower ordered the 92nd Bomb Wing from Fairchild AFB on a 30-day deployment to bases in Japan, Okinawa, and Guam as part of Operation BIG STICK. Ten B-36s are visible in this photo of Okinawa on 25 August 1953. (National Archives College Park Collection)

The war in Europe ended officially on 8 May 1945, but the Allied Forces, including the United States, continued to maintain a military peacekeeping presence in most of the defeated territories. During the war, the United States had established numerous air bases throughout Europe, North Africa, and parts of the Middle East, and opted to maintain control over them to provide communication and supply lines for its postwar occupation forces. When it became clear the Soviets intended to force the Allied Powers out of Berlin before overthrowing Turkey and Greece, the United States began transforming its occupation forces into a combat-ready organization. The new organization, composed of the Eighth Air Force and Fifteenth Air Force, was named "United States Air Forces in Europe" on 7 August 1945 – one day after the atomic bombing of Hiroshima, and one month before the XB-36 rolled out at Government Aircraft Plant 4.[1] The U.S. Air Forces in Europe (USAFE), and its many air bases near the Soviet Union and the Middle East, would soon become vital components of Cold War B-36 operations.[2]

In November 1945, Fort Worth Army Air Field was assigned to Headquarters, Second Air Force in Colorado Springs, Colorado. Personnel from various Combat Crew Training Schools around the country were relocated to Fort Worth and the first contingent of Second Air Force B-29s arrived on 1 December 1945. By the end of the year, all of the B-32s were gone and 53 B-29s were assigned to the base. Headquarters, Training Command, was transferred from Fort Worth to Barksdale Field, Louisiana, on 25 February 1946 after having directed the training of more than two million aviation officers and enlisted personnel during its tenure at Fort Worth.

Peace In Europe – An Impossible Dream

Two weeks later, on 5 March 1946, British Prime Minister Winston Churchill delivered his now-famous "Iron Curtain Speech" that confirmed a serious ideological breach between the Soviet Union and the Western democracies. This speech permanently galvanized east-west relations and is credited by some historians as the beginning of the Cold War.[3]

On 21 March 1946, the Army Air Forces was divided into three primary operating commands: Air Defense Command (ADC), Strategic Air Command (SAC), and Tactical Air Command (TAC). Of importance to this story, Gen. George Churchill Kenny (1889–1977), an air tactics planner during World War II, was selected as the first commander of SAC. As expressed by Gen. Carl A. Spaatz, commander of the Army Air Forces,

"The Strategic Air Command will be prepared to conduct long-range offensive operations in any part of the world, either independently or in co-operation with land and naval forces; to conduct

maximum-range reconnaissance over land or sea, either independently or in co-operation with land and naval forces; to provide combat units capable of intense and sustained combat operations employing the latest and most advanced weapons; to train units and personnel of the maintenance of the Strategic Forces in all parts of the world; to perform such special missions as the Commanding General Army Air Forces may direct."

The Berlin Blockade (24 June 1948 – 11 May 1949) was one of the first major international crises of the Cold War. The Soviet Union blocked the Western Allies' railway and road access to their sectors of Berlin. The Allies flew over 200,000 flights providing 13,000 tons of food daily to Berlin in an operation lasting almost a year. By the spring of 1949, the effort was clearly succeeding, and by April the airlift was delivering more cargo than had previously flowed into the city by rail. (National Archives College Park Collection)

Five days after the creation of the Strategic Air Command, on 26 March 1947, Consolidated chief test pilot B. A. Erickson and co-pilot G. S. (Gus) Green safely landed the XB-36 after a hydraulic cylinder ruptured in the aircraft's right main landing gear during a test flight. Of the twelve-man crew who bailed out of the crippled bomber before it landed, eight were injured. So appreciative were Consolidated officials for Erickson's saving the XB-36, and possibly the entire program as well, Erickson was awarded a special skiing vacation to Sun Valley, Idaho. The aircraft was repaired and flew again only three weeks later.

With much of Europe and Japan in ruins and their economies devastated following World War II, the United States and its European allies engaged in meetings to develop a plan of postwar reconstruction. The United States instituted the European Recovery Plan, usually referred to as the Marshall Plan, on 12 July 1947 to provide massive aid to former enemies in return for political reforms and strict oversight within their governments. The Soviet Union, claiming it was determined to prevent future threats from countries on its borders, objected to most parts of the Marshall Plan and claimed it was simply a ploy by the United States to buy a permanent military presence in Europe and Japan by trading financial aid for military bases. Further to the Soviets, the Marshall Plan called for a complete rebuilding of Germany whereas Stalin demanded that Germany remain economically impotent to prevent it from ever again becoming a threatening military power.

On 26 July 1947, President Truman signed the National Security Act of 1947, establishing the United States Air Force as a separate military branch under the newly formed Department of the Air Force. In addition to replacing the green Army Air Forces uniforms with ones of dark blue, all Army Air Fields were renamed Air Force Bases. A general reorganization of the Air Force, largely to comply with the Unified Command Plan issued by the Joint Chiefs of Staff, followed, although the three primary

The United States was the only air force to have developed truly successful heavy bombers during World War II, and the Soviets were anxious to catch up. Lacking resources to develop a new airplane, Soviet engineers reverse-engineered an interned B-29 and created the Tupolev Tu-4. The airplane was first displayed during a flyover at the Aviation Day parade on 3 August 1947 at the Tushino Airport in Moscow. A total of 847 were manufactured between 1949 and 1952. (Jay Miller Collection)

operating commands were retained largely unchanged. Gen. Carl A. Spaatz became the first Chief of Staff of the Air Force on 26 September 1947.[4]

A Massive Arms Race Begins

On 3 August 1947, only eight days after Truman established the U.S. Air Force, Soviet Premier Joseph Stalin dramatically revealed to the world, during the Aviation Day Parade at Moscow's Tushino Airport, the first of a planned fleet of Tupolev Tu-4 (NATO reporting-name Bull) long-range heavy bombers. The Tu-4 had made its maiden flight on 19 May 1947 with test pilot Nikolai Rybko at the controls, and was, for all intents, a copy of

Before the advent of ballistic missiles and nuclear weapons, the XB-36 (41-13570) was the ultimate statement of strategic deterrence. It was as much a statement to the United States Navy as it was to the Soviet Union, a fact that did not escape the admirals, or Congress. (Lockheed Martin)

Given the fact the airplane was designed and manufactured in Fort Worth, and that what became Carswell AFB was its primary home for much of its early career, it is not surprising that three B-36As and a single B-36J were named City of Fort Worth *at various times. This is the first B-36A (44-92004) at the Army Air Forces Day open house. This airplane only made two flights – one around the pattern and one to Wright Field, Ohio, where it was used as a structural test article.* (Don Pyeatt Collection)

the Boeing B-29 Superfortress.[5] When the new bomber became operational, it would allow the Soviets to strike any target in Europe and Asia and return to bases inside Russia. By launching one-way "suicide" attacks, the bombers could strike cities within the continental United States. Even though it was believed the Soviets were still many years away from having a nuclear weapon, the realization that they had developed capabilities to produce long-range heavy bombers was an alarming revelation to Western military planners. Nevertheless, the Tu-4 would not enter active service until 1949.

The impact of Stalin's propaganda spectacular was short lived on that same Sunday in 1947. As the sun rose over Texas only a few hours later, a crowd in excess of 50,000 people began arriving at the Army Air Forces Day open house that would showcase the YB-36A (44-92004), which had been towed from the Consolidated plant for the event. At the time of the open house, only two B-36s had been manufactured, the original XB-36 and the YB-36A, so the more production-looking airplane was selected for the ceremony.

The event, marking the 40th anniversary of the Army Air Forces, provided many static military exhibits and a spectacular airshow that included mock air battles with Lockheed P-80 Shooting Star jet fighters, a hands-free takeoff and landing by a remote controlled C-47, and fly-overs by P-82s, B-17s, B-24s, B-25s, B-26s, and B-29s.[6]

Following a demonstration by the base's "all-Negro" precision drill team and music provided by the Eighth Air Force Band, the ever-growing crowd converged on a speaker's stand that was erected near the nose of the YB-36A. The aircraft sported the words "CITY OF FORT

WORTH" painted in foot-tall letters on both sides of the forward fuselage extending from below and in front of the cockpit rearward to the forward sighting blister.[7] Affixed to the aircraft was a plaque reading:

*Dedicated to the City of Fort Worth Texas
Where it was built by Consolidated Vultee
Aircraft Corporation 1947*

Col. Alan D. Clark, commander of the newly redesignated Fort Worth AFB, began the ceremony by introducing many of the guests on the stand. Among those present were 8th Air Force Chief of Staff Thomas J. DuBose, Consolidated Division Manager Roland G. Mayer, mayors of dozens of surrounding towns and Amon G. Carter. Accompanying Carter were his long-time friends Raymond E. Buck (Southern Council for American Airlines, Division Council for Consolidated Vultee, former Fort Worth City Attorney and personal attorney to Carter) and Cyrus R. Smith (former deputy commander of the Air Transport Command and then-current board chairman of American Airlines), both of whom were instrumental in establishing Consolidated and the Air Force in Fort Worth.

Brig. Gen. Roger M. Ramey[8] had agreed to name a B-36 for Fort Worth, "because Fort Worth is the home of the B-36 and the plant which makes it, and is also home of the Very Heavy Bombing [*sic*] Group which will fly it."[9] While presenting Carter to unveil the dedication plaque, Ramey explained that Carter was selected for the honor "because of his international popularity, his general concern for community, state and international welfare, and his long and valuable service to both civil and military aviation."[10] After removing a seal from the plaque, Carter, Buck, and Smith joined the other speakers in extending congratulations to the Army Air Forces on its fortieth anniversary.

After the open house, the YB-36A was towed back to the Consolidated plant and made ready for its maiden

The shadow of a B-36A as it lands at Biggs AFB on 5 December 1948. This was Frank Kleinwechter's first B-36 flight, and the aircraft was commanded by Jack Risher. (Frank F. Kleinwechter)

flight on 28 August 1947. Unfortunately, the YB-36A was the dedicated static-test aircraft that would be tested to destruction at Wright-Patterson AFB, so its tenure as the *City of Fort Worth* would be short-lived.

A year earlier, the Eighth Air Force had moved from MacDill Field to Fort Worth AAF under the command of Ramey. The 7th Bombardment Wing (Very Heavy)[11] was established on 3 November 1947 as part of the Eighth Air Force, and was organized on 17 November under the command of Col. Clark, flying B-29s in a training role.[12] The new wing was composed of the already-formed 7th Bombardment Group and three new groups: 7th Airdrome Group, 7th Maintenance and Supply Group, and 7th Medical Group. The mission of the 7th Bombardment Wing was to:

> *"... organize and train a force capable of immediate and sustained long range offensive warfare and operations in any part of the world, utilizing the latest technical knowledge and advanced weapons (including the atomic bomb), to include long range offensive bombardment, reconnaissance, photographic, mapping photography, sea search, anti-submarine patrol, either independently or in cooperation with land and naval forces; to support such national guard and air reserve training units as were located on the station with personnel, equipment, and supplies as were available and would not detract from the accomplishment of the primary mission; to train the 1st Air Transport Unit to provide air transportation for special weapons technical equipment, and scientific personnel concerned therewith, as well as provide transportation support for Eighth Air Force and other tactical units of the Strategic Air Command in conjunction with their assigned mission; to train and prepare for overseas movement the 2nd Aviation Squadron, and to perform such special missions and assignments as the commanding general, Eighth Air Force may direct."*

On 13 January 1948, Fort Worth AFB was renamed Griffiss AFB in honor of Lt. Col. Townsend E. Griffiss, the first airman to die in the line of duty in Europe during World War II. The change lasted 17 days until 30 January 1948 when the base was renamed in honor of Maj. Horace S. Carswell, Jr., a native of Fort Worth and Medal of Honor recipient who was killed in combat during World War II.[13]

The U.S. Again Mobilizes For War

Czechoslovakia was the last remaining democracy bordering Russia after World War II until 25 February 1948 when the country fell under Soviet control through a "bloodless coup" led by Joseph Stalin's Communist Party. This event proved to Western European powers, and to the United States, that the Soviets intended to force communism on all of Europe. In the United States, the fall of Czechoslovakia created a painful awareness of the lack of a credible military deterrent in Europe that had been caused by the massive demobilization after World War II.

Reaction to the Soviet's advance into Europe was swift. With the signing of the Treaty of Brussels, France, Great Britain, Belgium, the Netherlands, and Luxembourg, formed a military self-protection alliance on 17 March 1948, becoming known as the Western European Union.

On 18 March 1948, President Truman announced plans to increase the capability of the armed forces, stating that the United States was, "the principal protector of the free world

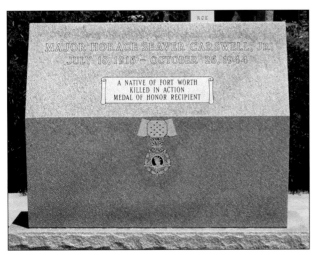

Grave marker of Horace Carswell at Oakwood Cemetery, Fort Worth. Medal of Honor recipient Carswell was a Fort Worth native who was killed in combat during World War II. Griffiss AFB was renamed Carswell on 30 January 1948. (Don Pyeatt)

Carswell AFB became the primary training base for SAC's nuclear mission. Shown here, Capt. Cassagrande conducts survival training for the 9th Bomb Squadron. (U.S. Air Force via Frank F. Kleinwechter)

This is the last group photo of 7th Bomb Group (M), 492nd Squadron in October 1947, before the unit was reorganized into the 7th Bombardment Wing (VH). Note the black-bottom B-29s lined up on the Carswell AFB ramp. (U.S. Air Force via Kathy Fowler)

and must pledge its military, economic, and moral strength to stop any further Communist gains." Present with Truman was Secretary of Defense James V. Forrestal, who said, "With Soviet military manpower unchanged from World War II levels of 4,050,000, and U.S. levels of only 1,392,000, if Russian forces should move into Germany or other parts of Europe, we could not stop them."[14]

On 22 March 1948, Headquarters, Eighth Air Force, announced that the 7th Bomb Wing at Carswell would become the first operational B-36 unit by receiving the first "war-ready" B-36A sometime during that week.[15] (Carswell was a logical place to assign the initial B-36s since Air Force Plant 4 was located on the other side of the runway.) The 7th Bomb Wing responded to this announcement by sending four flight engineers and five crew chiefs to Consolidated for additional training.[16]

Unfortunately, engine modifications placed the aircraft's delivery on indefinite hold.

During the following day, a little-known air base southeast of Fairbanks, Alaska, was highlighted in the press when it became known it was being prepared to accommodate the B-36. The press reports indicated that until B-36s were available, the base would host B-50s that "could make bomb runs over any portion of the Soviet Union."[17] The press report also reported that the "secret" base was just being built but, in fact, construction of the facility had begun on 25 August 1943 as part of the Alaska-Siberia Ferry Route. Nevertheless, it appears that the base, known as Mile 26 because of its proximity to an Army Signal Corps telegraph station, saw little use during the war and was briefly closed in 1945. On 1 December 1947, Strategic Air Command B-29s arrived at 26-Mile Airfield with the

One of the early B-36s (44-920019) takes off from Carswell AFB. Despite being called "war ready," the B-36A fleet was mostly useless except as trainers. This airplane was later remanufactured into an RB-36E, and then modified into a Featherweight II. On 22 August 1951 it was involved in a ground collision at Travis AFB, California, where its entire forward fuselage was severed. The airplane was rebuilt and returned to service. (National Museum of the United States Air Force Collection)

deployment of the 97th Bombardment Wing from Smoky Hill AFB, Kansas. Ironically, the wing returned to Kansas on 12 March 1948, ten days before the press report, leaving the base with no assigned aircraft. In the meantime, on 13 January 1948, the base had been named Eielson AFB.[18]

The Soviets Raise The Stakes

World tensions increased dramatically on 9 April 1948, when the Soviets sealed parts of West Berlin from access by its American, British, and French occupiers. The Allied response was swift, and Truman ordered a massive airlift of food and essential supplies for the isolated city under the direction of Maj. Gen. Curtis E. LeMay. The airlift continued for nearly a year and brought the world to the brink of war. It also increased the American resolve to increase its military capabilities to prevent any future Soviet expansion into Europe. The Cold War was quickly warming.

The first B-36A to be delivered to an operational unit (B-36A-5-CF, 44-92015) taxied under its own power from Air Force Plant 4 to Carswell AFB on Saturday, 26 June 1948. Consolidated or the Air Materiel Command had retained the eleven previous aircraft for further testing.

Since the original *City of Fort Worth* had been the short-lived YB-36A structural test article, temporary markings had been applied to another B-36A (44-92006) for use when showing dignitaries around Air Force Plant 4. However, it seemed fitting that the first "operational" airplane should have the honor of representing its host city, so factory-applied dedication markings were present on B-36A (44-92015) as it taxied across the field.

A short acceptance ceremony followed with R. G. Mayer, Consolidated's Division Manager, presenting the aircraft to Brig. Gen. Ramey, Commander of the Eighth Air Force and to Col. Clark, Base Commander, for the 7th

Eielson AFB – known as Mile 26 Airfield after the highway mile marker it was near – was built during World War II. On 13 January 1948 the base was named for Carl Ben Eielson, an Alaska aviation pioneer who was killed, along with his mechanic Earl Borland, in the crash of their Hamilton aircraft in 1929. The base became one of the northern staging areas for the B-36 fleet. (Ed Calvert via B-36 Peacemaker Museum, Inc.)

Bomb Wing. Onboard the aircraft as it taxied to Carswell was Amon G. Carter who hand-carried a new gold plaque. During the short delivery ceremony, Carter affixed the plaque to the airplane.

Three additional B-36s were delivered to the 7th Bomb Wing during the last three days of June. The first long-range flight by an all-Air-Force crew was on 22 August when the 492nd Bomb Squadron took a B-36A (44-92007) on a 15,500-mile, 26-hour flight that used 14,000 gallons of fuel. The crew found the B-36 much more comfortable than the B-29s it was replacing.[19]

At Shady Oak Farm, Consolidated presented Amon Carter with a hand-carved and polished scale-model of the first B-36 delivered to the Air Force. From the left, Gen. George C. Kenny, A. G. Carter, La Motte T. Cohû (Consolidated president and general manager), and Maj. Gen. Roger M. Ramey. (Consolidated)

The City of Fort Worth (B-36A, 44-920015), minus the name on the nose, landing at Walker AFB in Roswell, New Mexico. The public was very interested in the giant airplane, evidenced by the crowd at the side of the road. Walker was only three miles from the city center. (Don Pyeatt Collection)

The end was in sight for propeller-driven aircraft even as the B-36A (44-92017) was entering service. The Republic P-84B Thunderjet (46-553) shown here was advanced for its era, but like its contemporaries could not compete with the B-36 at altitude. This situation would change quickly, and by the middle of the 1950s the jet fighters and surface-to-air missiles posed a serious threat to the B-36. (Peter M. Bowers Collection)

Concurrently with this flying propaganda blitz, Consolidated placed advertisements in many major newspapers and magazines around the world. Full page ads were bought to display pictures and descriptions of the new bomber. Aviation Week, in particular, was a recipient of a great deal of Consolidated's advertising budget. As deliveries of B-36s from Air Force Plant 4 continued, SAC began displaying its new might.

In addition to participating in airshows, the 7th Bomb Wing flew six B-36As on a maximum effort mission on 17 and 18 September 1948 to key cities in the United States, giving the public – and Soviet spies – a first look at the world's largest bomber. Five routes were flown, each terminating back at Carswell:

- Two B-36s flew over El Paso, Tucson, Los Angeles, San Francisco, Seattle, and Salt Lake.
- One B-36 flew over Kansas City, Omaha, Denver, Abilene, Oklahoma City, and Tulsa.
- One B-36 flew over Des Moines, Minneapolis, Duluth, Chicago, Detroit, Ft. Wayne, Indianapolis, and St. Louis.
- One B-36 flew over Boston, New York, Philadelphia, Washington D.C., Buffalo, Cleveland, Pittsburgh, Cincinnati, Louisville, Nashville, and Memphis.
- The last B-36 flew over Birmingham, Atlanta, Charleston, Jacksonville, Miami, Tampa, Montgomery, New Orleans, Shreveport, Houston, Galveston, and San Antonio.

While campaigning for a seat in the U.S. Senate, then-Congressman Lyndon Baines Johnson (1908–1973) flew to Fort Worth on 19 July 1948 to deliver a speech to aircraft workers detailing the urgency of military preparedness. Speaking to thousands of workers, he said, in part, "Fort Worth is destined to become the No. 1 aviation center of the nation. The same Texas labor and management that made planes that won World War II now have the same job to prevent World War III." Johnson, continuing the propaganda war that had started between the two superpowers, told the crowd that "Russia has 260 divisions and the United States only 8;" and that "Russia is building 14,000 combat planes a year, the United States only 1,000." The numbers were complete fabrications, but accomplished their intended mission of scaring the populace.[20]

A B-36A from the 7th Bomb Wing making a "show off" pass over Galveston Island. Everybody who ever heard a B-36 commented on how loud it was; at this altitude it must have been deafening with six roaring R-4360s and six propellers churning the atmosphere. (Herb Cavanaugh Collection)

The main boarding hatch to the forward pressurized compartment was in the nose gear well, as shown on this B-36A (44-92010). Note the empty nose turret, the lack of a nose gunsight, and the glazed panel (with windshield wiper) over the Norden bombsight. (San Diego Air & Space Museum Collection)

A Strange Love Affair: LeMay and SAC

On 20 September 1948, Gen. Kenny was replaced as head of SAC by Lt. Gen. Curtis E. LeMay (1906–1990). Kenney then became head of the Air University at Maxwell AFB, Alabama. LeMay took control of SAC following his successful organization of air operations for the Berlin Airlift. Well known for commanding fire-bombing raids on Japan during World War II, LeMay was a stern commander who demanded absolute obedience to his orders. LeMay moved SAC Headquarters to Offutt AFB, Nebraska, and placed all air bases under his command on permanent alert status and ordered his commanders to prepare for war. B-36 propaganda flights continued under LeMay, but usually included a war-training mission before returning to base.

Not willing to tolerate the continued delays in B-36 deliveries, LeMay told Consolidated that it had to deliver 18 operational B-36Bs by the end of 1948. At Air Force Plant 4, Consolidated production managers shifted workers from all departments to the assembly line to ensure delivery of the aircraft before the end-of-year deadline. The new Consolidated Fort Worth division manager, Ray O. Ryan, held meetings with employees and told them the delivery "is important to Convair, to the Air Force, and to the nation." He continued that, "It may seem remote, but delivery of this group of airplanes might be the difference between winning the peace or losing it."[21] This statement was an obvious reference to the confrontation over Soviet-blockaded Berlin.

On 18 November 1948, the 11th Bomb Group at Carswell became the second B-36 unit. The group was attached to the 7th Bomb Wing, giving the wing six squadrons of B-36s. On Thanksgiving Day, 25 November 1948, the first "combat capable" B-36B was delivered to Carswell, and the remaining 17 aircraft were delivered before the end of December.

The Air Force continued exercising the B-36, and on 10 March 1949, a B-36B (44-92035) began a 9,600-mile, non-stop flight that lasted just over 44 hours. Conducted by the 492nd Bomb Squadron, the flight stayed entirely within the borders of the United States and was the longest recorded to date in a B-36.

"Peacemaker"

During the effort to deliver the first 18 B-36Bs, Consolidated announced a company-wide contest to name the B-36. The aircraft was known at Consolidated at that time only as the "Battleplane." The announcement said that, "preference will be given to names that relate to the size, weight, power, range, purpose, and mission of the B-36."[22]

The "Name the Plane" contest winners were announced on Wednesday, 14 April 1949. Amon Carter, Maj. Gen. Ramey, and LaMotte T. Cohû, President of Consolidated Vultee judged the contest. Prizes and certificates were awarded to the winners of the contest. The certificate read, in part, "Since the ultimate purpose of the B-36 aircraft is to secure and maintain peace throughout the world, we, the undersigned judges, have unanimously selected 'Peacemaker' from more than 600 suggestions and have respectfully recommended that the United States Air Force adopt the name as official for the B-36." The name, however, never became official. All aircraft names must be vetted and approved by the Department of Defense. Several religious groups objected to the name "Peacemaker," arguing there is only one true peacemaker, and "He was not built by Consolidated Vultee." In the end, the Air Force disapproved the name, and the B-36 served its career with only a designation.[23]

A gaggle of B-36Bs (44-92060 on the left) on the ramp at Carswell AFB. Unlike several of the other B-36 bases, Carswell never built a hangar large enough to house a B-36, and all maintenance was accomplished in the open air on the ramp. Although snow was seldom a major issue in Fort Worth, the summer heat took its toll on the ground crews, and eventually, a series of mainte-nance docks were built that afforded, at least, a bit of shade from the Texas sun. (Lockheed Martin)

"PEACEMAKER"

The Convair "Name the Plane" contest received 60 entries for the name "Peacemaker." According to Evatts Haley, of Canyon, Texas, historian and authority on early Texas, the word Peacemaker almost certainly referred to the Colt 0.45-caliber revolver used to settle disputes in the old west. The idea was echoed in the 13 April 1949 edition of the company newspaper, Convairiety. *It was not to be.* (Ed Calvert Collection)

On 22 April 1949, two B-36Bs flew to Muroc AFB, California, to perform an accelerated service test at 40,000 feet. The mission tested the suitability of the B-36 as a platform for very-large bombs. This was essentially a duplicate of the 29 January 1949 mission flown by Maj. Stephen Dillon and Doc Witchell, but using an all-military crew. Two dummy 43,000-pound bombs were dropped, the first from an altitude of 35,000 feet, the second from 41,000 feet.

The Berlin Airlift ended on 12 May 1949 with the Soviet Union lifting all restrictions on access to the city. The harrowing brush with World War III strengthened the resolve of the United States to maintain an effective military deterrent to the Soviets. Part of this resolve included the continued production of the B-36 beyond the initial 100-airplane order.

On 26 May 1949, the 7th Bomb Wing took delivery of the XC-99 (43-52436) and assigned it to the 436th Bomb Squadron. Although the cargo aircraft had been built as a way to test systems for the B-36, it quickly found operational uses carrying outsized cargo. The aircraft stayed in Fort Worth for less than a year before it was reassigned to the San Antonio Air Materiel Area at Kelly AFB, Texas.

The crew of a B-36A (44-92013) after a 33-hour, 10 minute flight that covered 6,922 miles on 8–9 April 1948. Kneeling, from left: C. J. Driskell, M. Hemby, J. D. McEachern, W. B. Easley, and J. P. Maffatt. Standing, from left: B. A. Erickson, A. S. Witchell, Walling R. Hernlud, A. W. Gecman, and W. D. Morris. (Convair)

The main gate sign for Carswell AFB. The sign had been recently repainted at this point, covering lettering that proclaimed, "Headquarters Eighth Air Force and 7th Bombardment Wing." Since the base was still home to both organizations, it is unclear why it was painted over. (Frank F. Kleinwechter)

The B-36As (44-92022 here) flew across great swaths of the country on their training flights, which averaged over 5,000 miles and could take 20–30 hours. Here the airplane makes a low pass over Lowry AFB, between Aurora and Denver, Colorado. Initially, the B-36 was not an overly comfortable airplane since many creature comforts had been removed from the production airplanes to save weight and extend range. Beginning with the B-model, these items began to reappear, only to disappear again as part of the Featherweight modifications. The two hangars (Hangar 1 and 2, Building 401 and 402, respectively) currently house the Wings Over the Rockies Air and Space Museum. (National Archives College Park Collection)

Cold War Peacemaker

The 7th and 11th Bomb Groups at Carswell had been the exclusive operators of the growing B-36 fleet until 1 May 1949 when the 9th Strategic Reconnaissance Wing (SRW) at Fairfield-Suisun (later Travis) AFB, California, became the third B-36 wing, followed quickly by the 28th SRW at Rapid City (later Ellsworth) AFB, South Dakota on 16 May. The fact these were reconnaissance wings spoke highly of the priority Curtis LeMay placed on intelligence gathering. With approximately 30 aircraft per wing, the B-36 fleet was expected to exceed 300 aircraft by the end of 1953 when the last of eleven planned wings was established.[24]

Threats and Countermeasures

On 29 August 1949, the Soviet Union conducted its first test of a fission bomb. The public met this announcement with great interest, but U.S. military strategists were not particularly alarmed by the development. At that time, it was known the Soviets had no reasonable means of deploying the weapon and it would be several years until they could.[25]

Of greater concern to the U.S. military was the awkward procedural limitations imposed by President Truman on access to fissionable weapons material. The AEC maintained possession of all bomb cores[26] and would release them to the military only by presidential order in time of a declared war. This arrangement resulted in a very complex and time-consuming procedure for transferring bomb cores to the military. The Air Force felt this procedure could have had disastrous effects on wartime strategic bombing missions.

Central to SAC's ability to retaliate was the use of pre-strike staging bases where B-36s would land to refuel and obtain bomb cores while en route to their targets. The staging bases were located in remote areas of Alaska, Canada, and Greenland. Upon receiving a war alert, the AEC would load bomb cores into transport aircraft and fly them, with fighter escort, to a staging base where the bombers would be waiting to receive them before departing for their targets. These arrangements were fraught with many opportunities for failure since the Soviets could intercept the cores en route or conduct a first strike on the staging bases. Additionally, weather conditions at Eielson AFB, the Alaskan staging base, were so severe that special cold weather equipment and procedures had to be developed to ensure the bombers could operate. Added to this was the need to train all flight crews in cold weather procedures.

Nevertheless, this was the chosen concept, and in August 1949, the 492nd Bomb Squadron began a series of B-36B polar training missions out of Eielson. For instance, one B-36B flew a navigational training flight to Eielson on 14 September, conducting simulated radar bombing on Stockton, California, and Geiger Field, Washington, before returning to Carswell on 16 September.[27]

7th BW Commanders During the B-36 Era

Name	Date of Command[54]
Col. Alan D. Clark	17 November 1947
Col. William P. Fisher	11 May 1949
Brig. Gen. Clarence S. Irvine	3 January 1950
Col. John A. Roberts	16 February 1951
Col. George T. Chadwell	29 October 1951
Col. John A. Roberts	14 April 1952
Col. George T. Chadwell	2 January 1953
Col. Clarence A. Neely	1 May 1954
Col. Raymond S. Sleeper	1 July 1955
Col. Frederick D. Berry, Jr.	3 July 1957
Col. John A. Roberts	16 July 1957

11th BW Commanders During the B-36 Era

Name	Date of Command[54]
Brig. Gen. Thomas P. Gerrity	16 February 1951
Col. Louis W. Rohr	15 November 1952
Col. William T. Seawell	2 March 1953
Col. Howard W. Moore	7 August 1954
Col. John S. Samuel	16 July 1957

This is the step leading to the cockpit from the airplane entrance. There was a circular hatch on the left side of the lower fuselage that provided the primary entrance to the crew compartment. As you climbed in, you could either crawl forward to the nose compartment, or climb this step to the cockpit. The tape measure gives a sense of scale. (Walt Jefferies Collection via Mike Machat)

Revolt of the Admirals

On 15 January 1949, five B-36A/Bs from the 7th Bomb Wing participated in an air review over Washington D.C., commemorating the inauguration of President Harry S. Truman. Several low-level passes were flown over the U.S. Capitol, resulting in a series of photographs that have been reproduced extensively, usually in conjunction with accounts of the "Revolt of the Admirals."[48]

When the B-36B first entered SAC's inventory in the fall of 1948, the Air Force had 59 groups, with an eventual goal of 70 groups. An unexpected decision by Truman to hold the 1949 defense budget to a ceiling of $11 billion was a serious blow. The problem was no longer how to procure additional aircraft for 70 groups, but how to whittle current forces to 48 groups with the least possible harm to national security. Cancelling the aircraft already on order, with minimum charges to the government, was a difficult task. In the end, over $573 million in contracts were cancelled, costing the government $56 million in penalties.[49]

Surprisingly, the B-36 actually gained from the crisis. The Air Force cancelled the purchase of various bombers, fighters, and transports, but at the same time, endorsed the urgent procurement of additional B-36s. A few months later, the Boeing B-54 (an improved B-50) was cancelled in favor of more RB-36s.

With funding becoming harder to obtain, the three military services began to squabble over which programs were most important. The Air Force and the Navy had long recognized that whichever service possessed the atomic mission would eventually receive a larger share of

This artist's concept of the USS United States (CVA-58) by Bruno Figallo shows the configuration in October 1948. Many details shown here, including the location of smoke stacks, elevators, and the retractable bridge, had not been finalized and likely would have changed. (Naval Historical Center Collection)

the budget. Thus, they had grown more critical of each other's strategic programs.

The B-36 program was the subject of a lot of criticism, especially from the Navy. The airplane was accused of being as slow as the B-24 and far more vulnerable to attack by modern fighters. Since the B-36 had been one of the few survivors in the mass cancellations of early 1949, anonymous reports had begun to circulate charging that undue favoritism and corruption were involved in awarding the B-36 contracts.

At the time, the Secretary of Defense was Louis A. Johnson, a former director at Convair.[50] On 23 April 1949, just a month after entering office, Johnson abruptly cancelled the Navy's first supercarrier, the 65,000-ton USS United States (CVA-58), which had been ordered by his predecessor to allow the Navy to develop a strategic-bombing capability. The decision was justified on the basis that the government could not afford both new strategic bombers and a new carrier force. Funds from the cancellation were used largely to order more B-36s. The Navy was enraged at the cancellation, but the Air Force insisted that strategic bombing was strictly an Air Force responsibility. The B-36 had already demonstrated it was capable of reaching targets inside the Soviet Union, while the entire concept of carrier-borne nuclear bombers had yet to be proven.

On 1 May 1949, however, the Soviets publicly demonstrated the jet-powered MiG-15 fighter, and there were serious doubts that the B-36 could continue to defend itself. Many expressed concerns that the Air Force had spent a fortune on what would turn out to be a sitting

As part of President Truman's inauguration, five B-36s (only a wingtip of the fifth airplane can be seen) flew over the White House on 19 January 1949. (National Archives via Stan Piet)

Workmen lay the ship's 15-ton keel plate and initial shell plate in a construction dry dock at the Newport News Shipbuilding and Dry Dock Company shipyard in Virginia, on 18 April 1949. The carrier was cancelled on 23 April and the steel used by the liner SS United States. *(Naval Historical Center Collection)*

duck. An anonymous document began making the rounds in press and congressional circles charging that the aircraft's performance did not live up to Air Force claims.

On 18 May 1949, the House Armed Services Committee sent a strongly-worded resolution to Johnson urging the Air Force to accept a Navy challenge to an 8-mile-high gun camera duel between a B-36 and Navy fighters. When the resolution was entered into the public record, the Navy quickly announced it would like to offer four Navy aircraft for the contest – a McDonnell F2H-1 and a Grumman F9F-2, both jet powered, and a Grumman F8F-2 and a Chance Vought F4U-4, both piston-powered. Secretary Johnson refused to comment, "… until he has a look at the Committee's proposal."[51]

While waiting for a decision from Washington, the Air Force staged an unannounced test at Muroc Base, California, between a B-36 and a "lightning fast" North American F-86 piloted by Capt. "Chuck" Yeager, the man who had broken the sound barrier two years earlier. Yeager managed to score a few hits on the B-36 but reported, "it's difficult to hold the jet steady for accurate firing at 40,000 feet." The B-36 did not attempt to "shoot" back at Yeager but attempted evasive maneuvers only. The test was deemed to be inconclusive.[52]

In June 1949, the House Armed Services Committee opened an investigation of what came to be known in the press as the "B-36 Affair." On 25 August, the House committee cleared the Air Force and Convair of any misconduct. In its final report, the Committee found no substance to the charges relating to Johnson's role in the procurement of the B-36. Although the B-36 contract

survived unscathed, one of the results of these hearings was an amendment to the National Security Act of 1947 that enlarged and strengthened the office of the Secretary of Defense and severely weakened the authority of the individual service secretaries.[53]

It was not over. In October 1949, congressional hearings resumed, this time on the question of whether the defense of the United States should rely on the Air Force's strategic bombers or the Navy's proposed fleet of aircraft carriers. This debate resulted in nearly open warfare between the Air Force and the Navy over who would control the nuclear mission. The Air Force argued that it had already demonstrated its ability to perform the mission, while the Navy continued to argue over the technical obsolescence of the B-36. The Navy was still enraged at the cancellation of the *United States*, and Adm. Arthur W. Radford, Commander-in-Chief (CinC) of the Pacific Fleet, denounced the B-36 as a "billion dollar blunder," a quote that was picked up by many newspapers across the country. Although there were still doubts about the B-36's ability to survive enemy fighter attack, the program once again survived uncut.

Thankfully, the B-36B was proving to be a capable, if somewhat slow aircraft. The Air Force and Convair were both looking for ways to improve the speed of the B-36, and everybody concerned was working on improving the reliability of the aircraft and its systems. It was now obvious that the B-36 would be the Air Force's primary nuclear delivery aircraft until development of the jet-powered B-52, and its supporting infrastructure (tankers, etc.), was completed.

From left, VADM Arthur W. Radford, VADM Forrest P. Sherman, ADM Chester W. Nimitz, and James V. Forrestal meet at the White House. (National Archives College Park Collection)

A distinguished group gathers in front of a B-36B (44-920078) on 19 November 1949 at Carswell AFB. From the left, Lt. Gen. Curtis LeMay, Senator Richard B. Russell, Jr. (D-GA), Maj. Gen. Roger M. Ramey, Maj. John Bartlett, Secretary of the Air Force W. Stuart Symington, Senator Lyndon B. Johnson (D-TX), and Representative William Homer Thornberry (D-TX). (Air Force photo via Frank F. Kleinwechter)

During the late 1940s, SAC sent B-36s to most of the air shows around the country as a ruse to convince the Soviets that the B-36 fleet was more extensive, and more useful, than it really was. Here is a formation of early airplanes at the Cleveland Air Races on 1 September 1949. (National Archives)

From 7 to 18 November 1949, the Eighth Air Force conducted the annual Air Inspection of Carswell. In general, the inspection team was satisfied with the overall condition of the base. The day the inspection closed, 18 November, Secretary of the Air Force W. Stuart Symington arrived to inspect the Eighth Air Force and fly in a B-36. After his flight, Symington stated that the B-36 was "the best bomber we have." Other honored guests in Symington's party included Senator Lyndon B. Johnson from Texas; Senator Richard B. Russell, Jr., of Georgia; D. Harold Byrd, National Vice Chairman of the Civil Air Patrol; and Amon Carter.[28]

"As Real As It Gets Short Of War"

On 14 February 1950, a B-36B (44-92075) from the 436th Bomb Squadron crashed while returning from the first full-scale practice of an all-out nuclear strike against the Soviet Union. The airplane's mission profile included simulated bombing strikes on American cities before returning to Carswell. Years after the incident, the copilot remembered that, "this mission was to be as real as it gets short of war."[29] This was the second 7th Bomb Wing B-36 lost in six months.

One purpose of the operation was to determine if outfitting and arming of the airplanes could be accomplished at Eielson in weather conditions so harsh that the engines had to be kept running at all times because they could not be restarted if they were shut down; the ground temperature was –40 degrees F. Six hours after leaving Eielson, the airplane was losing altitude because three engines had quit and were burning. The crew jettisoned and detonated an inert Mk 4 weapon over the Pacific and bailed out over one of many islands along the coast of British Columbia. Five of the seventeen crew members perished after bailing out, and the airplane was presumed to have sunk in the ocean. However, the wreck was accidentally discovered four years

The first loss came when a B-36B (44-92079) from the 7th BW/9th BS crashed in Lake Worth on 15 September 1949 while taking off from Carswell. Five of the 13 crewmembers were killed. The accident was attributed to two propellers unexpectedly going into reverse pitch. (Don Pyeatt Collection)

later on Mount Kologet, in an isolated region north of Smithers, British Columbia, about 50 miles from the Alaskan border. The airplane had apparently gained several thousand feet of altitude after being abandoned and flew 200 miles inland before crashing. An Air Force demolition team subsequently destroyed all sensitive parts of the airplane, but sections of it remain for the adventurous to explore.[30]

Subsequent investigation showed that icing was most likely responsible for the engine problems that led to the crash of the airplane, but many valuable lessons were learned from the tragic mission. One disturbing deficiency uncovered by the mission was that 64 hours were required to refuel the B-36 fleet at Eielson, way too long to be useful for an actual combat mission. Within a month's time, more than $11 million were appropriated to upgrade Eielson's refueling capabilities.[31]

Four months later, the world would again be brought to the brink of global war when North Korean troops invaded South Korea on 25 June 1950. Responding to a request from the United Nations, the United States ordered defensive ground forces into South Korea and authorized the Air Force to begin bombing targets within North Korea. The B-36 was withheld from direct participation in Korea, concentrating instead on its nuclear deterrent role.[32]

The 5th Strategic Reconnaissance Wing at Fairfield-Suisun AFB became the fifth B-36 wing on 14 November 1950. This was the second B-36 wing to be located at Fairfield-Suisun.

During January 1951, a B-36D (44-92098) from the 7th Bomb Wing participated in a cold weather test of the new jet engines and K-1 bomb-nav system. The test, conducted by the Air Proving Ground was performed at Eielson in temperatures that reached –55 degrees F to determine if the B-36D could successfully operate from Eielson in wartime conditions. Except for a few minor problems, the aircraft performed as expected and showed that the B-36D could operate at the northern pre-strike staging bases.

Five B-36s from the 7th BW approach Chicago from over Lake Michigan on 3 July 1949. During 1949, SAC rarely had more than 40 B-36s on hand, and only 5–8 of these were considered operationally capable. Because of maintenance problems and continued modifications, it is unlikely that the 7th BW could have launched more than a handful of sorties if the Cold War had turned hot. (Frank F. Kleinwechter)

The 7th Bomb Wing conducted the first B-36 deployment to the United Kingdom in January 1951. The purpose of the mission was to evaluate the B-36D under simulated war plan conditions, evaluate the equivalent airspeed and compression tactics for heavy bombardment aircraft, and evaluate select crew capability for bombing unfamiliar targets. Eleven bombers launched out of Carswell on 14 January, landing at Limestone AFB, Maine, later the same day; only six airplanes were required for the missions, and the other five were launched as spares. Departing Limestone on 15 January, two airplanes aborted shortly after takeoff for engine failures, and three others returned to Carswell. The remaining six landed at RAF Lakenheath

The second loss was a B-36B (44-92075) that crashed in British Columbia on 14 February 1950 after the crew bailed out over the Pacific. This was the only B-36 crash where the airplane was known to be carrying a nuclear weapon. A pair of 20mm cannon are visible in the center photo, while the photo at right shows the left wing. The wreckage was discovered in August 1997 with Scott Deaver visiting it on the 10th and Doug Craig and Doug Davidge on the 11th. (Doug Davidge)

on 16 January following a night radar bombing attack on Helgoland, Germany. For the next four days, the B-36s flew sorties out of England, including simulated bomb runs on the Heston Bomb Plot outside London, before returning to Carswell on 21 January.

On 16 February 1951, the 11th Bomb Wing was activated at Carswell under Brig. Gen. Thomas P. Gerrity. The new wing assumed control of the 11th Bomb Group, which had been attached to the 7th Bomb Wing since 18 November 1948. Brig. Gen. Clarence S. Irvine, the commander of the 7th Bomb Wing, became the 19th Air Division commander over the 7th and 11th Bomb Wings the same day. Col. John A. Roberts replaced Irvine as commander of the 7th Bomb Wing.

The long-running debate over the control of nuclear weapons finally ended in April 1951 when President Truman assigned control of nine Mk 4 bomb cores to Gen.

Hoyt S. Vandenberg, the Air Force Chief of Staff. By permitting the Department of Defense to possess a small number of the fission assemblies in addition to the non-nuclear bomb components, the awkward requirement of coordinating with the Atomic Energy Commission (AEC) during the opening phases of a retaliatory strike was eliminated. Nevertheless, the AEC still maintained control over the vast majority of the nuclear arsenal. Shortly afterward, Curtis LeMay announced that the B-36 was "now a mature weapon system."

SAC Continues Developing a Global Strike Force

A survey team from the 7th Bomb Wing deployed in a Douglas C-124 Globemaster II transport on 14 May to assess the facilities at Goose Bay, Labrador, Canada, for its use as a forward-operating base. The team returned 10 days

The 7th BW conducted the first B-36 deployment to the United Kingdom in January 1951 as Operation UK. Six B-36Ds (49-2658 shown) landed at RAF Lakenheath in Suffolk, England, on 16 January following a night radar bombing attack on Helgoland, Germany. For the next four days, the B-36s flew sorties out of England, including simulated bomb runs on the Heston Bomb Plot outside London, before returning to Carswell on 21 January. (National Archives College Park Collection)

later, fairly enthusiastic about the facility. Although the need to arm B-36s at pre-strike staging bases had been largely eliminated by Truman's decision to allow the Air Force to have weapons, the distance to targets in the Soviet Union still dictated that forward-operating bases be retained.

The 92nd Bomb Wing at Spokane AFB, Washington, became the sixth B-36 wing on 16 June 1951. The base was renamed in honor of Gen. Muir S. Fairchild on 20 July 1951 in a formal ceremony timed to coincide with the arrival of the wing's first B-36.[33]

On 17 July 1951, the 492nd Bomb Squadron dispatched six B-36s to Goose Bay for the first deployment since the May assessment. The purpose of the mission was to familiarize the squadron with the capabilities of the forward-operating base, test these capabilities, and provide an opportunity for crews to obtain actual polar flight experience. En route, a partial war plan profile was conducted as the bombers attacked Tampa, Florida; Birmingham, Alabama; Memphis, Tennessee; Little Rock, Arkansas; and Dallas, Texas, before returning to Carswell on 24 July.

The 7th Bomb Wing conducted a simulated radar-bombing mission against a commercial center target in Binghampton, New York, on 4 and 9 August. The exercise was flown to compare the radar bombing accuracy of aircrews using radar predictions based on eight-year-old photography against the bombing accuracy of crews using recent radar reconnaissance, and to determine the ability of crews to accomplish celestial navigation and electronic countermeasures reconnaissance. Unsurprisingly, the crews using the more current intelligence scored higher.

The 436th Bomb Squadron flew the second familiarization flight from Carswell to Goose Bay on 16 September 1951 using six B-36Ds. While at Goose Bay, the aircraft flew a polar navigation sortie to Thule, Greenland. The bombers returned to Carswell on 23 September.

A month later, on 11 October, six B-36Ds from the 9th Bomb Squadron deployed to Goose Bay for familiarization training. Two days later, the squadron flew a polar navigation mission to Thule and back. The six aircraft departed Goose Bay on 17 October, and flew a modified war plan profile mission en route to Carswell. With this deployment, each of the three 7th Bomb Wing squadrons had made a familiarization flight to Goose Bay.

By August 1950, operational storage sites for nuclear weapons were under construction in French Morocco at Ben Guerir AB,[34] Nouasseur AB, and Sidi Slimane AB, and all were completed by the end of 1951. The first B-36 deployment to French Morocco was made on 6 December 1951 when six aircraft from the 11th Bomb Wing landed at Sidi Slimane, having flown 5,000 miles nonstop from Carswell. During the 20-hour flight, the crews made good use of the recently installed bunks and galleys and reportedly ate steaks, bacon, and eggs. For the next five years, it would become relatively routine for B-36s to deploy to Sidi Slimane and nearby Nouasseur.[35]

B-36s from the 7th BW dot the flight line at Novasseur in French Morocco. The United States built three large air bases in North Africa during the late 1940s, mostly to support B-36 and B-47 squadrons. (Max Campbell)

Frank F. Kleinwechter, Jr., at Goose Bay with his B-36D (49-2680) on 23 January 1952. Note the hoses ducting warm air into the engine air intakes and the snow covering the top of the fuel truck in front of the wing. (Frank F. Kleinwechter)

Convair had an extensive B-36 exhibit at the National Air Show, held in September 1954 at Cox municipal Airport, Vandalia, Ohio. Boeing had a similar B-52 exhibit, but it appears the most popular item was the David Clark Company S-2 partial-pressure suit. (National Archives College Park Collection)

In 1949, the B-36 was featured in the documentary film, Target: Peace, which was centered around the operations of the 7th Bombardment Wing at Carswell AFB. Other scenes included B-36 production at the Fort Worth plant. (San Diego Air & Space Museum Collection)

A B-36A (44-92014) was displayed at the St. Louis Air Show on 17 October 1948. This is the view from the bombardier's compartment looking through the glazed nose. Note the two circular glass areas in the center of the glazed panels. The smaller one to the right is where the nose gunsight should be, but this item was missing from the A-models. The larger circular area is where the APS-54 radar warning receiver would be located on later aircraft. (National Archives College Park Collection)

This is the view out of the lower rear sighting blister. In addition to housing the gunsight, these blisters were used to visually monitor the engines and were retained even on Featherweight III airplanes. The diamonds on the engine cowling showed the position of the air plug that regulated cooling air. (Max Campbell)

Refueling in Alaska was an interesting exercise in the best of weather, and outright dangerous during storms. Note the crew walking on top of the wing, a hazardous activity when ice was present. Unlike modern aircraft, the early B-36s did not have single-point refueling. (Fairchild Heritage Museum Collection)

A view of the Rapid City (Ellsworth) AFB, South Dakota, flight line from atop the arch hangar. Note the two sets of maintenance docks, one of which is occupied. At Fort Worth and San Antonio the docks provided shade from the scorching Texas sun; at Ellsworth they provided a heated area to escape the bitter cold of winter. Major maintenance was done in the arch hangar where the entire airplane could be worked on out of the elements. (National Archives College Park Collection)

Given the freezing winters in Maine, the Air Force constructed an "arch hangar" large enough to house a couple of B-36s while they were undergoing maintenance. Similar hangars were built at Rapid City AFB, and surprisingly, at the Idaho test site. No attempt was made to construct enough hangars to house the B-36 fleet under normal conditions. This is the hangar, Building 8250, as it appeared when it was photographed for the Library of Congress during the 1990s. The Federal government has a long-standing program of photographing important buildings to document them for posterity. (Library of Congress Collection)

The 42nd Bomb Wing at Loring AFB, Maine, became the seventh B-36 wing on 25 February 1952. Loring had been built specifically to operate as a pre-strike staging base for the B-36, and included a large, arched hangar capable of housing two B-36s for maintenance (something no other B-36 base could do). Loring was the largest SAC base in the United States, with over 14,300 acres of overall area and 1.1 million square yards of ramp space. A remote area on the northeast corner of the property, originally called Caribou Air Force Station, was the first site specifically constructed for the storage, assembly, and testing of atomic weapons.[36]

The 6th Bomb Wing at Walker AFB, New Mexico, became the eighth B-36 wing on 16 June 1952, followed on the same day by the 72nd Bomb Wing at Ramey AFB, Puerto Rico. From 1941 to 1948, Walker AFB was known as Roswell Army Air Field, the location of the infamous Roswell UFO incident, an event that supposedly took place on 7 July 1947 while the base was under the command, ironically, of Roger Ramey. Borinquen Army Air Field had been established in 1939 to defend Puerto Rico and the Panama Canal, but the base took on new-found importance when SAC took it over after World War II.[37]

The snow-covered flight line at Loring AFB, Maine, sometime during 1956. In addition to the three B-36s in the foreground, note the Boeing KC-97 tankers in the background. These supported the B-47 and B-52 fleets on their strike routes over the **North Pole.** (National Archives College Park Collection)

Loring sometime during the B-52 era – note the five Stratofortresses standing alert in front of the old B-36 hangar. Loring AFB was carved out of the woods in 1953 and could accommodate 100 B-36s. It was named after Charles J. Loring, Jr., who was killed in Korea. (Library of Congress Collection)

Tornado!

Probably the most serious setback to the readiness of the B-36 force came on Labor Day, Monday, 1 September 1952, while B-36s from the 7th and 11th Bomb Wings sat parked at Carswell AFB. Surprisingly, the attack came not from the Soviet Union, or even the U.S. Navy, but from a source much deadlier and harder to predict.

Various maintenance procedures were being carried out and most of the aircraft were parked and not tied down. The weather forecast called for thunderstorms and gusting winds, not unusual for Texas during the summer. At 6:42 p.m., a tornado made a direct hit on the base and scattered the aircraft as if they were toys.[55]

As the storm subsided, two-thirds of the American very-heavy bomber fleet lay incapacitated. Thankfully, most personnel were off base for the long Labor Day weekend and there were few injuries. The base was immediately closed from fear of a major fire as thousands of gallons of high-octane aviation gasoline spilled from ruptured fuel tanks washed across the airfield. Operations were hurriedly transferred to other bases and to nearby Meacham Field.[56]

Not surprisingly, the original news accounts of the damage were less than accurate. For instance, the Convair employee newspaper reported that one B-36 had been destroyed (correct) "… and a number damaged …" (a gross understatement) with total damage estimated at $250,000. The paper did report that nine B-36s at Convair had been damaged, including four that sustained severe damage after they were "… rocked back on their tail sections."[57]

One aircraft (B-36D 44-92051) had been virtually destroyed and 82 others were damaged – including 10 at the Convair plant across the runway. Twenty-four of these were considered "seriously damaged." Upon receiving the news, the Strategic Air Command removed the 19th Air Division from the war plan.[58]

After landing at Meacham Field throughout the night, Air Force officials began arriving at Brig. Gen. Thomas P. Gerrity's office (Commander of the 11th Bomb Wing) by 5:30 a.m. Tuesday morning. Starting at dawn and continuing through the day, the Air Force made a thorough assessment of damage and called for a meeting of upper Air Force staff to develop a repair plan. On Wednesday morning, a meeting was held with Gerrity, Brig. Gen. Clarence S. Irvine (Commander of the 7th Bomb Wing), Col. Carl Extrand, and Maj. Gen. Kingston E. Tibbetts.[59] The generals decided the repair work would be apportioned one-third to SAC personnel, one-third to a Kelly AFB repair team (provided they could get the money and necessary work platforms out of the War Reserve Stocks and shipped to Carswell), and the remaining one-third would be repaired at Convair.[60]

The Air Force approved the repair plan and later that day, Wednesday, held a meeting in August C. Eisenwein's (President of Convair Fort Worth Division) office and a one-page letter contract was executed by Col. Jim Ferry, Contracting Officer on Gen. Irvine's staff, and Eisenwein on behalf of Convair, for the repair of two aircraft. Six were covered under a Contract Change Notice to the production contract and nineteen under a repair contract. Never before had an Air Force Contracting Officer issued a one-page letter contract authorizing several million dollars worth of work. The contract issued by Ferry was immediately approved by Irvine who ordered the expenditure of monies in support of the repair. Later, a conventional contract was issued to replace the Letter Contract.[61]

Twenty-five of the damaged aircraft were turned over to Convair to repair as part of Project FIXIT. By the end of September, the Convair newspaper was reporting that the total cost of Project FIXIT was likely to exceed $48 million – a considerable increase from the original report. Interestingly, the paper still did not provide any real indication of just how widespread the damage had been, although it did publish a photo of the one aircraft that had been written off. Of the twenty-five B-36s returned to Convair, eight required the replacement of major portions of the airframes: two had from bulkhead 4.0 forward replaced, five had the empennage (bulkhead 12.0 and aft) replaced, and one had from bulkhead 10.0 aft replaced.[62]

The aircraft listed as destroyed (44-92051) had been blown completely off the pavement, across a field, and came to rest in a ravine adjacent to the South fence. Its fuselage was broken in half and the left wing and the tail assembly were severed. The aircraft was partially disassembled and a path was graded to the pavement to allow it to be moved back to the ramp. All serviceable equipment, including control surfaces, etc., were stripped off the aircraft and used to fix other damaged airplanes or returned to inventory. The remains of the airframe were later shipped to Sandia Labs in New Mexico where it was used to fit-check new atomic

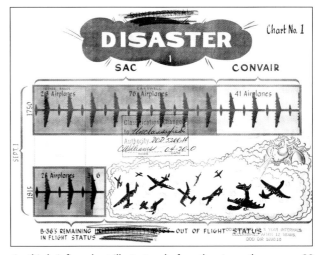

As this briefing chart illustrates, before the storm there were 28 airplanes at bases other than Carswell, 76 airplanes at Carswell, and 41 airplanes at Plant 4. Afterward, 83 of the B-36s were damaged beyond use. (Lockheed Martin)

bomb shapes and as a weapons loading trainer. Some reports indicate that at least part of the airframe was later used during various nuclear tests in Nevada.

Working jointly, Convair and the Air Force returned one aircraft to service the first week, and nine more in less than 2 weeks. Within 10 days of the storm, the 7th Bomb Wing was declared operationally ready. In fact, on 2 October, the 7th Bomb Wing dispatched six aircraft on a night tactics mission that included a simulated bomb run on Tampa, Florida, and actual armament firing on the Eglin test range. Interestingly, by the end of September the two Bomb Wings at Carswell were operating more aircraft than before the storm. Fifty-one more aircraft were back

in service by 5 October, and nineteen were at Convair awaiting repair. The last of the aircraft deemed repairable was back in the air on 11 May 1953.

The units at Carswell learned a lesson from the tornado. On 9 February 1953 high winds, thunderstorms, and hail again threatened the base, so the 7th Bomb Wing evacuated 22 of its 45 B-36s to Biggs AFB. The aircraft returned to Carswell the following day. On 19 February, the B-36s were again evacuated when high winds threatened the area. This time the aircraft went to Davis-Monthan AFB, Arizona, returning the following day. This scenario would be repeated many times to make sure the entire B-36 force was not exposed to severe weather at Carswell.[63]

Many of the airplanes lost their empennages during the tornado, perhaps showing a structural flaw in the B-36, but one that did not manifest itself in normal flight. This is a B-36D (44-92043) that was repaired by Convair and returned to service about a month after the tornado. (U.S. Air Force via Frank F. Kleinwechter Collection)

On the Carswell side, the maintenance docks proved destructive. Note the B-36F (50-1080) in the background missing its empennage. (U.S. Air Force via C. Roger Cripliver Collection)

This was the operations building for the 26th BS/11th BW. The maintenance dock is not supposed to be wrapped around the building. (U.S. Air Force via C. Roger Cripliver Collection)

The only airplane that was not returned to flying status was this B-36D (44-92051) that was blown into a field and severely damaged. (U.S. Air Force via C. Roger Cripliver Collection)

A large amount of damage was caused by maintenance docks blowing around. This is a B-36F (50-1076) and B-36H (51-5705). (U.S. Air Force via Frank F. Kleinwechter Collection)

This B-36H (50-1096) was the first airplane to be repaired by Convair and was returned to service only one week after the storm. (U.S. Air Force via C. Roger Cripliver Collection)

Photographed the night of the tornado, this B-36H (51-5705) and B-36F (50-1076) show the damage caused by a maintenance dock. (U.S. Air Force via C. Roger Cripliver Collection)

The first B-36B (by now a B-36D, 44-92026) got together with a B-36F (49-2675), resulting in significant damage to both airplanes. (U.S. Air Force via C. Roger Cripliver Collection)

Cleaning up the mess around a B-36D (49-2653). Despite the appearance, the damage was slight and was repaired by an Air Force team. (U.S. Air Force via Frank F. Kleinwechter Collection)

In addition to the single aircraft destroyed in the storm, one additional aircraft (B-36H 51-5712) was not returned to SAC – its damage was considered severe enough to not warrant repair. This aircraft was later converted into the NB-36H.

SAC Calls a Time-Out to Honor Amon G. Carter

The 95th Bomb Wing at Biggs AFB, Texas, became the tenth B-36 wing on 8 November 1952.[38]

Dwight David Eisenhower became President of the United States on 17 January 1953. A week later on Saturday, 25 January 1953, a crowd of thousands attended the opening of Fort Worth's Greater Southwest Airport – Amon Carter Field. The crowd listened to Secretary of the Air Force Harold E. Talbott give the dedication address and read a telegram from Eisenhower to Amon Carter who could not attend the event due to an advancing heart ailment. Present with Talbott were Walter S. McKee, Air Force Assistant Vice Chief of Staff and Lt. Gen. Roger M. Ramey, former Eighth Air Force Commander at Carswell. Also present were a B-36H (51-5736) and the XC-99 (43-52436), which were parked on the ramp for the ceremony.[39]

On 27 January 1953, the *Fort Worth Star-Telegram* reported that on 1 November 1952, a B-36 from Carswell had dropped a thermonuclear weapon (H-bomb) at Eniwetok Atoll[40] in the Pacific. The newspaper said the freshly painted airplane was scarred and blistered upon its return to Carswell. Unfortunately, as with many things reported in newspapers, this was not completely correct. There, indeed, had been a test of a thermonuclear device on 1 November – Shot Mike of Operation IVY was detonated at Eniwetok. However, the 10.4-megaton device was too heavy to be air dropped and was detonated on the

In addition to the B-36D sent to Sandia, one other airplane was not returned to operational service. This forward fuselage and cockpit of this B-36H (51-5712) was extensively damaged, and the aircraft was converted into the NB-36H nuclear test aircraft (NTA). (U.S. Air Force via C. Roger Cripliver Collection)

A B-36H and the XC-99 were featured at the opening of the Fort Worth Greater Southwest Airport – Amon Carter Field. Unfortunately, Carter was too ill to attend the dedication of the airport that bore his name. (Courtesy, Fort Worth Star-Telegram Collection, The University of Texas at Arlington Library)

The only airplane completely destroyed by the tornado was a B-36D (44-92051) that was largely ripped apart. The damage was sufficiently severe that the Air Force decided not to repair the airplane. Instead, all serviceable parts were removed for use on other B-36s, and the fuselage was used as an engineering mockup and training fixture at Sandia Base. Located on the southeastern edge of Albuquerque, New Mexico, for 25 years, the top-secret Sandia Base and the nearby Manzano Base carried on the atomic weapons research, development, design, testing, and training. The base was adjacent to, but separate from, Kirtland AFB. The photo at left shows the airframe being stripped for shipment and the photo at right shows the fuselage at Sandia. (Left: Lockheed Martin; Right National Museum of the United States Air Force Collection)

ground. It created a crater 164 feet deep and 6,240 feet across, with a fireball 3.5 miles in diameter. Nevertheless, a B-36H did conduct the first drop of a live thermonuclear weapon on 16 November as Shot King. The prototype Mk 18 super oralloy bomb was released from 40,000 feet using the Y-3A periscopic bombsight. Remarkably, the bomb was only 215 feet from the aiming point when it exploded at an altitude of 1,480 feet. Measurements showed the device had a yield of 500 kilotons.[41]

"Streamlined Crowbar"

As part of a simulated combat mission to RAF Fairford, United Kingdom, eighteen B-36s flew from Carswell to the staging base at Goose Bay on 2 and 3 February 1953; seventeen of the airplanes departed on 6 February, with one B-36 returning to Carswell. En route to Fairford, the formation encountered adverse weather conditions. One B-36, piloted by Capt. Richard S. George, experienced an equipment failure that nearly resulted in the loss of its crew. George later recounted the story of "A Streamlined Crowbar:"

"We left Carswell AFB in B-36H 51-5742 and flew to Goose Bay, Labrador, for staging the mission to England. The mission's targets were in a restricted area over the sea south of England where the simulated nuclear shapes (bombs) could be dropped.

"The profile called for cruising at around 7,000 feet for several hours before climbing to 25,000 feet for a few more hours of cruising before climbing to our bombing altitude of somewhere around 46,000 feet. All went very well up to this point.

"Night had fallen when we started the climb to bombing altitude. It was one of those cloudless, moonless nights when no visual horizon could be determined. The sky and the sea were as one. Thus, all flight operations were conducted by reference to the electric driven instruments. As we approached Iceland and turned toward the United Kingdom, the jets were restarted and the climb began. As we climbed through 42,400 feet, all ten engines abruptly quit and all lights in the aircraft went out – cause unknown at the time.

"Flame was streaming from the jets beyond the tail of the airplane from the small stream of fuel going into the hot combustion chambers. Flashlights illuminated the instruments for control; however, without electric power the gyros were operating strictly on inertia and were going to tumble in a very few minutes. We discovered the B-36 had the glide characteristics of a streamlined crowbar.

A large arch hangar was also built at Rapid City AFB, South Dakota. On 13 June 1953, President Dwight D. Eisenhower made a personal visit to dedicate the base in memory of Brig. Gen. Richard E. Ellsworth, commander of the 28th SRW, who lost his life in a B-36 crash in Newfoundland. (Fred Johnsen Collection)

"Ed Kieschnick and Robert Hardwick, the Flight Engineers, worked frantically to restore power. They split the electrical buss and began trying to put the alternators on the line. One alternator was excited and put into operation at around 39,000 feet and an engine start was attempted. By the time we reached 36,700 feet, two recip engines were running and the other four in various stages of being started. No attempt was made to restart the jets since the only goal was to get the machine on the ground.

"At Fairford RAF Base [sic], aircraft mechanics went over all systems on my B-36, searching for the cause of the loss of all ten engines during the

An incomplete B-36H (51-5702) being towed by the ubiquious Clark tug at Plant 4. Note that the nose turret is lacking its cannon and the APS-23 search radar and radome are not installed. Note the paper taped across the Convair line number (which was 222) on the nose, although the official data block a few feet aft is left uncovered. The censors scratched out the line numbers until the end. (National Archives College Park Collection)

flight from Goose Bay. No malfunction was discovered that could have caused the power failure. As a result, our crew was directed to prepare to fly a return Unit Simulated Combat Mission (USCM) to Goose Bay on February 12th. The crew's apprehension grew and there was even talk about refusing to fly since the cause of the malfunction had not been identified. Some crewmembers wrote letters to their families expressing their concern that they had been directed to fly without correcting the malfunction. We made the decision to set aside our fears and risk flying the mission as briefed.

"The preflight on the morning of departure was probably the most thorough ever performed. Everything checked out until the propeller reverse check was initiated. Both outboard props would not come out of reverse. All efforts to correct the malfunction by the flight crew failed. We taxied to the opposite side of the runway where a maintenance launch team began to work on the problem. This cleared the taxiway for the trailing aircraft in line so they could takeoff.

"At last, the master prop reverse switch was changed and, following five successful reverse propeller cycles, we were cleared for launch. A direct flight to Goose Bay was flown and we landed 10 hours 40 minutes after takeoff. The malfunction that caused the loss of ten engines on the flight to Fairford had still not been found when we launched for Carswell on February 15th. Four days after recovery at Carswell AFB, the cause of the malfunction was discovered.

"There were several large electrical panels in the bomb bay, each with three lights, each light was connected to one phase of the electrical system. These bus monitor lights were inserted through a hole in the face of the box and secured with a lock nut inside the box. A wire ran from the light and was attached to the main buss. The nut came loose, slid down the wire until it contacted and shorted the buss, disconnecting the alternators from the busses. The nut eventually burned in two, ending the short. This is what allowed the flight engineer to put the alternators back on line and resume normal operation."

From 20 to 24 March 1953, the 7th Bomb Wing supplied 12 B-36s to the AEC to provide photographic coverage of nuclear tests at Frenchman Flat, Nevada. Some of the aircraft were also equipped with sampling equipment to measure radioactivity at high altitudes around the tests.

The 99th SRW at Fairchild AFB, Washington, became the eleventh and last B-36 wing on 1 June 1953. The age of the piston-engine bomber was nearing its end.

A couple of B-36Fs (49-2683 near camera) from Walker AFB, New Mexico, in 1956. By this time, the entire active fleet had received the white anti-flash paint on the lower surfaces. (National Archives College Park Collection)

Six R-4360 engines sit behind a B-36H (51-5739) awaiting installation. Note that a maintenance dock surrounds the wings. Shipping the engines as a power-pack greatly reduced the time it took to install one on the airplane. (Lockheed Martin)

A Featherweight III B-36H (51-5727) undergoing maintenance at Fort Worth. Note that the upper sighting blister has been replaced by an aluminum cover – a clear indication of a Featherweight airplane with no gun turrets. (Lockheed Martin)

SAC's "Big Stick"

Hostilities in Korea ended on 27 July 1953 after claiming more than 50,000 American lives. The North Koreans had participated in cease-fire negotiations on three previous occasions, only to be followed by major military offensives. It appeared their "peace talks" were part of an on-going ploy to win military victory in the conflict by gaining time to re-arm. To prevent this from being repeated, one month after the truce was signed, President Eisenhower ordered SAC to deploy B-36s from the 92nd Bomb Wing at Fairchild to the Far East, visiting bases in Japan, Okinawa, and Guam. Operation BIG STICK was a

An RB-36H (51-5743, below) at Kirtland AFB to participate in Operation TEAPOT, a series of fourteen nuclear tests at the Nevada Test Site in the first half of 1955. B-36s dropped three weapons during the tests: 1.2-kiloton Mk 12s in Shot Wasp (above) and Wasp Prime, and an experimental 3.2-kiloton warhead in Shot HA (high altitude). (National Archives)

One of the B-36 crews during Operation Teapot. From left: Lt. Col. Eugene W. Cox, (standing) Capt. Earl R. Follensbee, Capt. Paul Eichenberg, 1Lt. Byron D. Miller, 1Lt. Dwight D. Odom, SSgt. Norman O. Whitmer; (kneeling) Maj. Fain H. Pool, 1Lt. Jackie L. Harvey, MSgt. Merlin D. Martin, TSgt. C.O.P. Canada, and SSgt. Paul J. Spella. (National Archives)

30-day exercise that dramatically demonstrated U.S. determination to keep peace in the region. The operation also fulfilled Convair's stated purpose of the B-36: "The ultimate purpose of the B-36 aircraft is to secure and maintain peace throughout the world."[42] As a further demonstration of power, on 15–16 October 1953, the 92nd Bomb Wing made a 90-day deployment to Guam, marking the first time an entire B-36 wing had been deployed overseas.

In 1954, Hollywood descended on Carswell to produce what has since become a cult classic among military aviation fans. Paramount Pictures brought Jimmy Stewart, June Alyson, Frank Lovejoy, and Harry Morgan[43] to Fort Worth to film *Strategic Air Command*, a propaganda film that also starred the B-36. Opening day of the film was similar to that of other epic films of the time such as *Ben Hur*, *The Ten Commandments*, and *Spartacus*, with blocks-long lines forming for tickets long before showtime. Theaters enjoyed sold-out performances for several months after the film was released on 1 January 1955. At Shady Oak Farm, a special private viewing of the film was made available for Amon Carter.[44] The viewing of this film that featured actors who had been guests in his home was the last movie Mr. Carter ever saw.

Wing insignia from the 6th Bomb Wing (Heavy) at Walker AFB, New Mexico. This is a B-36F (49-2681) undergoing maintenance in Fort Worth. Note the striped nose wheel door with the "No Smoking" warning on it. Between high-octane aviation fuel and nuclear weapons, it is uncertain why anybody would want to smoke around the airplane. (Lockheed Martin)

Scenes from the filming of Strategic Air Command, featuring Jimmy Stewart as Lt. Col. Robert R. "Dutch" Holland. During World War II, Stewart had been a decorated B-24 pilot with the 8th Air Force. June Allyson played his wife, Sally. Gen. Curtis E. LeMay was personally involved in the film, explaining why the movie captured SAC Operations like no other. (Lockheed Martin)

This B-36F (49-2680) was a Featherweight II airplane, and the sighting blisters confirm it still has gun turrets under their retractable covers. Photographed in May 1956 above Walker AFB, the airplane has non-standard markings, with a small aircraft number ahead of the "U.S. Air Force" on the forward fuselage. Note the painted cowlings on the J47 pods. (National Archives College Park Collection)

A Featherweight III B-36H (51-5722) late in its career. The device on top of the fuselage is a bomb hoist. Cable ran from the hoist through holes in the fuselage and allowed crewmembers to lift bombs onto the bomb racks. Most of the B-36 bases were fairly austere, not like the well-equipped bases crews of the current Northrop B-2 Spirit are used to. (Lockheed Martin)

Part of a Far East Deployment on 28 August 1953 to Yokota Air Base, Japan. The facility that houses Yokota AB was originally constructed by the Imperial Japanese Army in 1940 as Tama Airfield, and used as a flight test center. Yokota was used as a bomber base during the Korean conflict, but other than periodic visits, no B-36s were based there. (National Archives College Park Collection)

Deploying the B-36 meant maintenance – lots and lots of maintenance, especially on the R-4360 engines. Very few facilities were equipped to maintain the big bomber, so the crews were good at making do with whatever work stands and service vehicles were available. The photo above and the two on the facing page show several airplanes on 25 August 1953 in Okinawa during a Far East Deployment. Note that most aircraft have their engine cowlings removed and the gun turrets deployed. (National Archives)

7th Bomb Wing Named Operations

12 July 1953. Operation TAILWIND. Three B-36Hs flew simulated attacks on three vital control centers of the Air Defense Command in Savannah, Georgia, and New York City.

14 March 1954. Operation PATHAND. Nineteen B-36s launched on a unit simulated combat mission to Goose Bay and flew strike missions on U.S. cities while returning to base.

30 April to 5 May 1954. Operation ALAMO. The 7th Bomb Wing, along with other SAC wings, conducted simulated night radar-bombing evaluation missions against an industrial complex in San Antonio, Texas.

26 May 1954. Operation GOODWILL POLICY FLIGHT. A formation of three B-36s flew a goodwill flight over Granada, Managua, Leon, and Matagalpa, Nicaragua.

9 July 1954. Operation CHECK POINT. Twenty-two B-36s conducted simulated strikes on industrial targets in northeastern United States and southeastern Canada before deploying to North Africa in August.

11 to 22 October 1954. Operation FAT CAT. Twenty-eight B-36s participated in a combined operational readiness and unit simulated combat mission.

3 March 1955. Operation BAGDAD BILLY. Eight B-36s bombed Bedford, Indiana.

20 July 1955. Operation DEEP ROCK. Twenty 7th Bomb Wing B-36s flew out of Nouasseur and conducted a test and evaluation mission for the Strategic Air Command against targets in the northeast and eastern United States.

13 and 14 September 1955. Operation PEPPER POT II. Returning from Nouasseur, B-36s from the 7th Bomb Wing conducted a unit simulated combat mission.

6 and 7 October 1955. Operation POST HOLE. Twenty-four B-36s took part in an evacuation mission.

14 to 28 February 1956. Operation STYLE SHOW. Twenty-five B-36s deployed to Nouasseur, after loading special weapons at Loring AFB, Maine.

28 February 1956. Operation SNOW BANK. Three B-36s from the 7th BW took first place in a SAC competition against other B-36 wings.

15 March 1956. Operation HORNET GULF. Thirteen B-36s conducted simulated bomb runs on San Antonio and Houston, Texas, and Little Rock, Arkansas.

21 March 1956. Operation HORNET HOTEL. Eight B-36s conducted simulated bombing raids on San Antonio, Springfield, Denver, Salt Lake City, and Phoenix. During the mission, Lockheed F-80 and North American F-86 interceptors from the Texas Air National Guard at Hensley Field in Dallas flew fighter intercepts on the bombers.

6 to 8 June 1956. Operation HORNET JULIET. Eleven B-36s flew simulated attacks against Canada and the eastern and southern United States.

26 and 27 June 1956. Operation BROAD JUMP. Twenty-four B-36s from the 7th BW flew an unidentified classified mission.

19 July 1956. Operation HORNET KILO. Eight B-36s attacked St. Louis, Kansas City, Omaha, Amarillo, and Oklahoma City.

27 November 1956. Operation HORNET MIKE. B-36s from the 7th BW flew simulated bombing strikes on targets in the central United States.

13 December 1956. Operation HAPPY BIRTHDAY. Nine B-36s tested the capability to successfully launch aircraft under simulated wartime conditions.

10 January 1957. Operation WEDDING ALPHA. Thirty B-36s flew bomber stream missions.

17 January 1957. Operation WEDDING BRAVO. Thirty B-36s flew bomber stream missions.

24 January 1957. Operation WEDDING CHARLIE. Thirty B-36s flew bomber stream missions.

6 February 1957. Operation FIRST TEAM. The 7th BW flew 30 B-36 missions in a simulated combat exercise.

5 March 1957. Operation LAST STAND. Twenty-seven B-36s flew in a simulated combat exercise.

1 April to 1 July 1957. Project LONG RANGE. Training of 7th BW crews in a new type of mission.

5 April 1957. Operation BRIAR RABBIT. Six 7th Bomb Wing crews, two from each squadron, took part in a special weapons exercise.

20 April 1957. Operation SHOWDOWN. SAC Inspector General inspection. The 7th Bomb Wing was congratulated by the Commander-In-Chief, Strategic Air Command, and commended by the 19th Air Division commander for its superb performance in the exercise.

28 June 1957. Operation OVER EASY. The 7th Bomb Wing trained with new plans that were to become effective on 1 July 1957.

1 July 1957. Operation LOGBOOK ECHO. Thirteen B-36s flew bomber stream missions.

18 July 1957. Operation LOGBOOK DELTA. Thirteen B-36s flew bomber stream missions.

12 September 1957. Operation TREASURE CHEST. Twenty-five B-36s flew a unit simulated combat mission.

12 September 1957. Operation RED BALL began at Carswell requiring some crews to remain in base quarters at all times in case of a national emergency.

12 February 1959. Operation SAYONARA. Joint operation of the 7th BW at Carswell AFB and the 95th BW at Biggs AFB to retire the last B-36 to Greater Southwest International Airport – Amon Carter Field.

An unusual view looking directly up at a B-36 configured for landing. Note the location of the national insignia; these were moved outboard to these locations after the jet engines were installed. (Jay Miller Collection)

Dressed in heavy flight jackets and gloves, two 7th Bomb Wing officers at Goose Bay in March 1954. On the left is Lt. Col. George Burch, an aircraft commander, talking to Col. George T. Chadwell, 7th Bomb Wing Commander. (Frank F. Kleinwechter)

Snow covers several B-36s as they sit in Fort Worth. Note that the airplane in the foreground has had its propellers, and likely its engines, removed while it was undergoing maintenance or modification. (Lockheed Martin)

Retirement

Despite the 1951 proclamation by Curtis LeMay that the B-36 was "a mature weapon system," in reality it took several more years to reach that status. By the end of 1954, the B-36 was deployed with eleven operational Wings and routinely rotated through Fort Worth, San Diego, and San Antonio for major maintenance as part of SAN-SAN and SAM-SAC. The B-36 was the only aircraft capable of carrying any nuclear weapon in the inventory, particularly the first "stockpiled" thermonuclear weapons such as the Mk 17. Unfortunately, by 1954 it was obvious that the B-36 was also becoming quite venerable to the latest jet fighters, and that its high altitude capabilities were no longer sufficient compensation for its relatively slow speeds.

The end of the B-36 was much like the beginning – protracted and somewhat confused. By 1953, the Air Force had decided to phase out the B-36 in favor of the new Boeing B-52 Stratofortress. The B-36 was certainly outmoded by then and the B-52 promised a quantum leap in performance, but it would come at a tremendous cost in time and money, and its development lagged several years. In February 1956, the B-36 fleet finally began to be replaced by B-52s, but defense cutbacks in FY57 and FY58 slowed B-52 procurement and caused the final phase-out date for the B-36 to be changed from the end of FY57 to the end of FY59.

Nevertheless, in February 1956 the first early model B-36s began arriving at Davis-Monthan AFB, outside Tucson, Arizona. Over the next 39 months, a two-step process would reclaim everything useable from the airplanes. The first step removed parts from each aircraft that would eventually find use on still-operational B-36s and other aircraft types. The second step used a large guillotine to chop the airframes into pieces small enough to fit in portable ovens and smelted into ingots. Fortunately, four B-36s (51-13730, 52-2217, 52-2220, and 52-2827) and the

The storage yard at Davis-Monthan AFB showing reclaimed B-36s awaiting the smelter. Note the long row of propellers at lower left that have been removed from the aircraft. All of the airplanes are missing their R-4360 and J47 engines and whatever armament each still carried. The fleet was still young – less than 10 years on the oldest of the airframes – but the jet age had arrived and the piston-powered Peacemaker was obsolete. (AMARC/Teresa Vanden-Heuvel)

B-36 Wings

Wing	Tail Code	Location	Begin	End
5th Bomb Wing (Heavy)* [23rd, 31st, and 72nd BS]	Circle X	Travis AFB, CA	14 Nov 50	01 Jun 58
6th Bomb Wing (Heavy) [24th, 39th, and 40th BS]	Triangle R	Walker AFB, NM	16 Jun 52	01 Jun 57
7th Bomb Wing (Heavy) [9th, 436th, 492nd BS]	Triangle J	Carswell AFB, TX	01 Aug 48	01 Feb 58
9th Strategic Reconnaissance Wing [1st, 5th, 99th SRS] [1]	Circle X	Travis AFB, CA	01 May 49	01 May 50
11th Bomb Wing (Heavy) [26th, 42nd, 98th BS]	Triangle U	Carswell AFB, TX	18 Nov 48	01 Oct 57
28th Bomb Wing (Heavy)* [77th, 717th, and 718th BS]	Triangle S	Ellsworth AFB, SD	16 May 49	01 Feb 57
42nd Bomb Wing (Heavy) [69th, 70th, and 75th BS]	None+	Loring AFB, MN	25 Feb 53	01 Dec 55
72nd Bomb Wing (Heavy)* [60th, 73rd, and 301st BS]	Square F	Ramey AFB, PR	16 Jun 52	01 Jan 59
92nd Bomb Wing (Heavy) [325th, 326th, and 327th BS]	Circle W	Fairchild AFB, WA	16 Jun 51	15 Nov 56
95th Bomb Wing (Heavy) [334th, 335th, and 336th BS]	None+	Biggs AFB, TX	08 Nov 52	01 Jan 59
99th Strategic Reconnaissance Wing [346th, 347th, and 348th BS]	Circle I	Fairchild AFB, WA	01 Jan 53	04 Sep 56

* = redesignated from Strategic Reconnaissance Wing (SRW).

+ = the geometric tail codes were phased out before these Wings were activated.

Square was the 2nd Air Force; Triangle was the 8th Air Force; Circle was the 15th Air Force.

XC-99 (43-52436) were selected for preservation and given to various museums around the country.

With destruction of the B-36 fleet underway, Carswell's 11th Bomb Wing was reassigned to the Second Air Force, 19th Division, on 13 December 1957 and was moved to Altus AFB, Oklahoma. A transfer of Carswell's 7th Bomb Wing B-36s to various SAC wings began during January 1958 and ended on 30 May 1958 when the last B-36 left the base. On that day, a ceremony was held that featured a flyover of the B-36, its replacement B-52,[45] and Convair's new Mach 2 bomber, the B-58 Hustler. Making the ceremony's final speech was Amon Gary Carter, son of the late Amon G. Carter.[46]

By December 1958, only 22 B-36Js remained in the operational inventory, all with the 95th Bomb Wing at Biggs AFB. On 12 February 1959, the final B-36 built, B-36J (52-2827), flew the last official B-36 mission from Biggs to Amon Carter Field in Fort Worth, where it was put on public display at the end of Operation Sayonara.[47] The retirement of this B-36 marked the beginning of a new era – SAC became an all-jet bomber force on that day.

The first B-52 assigned to the 7th Bomb Wing arrived at Carswell on 19 June 1958. The wing continued deter-

rence operations until being transferred during 1965 to Southeast Asia in support of the Vietnam War, and later returned to Carswell at the end of that conflict. The wing then moved to Dyess AFB, Abilene, Texas, and Carswell AFB closed to later re-open as Naval Air Station Joint Reserve Base Fort Worth at Carswell Field.

After all serviceable and sensitive equipment had been stripped from the airplanes, the carcass was chopped up using a large blade suspended by a crane. The pieces were then loaded into a portable smelter. (Frederick A. Johnsen Collection)

Working on an R-4360 at Ramey AFB, Puerto Rico, in May 1956. Note how much paint is missing from the propeller hub, surprising given the pusher configuration used by the B-36. (National Archives College Park Collection)

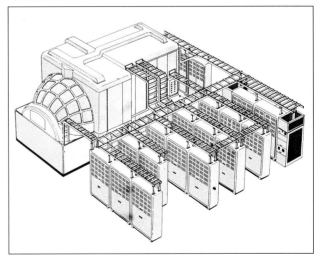

This photo from Biggs AFB in 1956 shows the air plugs on the J47 engines in the open (left) and closed positions. The jet engines were not used very much, and the streamlined air plugs minimized drag. (National Archives College Park Collection)

This early, fixed-based Curtiss-Wright Dehmal Flight Simulator was installed at Ramey, Fairchild, and Carswell. The unit was a systems trainer, and allowed instructors to insert failures in many of the systems. (National Archives College Park Collection)

This was a standard publicity photo for the B-36 for many years, showing a factory-fresh B-36D (44-92057). This airplane became the armament test ship shown on pages 90 and 110. This airplane also was used for J35 and J47 jet engine tests, four-blade propeller vibration tests, and was the first airplane equipped with R4360-53 engines. (Frank F. Kleinwechter Collection)

The upper aft turrets in their retracted position. This was an RB-36 at Ramey AFB in late 1956. The B-36 was the last American bomber with extensive defensive armament. (National Archives College Park Collection)

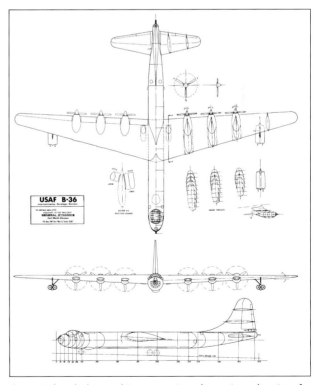

Convair handed out this poster-size three-view drawing for years, back when aircraft manufacturers did that sort of thing. Excepting the addition of jet engines and minor detail changes, all B-36s were essentially identical. (Lockheed Martin)

This B-36F (49-2677) carried the B-58 static-test airframe from Plant 4 in Fort Worth to Wright-Patterson AFB, Ohio, on 12 March 1957. Note the external bracing between the B-36 main landing gear well and the top of the B-58 wing. The inboard propellers were removed since they would have hit the B-58's wing, and the B-36 landing gear was left down for the entire cross-country flight. Surprisingly, preparing for this flight was not considered a major undertaking at the time. (Bill Shiner via James Baldwin)

In 1955 Leo A. Daly designed two buildings for SAC headquarters at Offutt AFB, Nebraska: the command post and the chapel. The new command post featured a four-story, reinforced-concrete and masonry office building above ground, and a reinforced-concrete, below-ground command post with 24-inch-thick walls and a 24 to 42-inch-thick roof. At right is the "big board" that showed the status of all SAC units – and the Soviets – around the world. (National Archives College Park Collection)

The first B-36A (44-92004) during its static testing at Wright-Patterson AFB. Hydraulic jacks and sandbags were used to apply pressure to the airframe to simulate flight loads. The fuselage skins buckled at 70 percent of the design load, but the primary structure was not damaged. Note the open aft turret bay. (National Archives College Park Collection)

A couple of B-36Bs (44-92012 in the background) at Carswell in May 1948. Note the missing rudder and the maintenance stands around the airplanes. The A- and B-models were never truly operational. (National Archives College Park Collection)

This B-36H (52-1362) poses in 1956 at Carswell with some of the dozens of stands needed to maintain the airplane. Although a reliable engine for its era, the R-4360 required a lot of maintenance. (National Archives College Park Collection)

A B-36D (44-92097) flies above Carswell AFB on 8 June 1951. Note the Triangle-J tail code on the vertical stabilizer. Note the forward fuselage markings. This airplane was written off on 28 August 1954. (National Archives College Park Collection)

A formation of three B-36s show the anti-flash white "high-altitude camouflage" the fleet received late in their careers. Note that only part of the underwing surface was painted. (San Diego Air & Space Museum Collection)

One of the RB-36Es (44-92012) at Ramey AFB on 30 September 1954. Note that the forward upper turret is deployed – this is before the airplane was converted to its final Featherweight III configuration. (National Archives College Park Collection)

This RB-36E (44-92023) was assigned to the 72nd BS/72nd BW based at Ramey AFB. It was photographed at Travis AFB in August 1952 with a Circle-X tail code. (National Museum of the United States Air Force Collection)

This B-36D (44-92067) was part of a large Far East deployment on 26 August 1953 to demonstrate U.S. resolve over Korea. Note the dust being blown up by the propellers and jet engines. (National Archives College Park Collection)

Another B-36D (44-92048) during the same 1953 Far East deployment. Of interest is the serial number on the tail, which appears to have been stenciled on instead of the normal neat paint job. (National Archives College Park Collection)

This RB-36H (51-13730) was on display at the National Aircraft Show in Philadelphia on 6 September 1955. Note the deployed aft upper turret and the location of the serial number on the forward fuselage. (National Archives College Park Collection)

This B-36D (44-92042) made a less-than-perfect landing at RAF Boscombe Down in the United Kingdom. The airplane attempted to land during bad weather and ran off the runway. It was subsequently repaired. (Kev Darling Collection)

Four B-36s from the 92nd Bomb Wing line up on the ramp at Fiarchild AFB. A couple of additional airplanes are undergoing maintenance in the background, including one mostly inside the hangar at the upper left. (Fairchild Heritage Museum Collection)

The B-36F (49-2672) in the foreground had not been converted to the Featherweight III configuration – note the deployed upper turret. This aircraft arrived in the graveyard in late 1956 and was scrapped during early 1957. (Frederick A. Johnsen Collection)

Two B-36Hs (51-1358 shown), sporting a wild red, white, and blue paint scheme, were used as high-altitude photography targets on the Atlantic Missile Range at Cape Canaveral, Florida. (Dave Menard Collection)

B-36 Hull Losses

	Date	Model	Serial No.	Unit	Location	Remarks
1	15 Sep 49	B-36B	44-92079	7th BW	Carswell AFB	Crashed into Lake Worth on take off. Five of 13 crewmembers killed.
2	14 Feb 50	B-36B	44-92075	7th BW	British Columbia	Returning from Alaska. Severe icing and engine fire. Abandoned by crew in-flight. Five of 17 crewmembers killed. Broken Arrow.
3	22 Nov 50	B-36B	44-92035	11th BW	Cleburne, Texas	Three engines – two on one side – failed. Crashed 20 miles south of runway. Two of 17 crewmembers killed.
4	27 Apr 51	B-36D	49-2658	7th BW	Oklahoma	55 miles northeast of Oklahoma City. Mid-air collision with F-51 fighter. F-51 pilot killed; 13 of 17 B-36 crewmembers killed.
5	06 May 51	B-36D	49-2660	7th BW	Kirtland AFB	Landing during high winds. Twenty-three of 25 crewmembers killed.
6	29 Jan 52	B-36D	44-92080	92nd BW	Fairchild AFB	Landed short. All crewmembers survived.
7	06 Mar 52	B-36F	50-1067	7th BW	Carswell AFB	Landing gear collapsed on touchdown. Burned at ramp. Only minor injuries.
8	15 Apr 52	B-36D	44-92050	92nd BW	Fairchild AFB	Crashed on take off. Fifteen crewmembers killed.
9	28 May 52	B-36F	50-1066	11th BW	Carswell AFB	Landed short. Seven crewmembers killed.
10	12 Jun 52	B-36D	44-92038	Convair	San Diego	Fuel fire on the ground during SAN-SAN. No one aboard.
11	04 Aug 52	B-36F	49-2679	7th BW	Carswell AFB	Fuel fire on the ground. Only minor injuries to three crewmembers.
12	05 Aug 52	B-36D	49-2661	Convair	Pacific near San Diego	Wing fire in flight. Two crewmembers killed.
13	01 Sep 52	B-36D	44-92051	11th BW	Carswell AFB	Tornado damage not repaired. No one aboard.
14	07 Feb 53	B-36H	51-5719	7th BW	RAF Fairford, England	Adverse weather caused the aircraft to run out of fuel. All survived.
15	12 Feb 53	B-36H	51-5729	7th BW	Goose Bay	Misguided by GCA – flew into hill. Two of 17 crewmembers killed.
16	18 Feb 53	RB-36H	51-13719	28th SRW	Walker AFB	Landing gear collapsed. Burned on ground. All survived.
17	18 Mar 53	RB-36H	51-13721	28th SRW	Newfoundland	Controlled flight into terrain. Twenty-three crewmembers killed.
18	05 Aug 53	RB-36H	52-1369	5th SRW	Atlantic off Scotland	Loss of power. Nineteen crewmembers killed, four survivors.
19	11 Dec 53	B-36D	44-92071	7th BW	El Paso	Controlled flight into terrain during approach. The crew of nine was killed.
20	27 Feb 54	B-36D	44-92069	92nd BW	Fairchild AFB	Landing gear collapsed. Burned on ground. All crewmembers survived.
21	29 Mar 54	B-36D	44-92032	92nd BW	Fairchild AFB	Takeoff practice abort. Seven crewmembers killed.
22	27 Aug 54	RB-36H	51-13722	28th SRW	Ellsworth AFB	Controlled flight into terrain. Twenty-six crewmembers killed, one survivor.
23	28 Aug 54	B-36D	44-92097	95th BW	Biggs AFB	Loss of power on landing. One crewmember killed.
24	08 Feb 55	B-36D	44-92029	95th BW	Carswell AFB	Pilot landed short after misjudged approach. Two crewmembers killed.
25	06 Mar 55	B-36D	44-92030	42nd BW	Loring AFB	Wingtip hit snowbank during landing. All crewmembers survived.
26	25 May 55	B-36J	52-2818	6th BW	Sterling City, Texas	In-flight breakup during overflight of thunderstorm. Crew of 15 killed.
27	27 Jun 55	B-36D	49-2653	11th BW	Carswell AFB	Delayed salvage. Aircraft damaged during Operation CASTLE atomic tests.
28	04 Jan 56	RB-36H	52-1387	28th SRW	Ellsworth AFB	Landing accident. Burned on ground. All crewmembers survived.
29	10 Jan 56	B-36D	44-92041	95th BW	Biggs AFB	Hard landing. Four longerons at Bulkhead 10.0 failed . All survived.
30	15 Nov 56	RB-36H	51-13720	28th SRW	Denver	Loss of power after takeoff; crash landed. Fire on ground. All survived.
31	07 Jun 57	B-36H	51-5741	7th BW	Carswell AFB	Aircraft heavily damaged on 25 April 1957 during a storm fly-through. No injuries. Delayed salvage on 7 June 1957.
32	09 Nov 57	RB-36H	51-5745	72nd SRW	Ramey AFB	Explosion and ground fire. All crewmembers survived.

This B-36D (49-2660) crashed while landing in high winds at Kirtland AFB, New Mexico, on 6 May 1951. Twenty-three of the 25 crewmembers were killed. A C-54 and four Bonanzas were also damaged. (National Archives College Park Collection)

On 28 May 1952, this B-36F (50-1066) from the 11th BW crashed during a contingency landing at Carswell AFB after an engine cowling came loose during take-off. Seven crewmembers died in the accident. (San Diego Air & Space Museum Collection)

Not a write-off, but an accident nonetheless. This B-36D (49-2649) made a rough landing at Fairchild AFB and the nose gear collapsed. Note that rescuers went through the forward blisters and the crew hatch. (Fairchild Heritage Museum)

On 28 May 1952, a B-36F (50-1066) burned after landing short of the runway at Carswell AFB. Seven crewmembers were killed in the accident. Note the number of people around the crash site. (Air Force photo via Ed Calvert)

This RB-36H (51-13720) lost power after taking off from Stapleton Airport outside Denver and crashed. Fortunately, all of the crewmembers survived, although the airplane was a complete loss. (National Archives College Park Collection)

Returning from a deployment on 12 February 1953, this B-36H (51-5729) crashed at Goose Bay when the GCA controller issued incorrect instructions during landing. Another B-36H (51-5719) had crashed in England a week earlier during the same deployment. (National Archives College Park Collection)

The last B-36J (52-2827) was loaned to the city of Fort Worth on 12 February 1959 and spent the better part of the next four decades on display at various locations around the city. Unfortunately, a proper museum never materialized, and in 2008 the Air Force (which still owned the aircraft) sent the B-36 to the Pima Air & Space Museum in Tucson, Arizona. The airplane was restored to a good condition and placed on display in October 2009. Nevertheless, there are a few details of the restoration that are incorrect, including the sighting blisters (this was a Featherweight III airplane and should not have upper blisters, but should have lower aft blisters) and the white anti-flash paint (which was masked when it was painted instead of being free-hand). The painted glazed panels protect the interior from the desert sun. (Don Pyeatt)

Pima is the only museum where it is possible to see the evolution of American heavy bombers in one glance. The facility has a B-17, B-24, B-29, B-36, B-47, B-52, and B-58 (although the last was a medium bomber). This is the NB-52A (52-003). (Don Pyeatt)

EPILOG

POLITICAL IDEOLOGY
AND ECONOMIC REALITIES

A B-36H or early B-36J (the twin APG-41 radomes are visible, and the airplane has sighting blisters so it is not a Featherweight III J-model) flies over Walker AFB, New Mexico in 1956. The contrails produced by the B-36 could be seen for miles, not an asset when attacking a heavily defended target. (National Archives College Park Collection)

World War II had simply served to put on hold a growing rift that began during the 1920s between the Stalinist Soviet Union and the western democracies. When Nazi Germany attempted to conquer Russia, the United States and United Kingdom were forced into an extremely awkward alliance with the Soviet Union to prevent its economic and military resources from being absorbed by the Third Reich.

When World War II ended, the democracies sighed in relief and immediately disarmed, furloughed their troops, and destroyed their weapons of war. A doomed effort by the Western democracies to work with the Soviet Union in the administration of defeated Axis countries immediately fell apart when Stalin, sensing a threat to his borders, tried to evict the Allies from Berlin. One result of the Berlin Crisis was that the Allies realized they were disarmed and incapable of preventing Stalin from overrunning all of Europe. The Allies needed a super weapon to stave off the perceived Soviet threat, and they needed it immediately. Unfortunately, the only super weapon available to Europe and the United States was a skillful use of intimidation – starring the B-36.

The B-36 was presented to the world as a larger-than-life machine fully capable of annihilating, with impunity, any enemy anywhere in the world – a claim that was simply not true. Nevertheless, as development continued, so did claims about the unimaginable performance of the aircraft. The U.S. Air Force flew the new bombers over heavily populated areas simply to be seen, and seen in numbers and in diverse locations. Sequence numbers were scratched from photographs of the airplanes to not reveal the actual numbers produced. The subterfuge, however, produced the desired result – it bought time to develop the airplane into what it was originally intended to be through a series of modification programs. As more time was gained, other weapons were developed, particularly the Boeing B-52 Stratofortress, Intercontinental Ballistic Missiles (ICBM), Air Launched Ballistic Missiles (ALBM), and Submarine Launched Ballistic Missiles (SLBM).

The Soviets attempted to match, and even overtake, the technical lead of the west by developing their own nuclear weapons and advanced delivery systems. As a means of slowing the western powers, the Soviets started a series of "proxy wars" in Korea, the Middle East, and Vietnam in order to divert U.S. military focus away from Russia. It almost worked. Ultimately, however, an unexpected force – the bank – overthrew the Soviet Union.

Over the forty-year epic called the Cold War, the United States spent more than $8 trillion on defense, with $2.2 trillion spent during Ronald Reagan's eight years as president alone.[64] The Russians simply went bankrupt trying to match this massive spending. Political ideology started the Cold War and economic ideology ended it.

Capitalism will always outperform socialism for two basic reasons: a capitalist is rewarded for hard work and innovation by an increase in discretionary personal wealth whereas a socialist is rewarded with a state-dictated food and shelter ration and another job assignment. For the same reasons, capitalists will fervently protect their freedoms on the battlefield. Ironically, capitalism has little bearing on the actual form of government it resides within; China is the latest example of capitalism mixing, mostly successfully, with communism.

Using the most perverted logic imaginable, the threat of nuclear devastation prevented nuclear devastation; it even had an ironically appropriate acronym – MAD, for Mutually Assured Destruction. When describing "global thermonuclear war," perhaps the computer in the movie War Games said it best, "A strange game; the only winning move is not to play."[65]

Fortunately, the Cold War produced many benefits for mankind. Technology advanced to the level it is today, space flight evolved from the conflict, and a healthier population now enjoys medical discoveries derived from atomic weapons research. Cities contributing to the conflict flourished into something they would have never become otherwise. This outcome was summarized in Amon Gary Carter's farewell speech when the last B-36 left Carswell on Memorial Day, 30 May 1958. As part of the Operation MILESTONE speech presented after re-enacting his father's then-famous B-36 ride from the Convair plant to Carswell in 1948, the younger Carter said:[66]

"Twice during the history of the B-36 in Fort Worth, Convair's employment passed 30,000.

"In 1940, before the Convair plant existed and before the B-36 existed, Fort Worth was a city of 177,622 people whose banks reported clearings of $355,864,409. The next census, in 1950 – right in the middle of the B-36 program – shows an increase of more than 100,000 people, to 278,778. And bank clearings had risen to $1,451,447,698.

"The B-36 was not solely responsible for this tremendous growth, of course, but it was perhaps a bigger figure than all the other factors put together.

"Let's take a quick look at the economic picture. Carswell's payroll and other expenditures approximate $39 million each year. Convair's Fort Worth payroll during the B-36 program averaged nearly $60 million annually, and at the peak in 1951, it was $11 million for the year.

"And we must take into consideration the other millions spent locally by both Convair and Carswell for materials, operating supplies, and parts connected with the B-36 program.

As the official publication of the West Texas Chamber of Commerce phrased it a few years ago, Convair, Carswell, and the B-36 put gold-plated hinges on the 'Gateway to the West.' "

THE FIRST WIDE BODY
THE SAN DIEGO-BUILT XC-99

Despite its massive size, the ground crew still manually pulled the prop through a cycle to circulate oil before starting the engines. This is the XC-99 (43-52436) and the crew has a rope around the inboard 19-foot-diameter propeller. Note the single 110-inch main gear, a feature initially shared with the XB-36 and YB-36. (Peter M. Bowers Collection)

While it is certain that Air Force Plant 4 was designed for production of aircraft larger than the B-24, the 60,000-pound B-32 that was produced did not compare to the 200,000-pound B-32 that was forecast before the plant opened. Perhaps the Consolidated spokesperson was confused, or perhaps his intention was to confuse the enemy. What we do know is that wind tunnel testing of a new "Model 37" passenger liner was reported in the 25 May 1945 edition of the plant's newspaper, *The Eagle*. Ostensibly described as an experimental passenger liner ordered by Pan American World Airways, the aircraft sported luxury seating and sleeping quarters. The aircraft, a cargo version of the B-36, was claimed to be in development for postwar commercial use.[1]

As early as May 1942, Consolidated had investigated a Model 37 cargo variant of the XB-36 that used the same wing, empennage, engines, and landing gear. The Army Air Forces ordered a single example (43-52436) on 31 December 1942 under a $4.6 million contract (W535-ac-34454) that specified the XC-99 project was not to interfere with the construction or delivery of the XB-36. Interestingly, the fact that an entire new fuselage needed to be designed was not considered high risk, and Convair viewed the XC-99 as an expeditious way of verifying several aspects of the B-36 design since no military equipment needed to be provided for the aircraft. The XC-99 would prove to be the largest piston-engine cargo aircraft ever developed.[2]

Even during the war, Consolidated pitched a commercial version of the aircraft to several airlines.[3] Pan American World Airways ordered 15 of the aircraft in February 1945, and production of the "Super Clippers" would begin as soon as the war ended. Each of the airliners could carry 204 passengers in relative luxury, along with 15,300 pounds of baggage and mail. Six 5,500-hp Wright T-35 turboprop engines would drive 19-foot three-bladed propellers. The interior arrangement featured a mixture of dayplane seats and sleeper berths, with spacious lounges located on each of the two decks, and large circular staircases located on each end of the aircraft. A full galley would offer gourmet meals, and the lavatory facilities resembled a fine hotel more than a modern airliner. However, it was not to be, and the "wide body" era would have to wait another 20 years until the Boeing 747 was introduced.

Pan Am also asked Convair to investigate a flying boat derivative of the huge aircraft.[4] The basic design of the aircraft was similar, except the six turboprop engines drove counter-rotating, three-bladed, 16-foot-diameter tractor propellers instead of the larger pushers. And, of course, the fuselage incorporated a hull design. The elimination of the landing gear and its supporting structure allowed a weight savings of 6,500 pounds, even after the modified hull and retractable wing floats were added. However, the additional drag generated by the hull and floats meant the flying boat would need to carry 3,000 pounds more fuel to achieve the same nominal range. The design had a range of

Consolidated's peacetime production planning relied on conversions of military designs to commercial applications. This is the Model 39 XR2Y-1 Liberator Liner, based on the wing and landing gear of a B-24 and the vertical stabilizer from a PB4Y Privateer. The fuselage was of new design. One prototype was produced after the war for the U.S. Navy but was eventually sold to American Airlines. (Don Pyeatt Collection)

4,200 miles at 25,000 feet and 332 mph – 10 mph slower than the conventional aircraft. Its maximum service ceiling was reduced from 30,000 feet to 29,100, and its takeoff distance increased from 4,760 feet (for the landplane) to 5,680 feet. It would take 48 seconds for the flying boat to clear the water after it started its takeoff run.

There appeared to be no reason a flying boat version of the Model 37 could not be developed. But the age of the flying boat was past, and Pan Am decided to concentrate on more conventional aircraft such as the Constellation and DC-7.

The single XC-99 was built at the Consolidated factory in San Diego, although the wings and other common B-36 parts were manufactured in Fort Worth and shipped

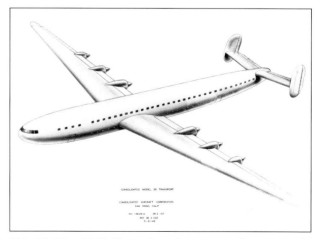

This 21 May 1942 illustration shows an early commercial passenger versions of the Model 36 transport. Note the two vertical stabilizers, streamlined fuselage, and square windows. (San Diego Air & Space Museum Collection)

to San Diego for installation. On 23 November 1947, the XC-99 made its maiden flight with Russell R. Rogers and Beryl A. Erickson at the controls.[5] The aircraft used the same 110-inch-diameter single main wheels as the XB-36, but the runway at Lindberg Field could tolerate these as long as the aircraft was lightly loaded. The dual-tandem, four-wheel main gear was retrofitted, and the XC-99 first flew with it on 24 January 1949. Initially the aircraft was fitted with R-4360-25 engines, but in early 1950 was fitted with -41 engines for commonality with the B-36 fleet.

The XC-99 could carry over 100,000 pounds of cargo, 400 fully equipped troops, or 300 litter patients. Total cargo volume was 16,000 cubic feet split between two decks in a fuselage that was 20 feet high, 14 feet wide, and 182.5 feet long. The aircraft could fly 1,720 miles with a 100,000-pound load, or 8,100 miles with 10,000 pounds.

Cruising speed was 292 mph, with a top speed of 335 mph at 30,000 feet. Eight crewmembers were required to operate the aircraft: pilot, copilot, two flight engineers, navigator, radio operator, and two scanners. The scanners were stationed on the lower deck in the aft section near windows to observe the operation of the engines and landing gear. The scanners doubled as cargomasters while the aircraft was on the ground.[6] The flight deck was carpeted and soundproofed, and black fluorescent lighting was provided at all crew stations for night flying.[7]

The XC-99 was equipped with two electrically operated sliding cargo doors on the bottom of the fuselage, one just forward of the wing and one in the aft fuselage. Two pairs of clamshell doors were installed immediately aft of the rear sliding cargo door although the rear sliding door had to be opened before them. Structural limitation

The pace of progress was rapid after World War II. The XC-99, still under construction in the upper left corner, with the XB-46 jet demonstrator being assembled in the foreground. The maiden flight of the sleek XB-46 took place on 2 April 1947 after a month of taxi testing, and lasted ninety minutes as the bomber departed the Convair plant in San Diego for Muroc Army Airfield in the High Desert. This was more than six months before the XC-99 made its maiden flight. The XB-46 was an unsuccessful competitor against the Boeing XB-47 Stratojet. The nose section is preserved at the Air Force Museum. (National Archives College Park Collection)

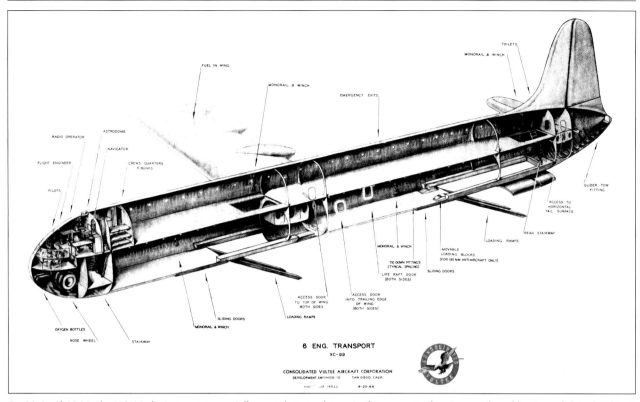

By 20 April 1944, the XC-99 design was essentially complete as shown in this cutaway drawing produced by Consolidated Vultee's Development Engineering Department in San Diego. Note that the navigator and radio operator sat one level above the pilot and flight engineer on the flight deck. The XC-99 was huge by cargo aircraft standards. (Convair)

prohibited the clamshell doors from being opened in flight, although the sliding doors could be opened to drop cargo. Either cargo opening could be fitted with angled ramps that permitted vehicles to be driven onto the lower level.

There were two cargo compartments on the lower deck, separated by the wing carry-through structure and a single long compartment on the upper deck. Cargo could be loaded, unloaded, or shifted within the cargo compartments by means of four electric hoists. The hoist in each of the lower compartments could be used to shift or drop cargo while the aircraft was in flight, but the two hoists in the upper compartment were normally restricted to ground operations. The hoists were set on tracks located in the ceiling of each compartment and could traverse the entire length of their compartment. Each hoist could lift up to 4,000 pounds single purchase, or 8,000 pounds double purchase. The lower decks were equipped with winches attached to the cargo floor to pull items up the ramps.[8]

The upper cargo compartment was accessed via two openings in its floor, one directly above the forward sliding door, and the other directly above the aft-most clamshell door. There was also a ladder at the front and rear of the fuselage to allow personnel access to the upper compartment. The flight deck was equipped with five canvas bunks, two of which could be reconfigured to provide "jump-type" seats along one of the outside walls.

A toilet and drinking water supply were also provided, but no galley was fitted. Provisions were made for five additional toilets (two on the upper deck and three on the lower deck) when the aircraft was outfitted as a troop carrier. Troop seating was on canvas benches along each side of the fuselage on both decks.[9]

The XC-99 was delivered to the Air Force on 26 May 1949 and was used extensively by the San Antonio Air

First flying on 16 March 1947, the CV-240 Convairliner was the major commerial product offered by Consolidated after World War II. Eventually, Convair produced almost 1,200 of the airplanes. (National Archives College Park Collection)

Materiel Depot at Kelly AFB, Texas. In June 1950, the XC-99 made several 1,150-mile flights carrying B-36 parts from Kelly AFB to San Diego as part of Operation ELEPHANT. On 14 July, a return trip from San Diego to Kelly included ten R-4360 engines and 16 propellers, as well as other material. The total payload was 101,266 pounds, and the aircraft had a ramp weight of 303,334 pounds. During the flight, the No. 6 engine began backfiring and was shut down – the flight was completed on five engines!

The XC-99 continued to provide useful service to the San Antonio depot, and flew more flight hours than any other Air Force experimental aircraft. By June 1957, it was obvious that structural fatigue was occurring in the wing and some fuselage bulkheads, and the Air Force did not want to spend the estimated $1 million to fix it. The XC-99 was permanently grounded. A few months later, title for the aircraft was transferred to the Disabled American Veterans, who put the aircraft on public display for the next 30 years. The aircraft fell into disrepair, and in 1993, the Kelly Field Heritage Foundation purchased it for $65,000 and donated it to the Air Force Museum. The museum is in the process of disassembling the XC-99 and transporting it to Wright-Patterson AFB. As of the end of 2009, most of the fuselage upper deck, the outer wing panels, and the empennage had been relocated using available (no cost) C-5 training flights. Given the fleet-wide issues surrounding the C-5s, and the heavy usage of the type to support the wars in Iraq and Afghanistan, it might be several years before the entire aircraft makes it to the museum.

By December 1949, Convair had designed a production version of the C-99. The most visible change was the raised "bubble" cockpit common with the production B-36. This included the same basic flight deck used on the B-36B. A new nose landing gear was located in a bulge located under the forward fuselage, looking much like the radome under the B-36. The new arrangement did not protrude into the cargo area, and its slightly longer stroke allowed a level floor (the XC-99 had a slight forward slope).[10]

A revised fuselage featured a rearranged cargo area with a pressurized upper deck that could accommodate 183 troops. The lower compartment remained unpressurized, but now featured large clamshell doors in the nose and tail that allowed vehicles to drive on and off at the same time. The doors provided an entrance measuring 12x13 feet and could accommodate the Army's 240-mm howitzer and M46/M47/M48 Patton battle tanks. The C-99 was designed to allow vehicles or tanks to be transported with their operating and maintenance crews directly to a combat area without the need for a staging area, a capability not realized until the advent of the Lockheed C-5A Galaxy.

The C-99 had 21,714 cubic feet of available cargo space, compared to the 16,000 cubic feet available on the XC-99. The Fort Worth-based design team believed that 100,000 pounds could be transported 3,800 miles, with an overload capability of 116,000 pounds over a somewhat shorter distance. If necessary the aircraft could carry 401 fully equipped troops (unpressurized) or 343 litters and 33 medical attendants. The aircraft shared the 230-foot wingspan of the standard B-36, but was 182 feet long and 57 feet high at the vertical stabilizer. The maximum gross takeoff weight was 357,000 pounds. Alternate designs were also prepared using the VDT engines proposed for the B-36C, and also using the track-style landing gear tested on the XB-36. Four turboprop engines or eight J57s in four nacelles would have powered a version using the swept wing from the YB-60.

However, for reasons that are not readily apparent, the Air Force decided against procuring the C-99. Instead, it bought large numbers of the Boeing C/KC-97 (a B-50 variant) and Douglas C-124 and C-133 transports. None of these aircraft were as capable as the C-99 would have been, but at the time it was not completely obvious how much the U.S. military would come to rely on air transport. Of course, much of the reliance would wait until the advent of workable jet transports such as the Boeing C-135 and Lockheed C-141.

The XC-99 undergoing maintenance in San Diego on 21 July 1950. Note the two B-36Bs on the left undergoing conversion to D-models. The XC-99 has not yet received its weather radar nose. (National Archives College Park Collection)

The XC-99 with its engines running on the day it was formally accepted by the Air Force. Note that the original 110-inch main landing gear has been replaced by the production 4-wheel bogies. (National Archives College Park Collection)

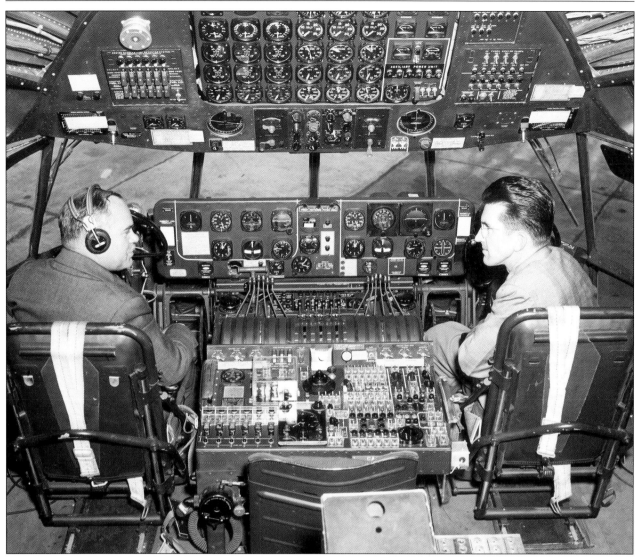

The flight deck of the XC-99 was unusual in that the flight engineer sat behind the center console and his instrumentation was on the overhead in front of him. Despite the width of the center console, the flight deck was roomy, and there were bunks and a rest area behind the cockpit. This 16 March 1949 photo shows (left) Russell R. Rogers, chief of flight test for Convair, and Robert R. Hoover, the XC-99 project engineer. (National Archives College Park Collection)

If they had been built, the Pan Am Super Clippers would have featured luxurious lounges and bathrooms. The lounges (shown above) were located amidships on each of the two decks. (San Diego Air & Space Museum Collection)

A far cry from the luxury promised by the Pan Am Super Clippers, here is the inside of the XC-99 on 29 June 1952. The load crew frequently played cards to pass the time during the long flights. (National Archives College Park Collection)

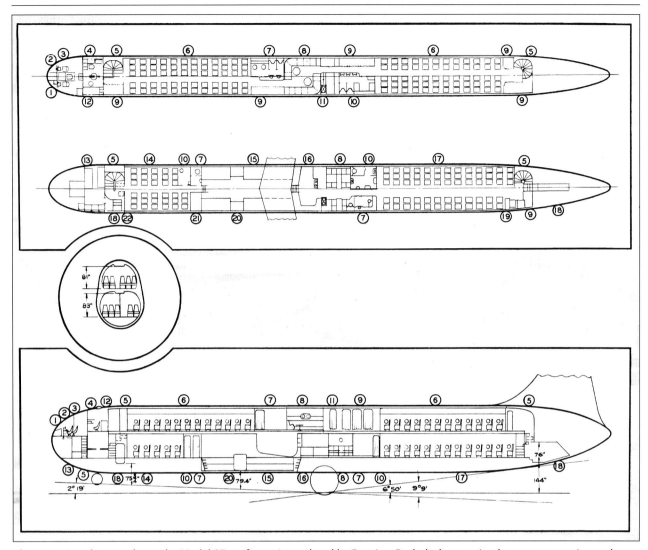

This May 1945 drawing shows the Model 37 configuration ordered by Pan Am. Both decks contained passenger seating and were connected by circular staircases front and rear. Seating was 3x2 on each deck, with the upper deck having 81 inches of clear height and the lower deck with 83 inches. A lounge and restrooms were located amidships on each deck. Note the outline of the single 110-inch main gear. (San Diego Air & Space Museum Collection)

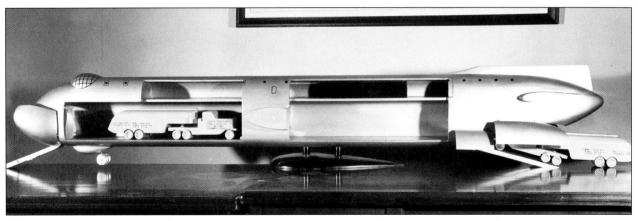

Consolidated continued refining the production C-99 concept for quite a while; this is a model manufactured in December 1950. Note the significant changes from the XC-99, including the forward and rear cargo doors and ramps and the B-36-style cockpit canopy. The C-99 would have provided a huge increase in capability over the Douglas C-124 Globemaster II that first flew on 27 November 1949. (National Archives College Park Collection)

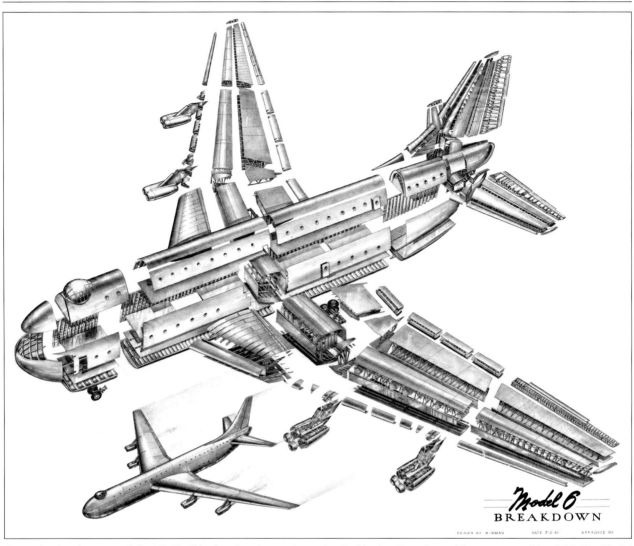

Given the development of the YB-60 all-jet bomber, it was almost inevitable that Convair would propose an all-jet C-99. The Model 6 was first proposed in 1950. This version had a pressurized upper deck, a nose cargo door and aft clamshell doors, allowing a drive-on/drive-off capability. Although the airplane would have still been fairly slow, it would have provided a C-141-like capability a decade sooner. The original art for this drawing was done on a 2x3-foot piece of vellum. (Convair)

After many years of neglect sitting in San Antonio, in 2007 the Air Force Museum disassembled the XC-99 and began transporting it back to Wright-Patterson AFB for eventual display. The effects of time were not kind to the airplane. At left is the center wing area – the humps on top were added after the airplane was built when the four-bogie main landing gear was added and needed additional space in the wing for clearance. At right is the upper forward fuselage including one window frame. (Dennis R. Jenkins)

APPENDIX B

UNWORTHY COMPETITOR
THE ALL-JET YB-60

Only the first YB-60 (49-2676) ever made it into the air and it looked exactly like what it was – a swept-wing B-36. The wing was huge and provided considerable area, but was still as thick as the B-36 wing and significantly restricted the top speed of the airplane. (National Archives College Park Collection)

It was clear early on that the B-36 replacement was going to be the Boeing B-52, although at the beginning it was not nearly as clear if the B-52 was going to be a turbo-prop or a pure-jet aircraft. By January 1951, the first two B-52s were being assembled and the general configuration of the eight-engine jet bomber was well known. Although the Air Force never conducted an actual competition for possible B-52 alternatives, both Convair and Douglas worked on various designs that could fill the role.

The most promising Douglas design was the 1211-J turboprop revealed in January 1951. This swept-wing aircraft had a design gross weight of 322,000 pounds, a speed of 450 knots at 55,000 feet, and an absolute range of 11,000 miles. The design looked similar to the Soviet Tu-95 Bear bomber.[1] Convair also wrestled with the question of pure-jet versus turboprop propulsion. At one point the Convair options included a six-turboprop design that had each engine housed in its own pod slung beneath the wings, and a pure-jet version that used a dozen J47 engines in six pods beneath the wings.[2]

On 25 August 1950, Convair submitted an unsolicited proposal for an all-jet, swept-winged version of the B-36. The Air Force was sufficiently interested that on 15 March 1951 it authorized (contract No. AF-33(038)-2182) Convair to convert two uncompleted B-36Fs (49-2676 and 49-2684) into B-36Gs. Since the aircraft was so radically different from the existing B-36, the designation was soon changed to YB-60. By the 20 August 1951 mockup review, it was noted that turboprop engines would replace the turbojet engines in June 1953. Production of either aircraft configuration could begin in March 1953 if authorization was received by 1 January 1952.[3]

In the interest of economy, many components from the B-36F were used to build the YB-60. The fuselage from aft of the forward cabin to near the end of the tail remained essentially the same as that of the B-36F. The aft fuselage was modified to house a braking parachute and a retractable tail wheel. At 171 feet, the fuselage was almost nine feet longer than that of the B-36F.[4]

A wing sweep of 38 degrees was accomplished by cutting each main wing spar outboard of the main landing gear and inserting a wedge-shaped structure at each location to angle the main spar 35 degrees. A glove was added to the leading edge of the center wing to continue the sweep line to the fuselage. The net result was a wing area to 5,239 square feet, an increase of almost 500 square feet. The wingspan was 206 feet, about 24 feet less than that of the B-36F. An entirely new leading and trailing edge was fabricated, including new flaps and ailerons. The aircraft was also fitted with swept vertical and horizontal stabilizers, making the aircraft slightly taller than the B-36F. Most of the structure inside the new horizontal and vertical surfaces were common with the B-36, simply angled appropriately, covered with new skin, and fitted with new control surfaces. Eight 8,700-lbf Pratt & Whitney J57-P-3 turbojets

The forward fuselage assembly of aircraft No. 151 carried the name Swept Wing Slugger *for a short time prior to being assembled into the first YB-60 prototype.* (Lockheed Martin)

were housed in four pairs suspended below and forward of the wing leading edge, using nacelles identical to the XB-52.[5]

The first YB-60 had only five crewmembers – pilot, copilot, navigator, bombardier/radio operator, and radio operator/tail gunner – seated in the pressurized forward compartment. All of the defensive armament was eliminated except the tail turret, which was remotely directed by an APG-32 radar. The K-3A bombing/navigation system, with its associated Y-3A bombsight, was retained. The maximum bomb load capacity of 86,000 pounds was the same as the B-36F.

The second prototype and production aircraft would have carried a crew of nine. The pilot, copilot-engineer, bombardier, navigator-gunner, engineer-gunner were in

Fitzhugh L. "Fitz" Fulton, Jr. (right), and Boyd L. "Danny" Grubaugh (left) in the hatch of the YB-60 at Edwards AFB during its brief Phase II testing. Fulton would go on to pilot faster aircraft, such as the North American XB-70A and Lockheed YF-12A. (Lockheed Martin)

the forward compartment, and a radio-ECM operation, tail gunner, and two gunners were in a pressurized aft compartment. The two lower aft sighting stations were positioned higher on the fuselage to improve crew comfort during use. Interestingly, the tunnel that B-36 crewmembers could use to move between the two compartments was deleted because "… the arrangement of equipment and functions of crewmembers make it unnecessary." Galleys, bunks, and lavatory facilities were installed in each compartment. Production aircraft were to include two upper forward turrets and two lower aft turrets, with standard B-36 optical sights located in four sighting blisters (two forward and two aft). The tail gun-laying radar would switch to the APG-41 scheduled for use on the B-36H, and a modified APG-41 would be incorporated in the nose to control the two upper forward turrets, in addition to "… furnishing information to the pilot for evasive maneuver tactics." For production aircraft, Convair also proposed using a new type of turret that retracted flush with the upper surface of the air-

craft, eliminating the doors found on the B-36. This would simplify maintenance, and decrease the time necessary to deploy the turrets when necessary.[6]

Production B-60s would have mounted the APS-23 search radar behind a flush radome in the nose. The packaging arrangement for the entire K-3A system was unique since all components, including the antenna and radome, were installed on a pallet that could easily be removed from the aircraft for maintenance. This arrangement also eliminated a variety of connectors and interconnecting cables that, it was hoped, would eliminate several areas that had proven troublesome in the B-36 installation. The entire K-3A pallet would be pressurized, and accessible by the crew during flight for maintenance. The designers were not terribly confident that this arrangement would improve the reliability of the K-3A, and they built in a complete set of test equipment and oscilloscopes on the pallet.[7]

Ten fuel tanks in the wings held 42,106 gallons of fuel. A little behind the times – the Boeing-designed flying boom was becoming operational by then – Convair included a probe-and-drogue refueling system in the production specification.[8]

The construction of the first aircraft (49-2676) began in the spring of 1951 in the Hangar Building at Fort Worth (not in the main production building). Major airframe sections and systems were built-up on the normal production lines, then brought to the Hangar Building for use on the two YB-60s, which progressed largely in parallel. The first aircraft was completed in only eight months, mostly because almost 72 percent of the parts were identical to the B-36F. However, the project was delayed by the late delivery of the J57 turbojets, which did not arrive at Convair until April 1952. The aircraft was rolled out on 6 April 1952, and was the largest jet aircraft in the world at the time.

The YB-60 made its maiden flight on 18 April 1952, with Convair chief test pilot Beryl A. Erickson and Arthur

Like Convair, Boeing toyed with many ideas for the B-52. This 15 November 1947 example shows a straight wing and four Wright T-35 turboprops. By this point, Boeing had spent $10 million on development. (Air Force Historical Research Agency)

The first YB-60 shows its clean lines. Like the B-36 it was derived from, much of the skin was dull magnesium. The shiny areas were aluminum, used to cover pressurized compartments and high-stress areas. (Air Force Historical Research Agency Collection)

S. "Doc" Witchell, Jr., at the controls. Also aboard were J. D. McEachern and William P. "Bill" Easley, who along with Erickson had been on the first flight of the XB-36 six years earlier. The aircraft lifted off at 4:55 p.m., landing back at Carswell 66 minutes later. As was procedure at the time, the landing gear was left down for the entire flight. Interestingly, the photographs released by the Air Force after the flight had the landing gear air-brushed out for security reasons that are not understood.

The Boeing YB-52 had taken to the air for the first time only three days earlier. Although there was never a formal competition between the YB-60 and the YB-52, the B-52 quickly exhibited a clear superiority. The YB-60 had a cost advantage over the B-52 because of its commonality with the B-36, but the B-52 clearly had superior performance. The top speed of the YB-60 was only 508 mph at 39,250 feet, more than 100 mph slower than the B-52. In addition, flight tests of the YB-60 turned up a number of deficiencies, including engine surge, control system buffeting, rudder flutter, and electrical system problems. The stability was rather poor because of the high aerodynamic forces on the control surfaces acting in concert with fairly low aileron effectiveness. The refined aerodynamics of the B-52, which had been designed from the beginning as a high-speed aircraft, quickly proved their worth.[9]

Consequently, the Air Force concluded that there was no future for the YB-60, and cancelled the flight test program on 20 January 1953 after only 66 flight hours. The second prototype was never flown, although it was 95-percent complete, basically only missing its engines.

The two YB-60s were shunted off to the side of the runway at carswell, where they sat out in the weather for several months. The Air Force formally accepted the aircraft on 1 July 1954, and the same day workmen took axes and blowtorches to them. By the end of July, they had both been scrapped, with some of the components that were common with the B-36F being scavenged for

spare parts and the J57 engines and nacelles sent back to the B-52 program. The cost of the YB-60 experiment was approximately $15 million.[10]

Convair considered adapting the YB-60 as a commercial jet airliner, to no avail. A proposed 380,000 pound gross weight commercial version was powered by eight P&W J57-P-1 engines, and carried 261 passengers, a flight crew of five, and a cabin crew of four. It was expected the aircraft would cost $7 million, plus an additional $1 million for engines. The aircraft would have had a maximum range of 3,450 miles, and would have been available in December 1956. Interestingly, although the aircraft could fly nonstop from New York to London with 261 passengers, it could only carry 22 passengers on the return flight because of the prevailing 100 mph east wind encountered at cruising altitude. But engineers also noted that the YB-60 derivative only had a projected speed of 432 mph, compared with 550 mph for the Boeing 707 and other competitors. In the end, Convair decided to concentrate on the 880 series of jet transports instead.[11]

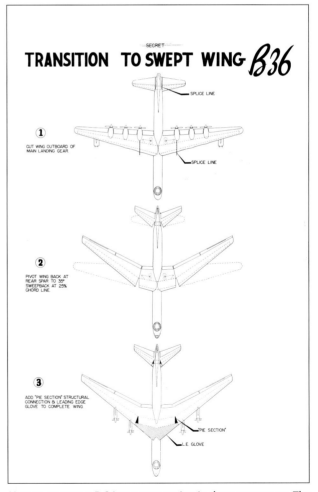

How to convert a B-36 to a swept wing in three easy steps. The majority of the structural pieces (spars, etc.) were common between the B-36 and YB-60, but the entire leading and trailing edges were different. (San Diego Air & Space Museum)

The jet engine test area at Fort Worth had a location for the General Electric J47 engines used on the B-36 (left) and the Pratt & Whitney J57s used on the YB-60. Note that the test stand was built to house two sets of engines. (Lockheed Martin)

Most Convair documents indicate that any production B-60s would have been powered by four turboprop engines, most likely the same Wright T35s being investigated by Boeing for the B-52. Turboprops were believed to offer significantly better fuel economy than the early turbjet engines, an important attribute for a long-range bomber. The photo at left was taken on 12 April 1954; fortunately, the model survived and was photographed again in 2008. (Left: Lockheed Martin; Right: photo by Don Pyeatt)

The entire trailing edge was covered in movable devices – multi-segment flaps inboard and mod-span, and a large aileron outboard. This photo does not show the tail wheel used by the YB-60 at certain gross weights and center-of-gravity conditions. Although the YB-60 was based on an F-model airframe, the rear-facing defensive radar is covered by a late H-model radome. The first prototype was unarmed and not equipped with any offensive or defensive systems. (Lockheed Martin)

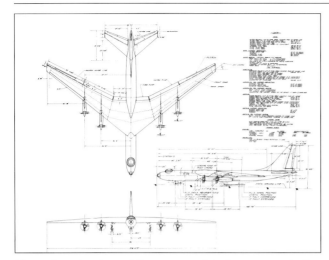

Three-view drawing of the proposed turboprop production model of the B-60. Each of the Wright T35 engines was slung under the wing in a separate nacelle and turned 11-foot, six-blade single-rotation transonic propellers. (Lockheed Martin)

Gen. Joseph T. McNarney (USAF, ret.), left, the new president of Consolidated during his first visit to Fort Worth on 22 May 1956. To McNarney's left are other Convair executives, A. P. Fontaine, August C. Esenwein, and L. W. Miller. (Lockheed Martin)

The first YB-60 being weighed before its first flight. Note the opening where the upper forward sighting blister was located on the B-36 and the open crew hatch. The nose carried a flight-test instrumentation probe and was not representative of the production configuration. This was one of the few B-36 type airplanes that carried factory-applied markings (the NB-36H was the other notable example). (Lockheed Martin)

The YB-60 departing Fort Worth on a test flight. As could be expected, the swept wing completely changed the low-speed handling characteristics of the airplane, and the jet engines were only marginally powerful enough for a comfortable take-off. (Lockheed Martin)

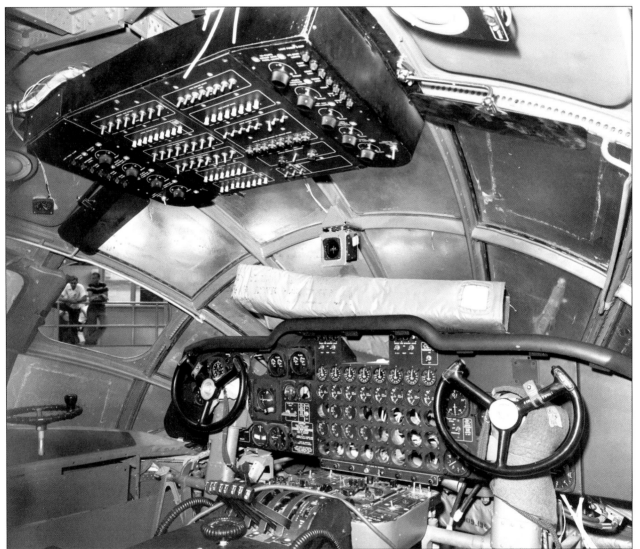

These 4 April 1952 photos (above and top right) show the flight deck and flight engineer's panel on the second YB-60 (49-2684). Unlike the B-36, the jet throttles were in a conventional location on the center console and the jet instrumentation was on the forward panel. It is unclear if the airplane ever received its full complement of instrumentation since it was decided fairly early that it would never fly. (National Archives College Park Collection)

The second all-jet prototype was different in many details from the first. Contrary to most published reports, the airplane would have carried two upper forward turrets, two lower aft turrets, and a tail turret. The entire nose forward of the canopy was removable to allow access to the bomb-nav system, which could be replaced as a module and repaired offline. The nose profile was also considerably different. Note the side of the fuselage says "B-60," not "YB-60" as on the first airplane. (Lockheed Martin)

The Story of Cowtown and the Convair B-36

APPENDIX C

DREAM UNREALIZED
ATOMIC-POWERED AIRCRAFT

A Boeing B-50 (48-058) chase plane accompanied every flight of the NB-36H where the reactor was installed. The B-50 carried an array of instrumentation to monitor radiation levels around the NB-36H. A C-97 also accompanied the bomber, carrying a platoon of Marines ready to parachute down to secure a crash site if needed. This is a flight on 18 August 1955. (National Archives College Park Collection)

n May 1946, the Air Force initiated the Nuclear Energy for the Propulsion of Aircraft (NEPA) project to support developing long-range strategic bombers and other high-performance aircraft. When the Atomic Energy Commission (AEC) was created in January 1947, the fate of the military NEPA effort became uncertain, and the program was continued mainly to allow time for the AEC to devise its own strategy. In May 1951, the Aircraft Nuclear Propulsion (ANP) program, a joint effort between the AEC and the Air Force to develop a full-scale aircraft reactor and engine system, effectively replaced the NEPA project. Another factor that led to the ANP program was a 1948 MIT study that concluded, "… nuclear aircraft (manned) were likely less difficult than nuclear ramjets, which, in turn, would be less difficult than nuclear rockets to develop." Ironically, this turned out to be the opposite of how events turned out. Although nuclear ramjets (Project PLUTO) and nuclear rockets (Project ROVER) were successfully tested at the levels needed for operational use, an operational-level atomic aircraft powerplant was never developed. During early 1951, the Joint Chiefs of Staff had endorsed the military necessity of an atomic powered aircraft, clearing the way to continue the program at a higher priority.

NB-36H

Despite its problems, the ANP program spawned plans for two flight vehicles. Both were to be B-36s modified by Convair as part of Project MX-1589. The first was an effort to more fully understand the shielding requirements for an airborne reactor by building a small reactor and flight-testing it aboard a B-36. The reactor would not provide any power to the aircraft, but both the reactor and its associated radiation levels would be carefully monitored during a series of flights. This would give designers actual flight data to use in determining the characteristics of the operational shielding, as well as insight into various operational factors. This was referred to as the Nuclear Test Aircraft (NTA).

The second flight vehicle envisioned by the ANP program would actually use the reactor to provide power for flight. The B-36 was to provide the basis for two X-6s since it was the only existing airframe large enough to carry the expected engine and shield weight, although some consideration was also given to using the two YB-60 airframes.[1]

The decision to use the B-36 for the initial experiments was based primarily on the ability of the bomber to carry the large reactor. Performance would not be outstanding given the speed limitations of the B-36 airframe, but it would serve as an adequate proof-of-concept. There was never any intention of producing more than the single NTA and two X-6 aircraft. No tactical requirements were levied on either design, and they were to be optimized for their test functions with no regard to future operational utility.

Convair built a plywood mockup of the NB-36H and X-6 crew compartment to work out equipment installation details. (National Museum of the United States Air Force Collection)

Convair constructed the Nuclear Aircraft Research Facility at Fort Worth to support MX-1589, and the AEC awarded Convair a contract on 29 June 1951 to support operations of the flight vehicles. Convair Fort Worth division manager August C. Esenwein made the first public announcement of the MX-1589 program on 5 September

The NB-36H was modified in the Hangar Building at Plant 4. By 27 December 1954 the airplane was mostly completed. The large opening on top of the fuselage is where the shielded crew compartment would be installed. (Lockheed Martin)

The classic shot of the NB-36H (51-5712) during its seventh flight on 23 December 1955. Note the large cooling scoop where the aft lower sighting blisters used to be. The entire crew was located in the forward, shielded crew compartment and what had been the aft compartment was loaded with equipment. Note the radiation symbol on the vertical stabilizer. (Lockheed Martin)

1951, and the contracts were signed on 11 November 1951. At the same time, Lockheed was awarded study contracts in case Convair ran into trouble. Separately, Boeing, Convair, Douglas, and Lockheed were studying requirements for an operational supersonic atomic-powered aircraft.[2]

A model of the ASTR reactor from the NB-36H. The reactor itself is at the left of the photo, followed by the pumps and radiators that cooled it in flight. There was a large scoop on each side of the fuselage to feed the radiators. (Lockheed Martin)

In preparation for the NTA experiments, Convair installed a small nuclear Ground Test Reactor (GTR) at the Nuclear Aircraft Research Facility during 1953. The initial public announcement of the reactor – the first in Texas – came on 20 August 1954. The GTR had gone "critical" on 17 November 1953. The Aircraft Shield Test Reactor (ASTR) – the unit that would be carried aboard the NTA – first went critical on 17 November 1954.[3]

Convair spent a surprising amount of time defining the crew compartment for the NTA. The preliminary design for an appropriate crew compartment – and its associated shielding – exceeded the structural limitations of the B-36 forward fuselage by a rather large margin, and was rejected. A decision on 4 June 1952 to delete most crew comfort items and to move some equipment to other locations on the aircraft resulted in weight estimates within the structural limitations of the aircraft. After evaluating seven alternatives, the final design had side-by-side pilot and copilot stations that were located lower in the fuselage than the standard B-36 (actually, at approximately the same level as the original XB-36). Two nuclear engineers

Parked over the reactor pit, the NB-36H is readied for another flight. Note the thickness of the open upper crew hatch. In addition to the airplane and reactor facilities, Convair built special ground equipment (such as the bulldozer to the left and tow tractor at right) that were heavily shielded to protect the ground crews. (National Archives College Park Collection)

were located immediately aft of the pilots, facing forward. The flight engineer was located in the extreme necked-down aft end of the compartment on the centerline of the airplane, also facing mostly forward.

Construction of a crew compartment mock-up began in July 1952. The new nose section would replace the nose on the B-36 forward of bulkhead 5.0 The contours of the nose changed substantially in detail – the cross section of the extreme nose was oval instead of round, for instance. However, from a distance the only major difference was that the "bubble" cockpit of the B-36 had been replaced by a more conventional "airliner" configuration. In addition, the nose landing gear was moved 6 inches forward to accommodate the entry hatch to the crew compartment. The construction of the flight-rated crew compartment took most of 1953, and the early part of 1954 was spent testing the module. These revealed the need for additional shielding materials, some revised instrumentation, and a new windshield. These modifications were completed in early 1955.[4]

Although the B-36 was a large aircraft, and the normal crew compartment provided a fair amount of room for the

The Aircraft Shield Test Reactor (ASTR) was a water-cooled, water-moderated, enriched-uranium thermal reactor installed in the NB-36H. The reactor was installed on 20 of the 47 test flights, but did not power the airplane. (Lockheed Martin)

crew, the NTA would not have this luxury. The amount of shielding required to protect the crew greatly decreased the space available, and the final result was very cramped. The station arrangements were carefully planned to obtain the maximum efficiency from the crew and their equipment within the confined area of the compartment. For example, one problem concerned the placement of the nuclear engineer's oxygen regulators and interphone panels. It was finally decided that the instruments could be mounted on a drop-door hinged to the base of each nuclear engineer's seat. When let down, the door fell between the engineer's legs just above his feet, allowing him to see the instruments. When not in use, the door was pushed upright against the seat, out of the way.

At the pilot's stations, there was only a single set of instruments, located in the middle of the panel since there was not sufficient room behind the panel for all the normal plumbing and electrical wiring. The engine scanning normally performed by crewmembers in the aft compartment was performed instead using television cameras. A location for the television monitor could not be found, however, until it was decided to locate it in the overhead area between the two nuclear engineers, where the flight engineer could see it relatively easily. Although the two pilots had movable seats, the other three seats were fixed

This B-36H (51-5712) was damaged in the 1 September 1952 tornado that tore up much of the B-36 fleet. (Another photo is on page 152.) (U.S. Air Force via C. Roger Cripliver Collection)

since there was insufficient room. The area underneath the seats was used for storage.

A drinking water container was provided in the aft portion of the copilot's seat, while the aft side of the pilot's seat contained a relief tube. This location was chosen since it allowed crewmembers to stand at the only location in the compartment that was full-height. A chemical toilet was located outside the crew compartment in the fuselage near the entrance hatch.

The 6-inch-thick plexiglass windshield had excellent optical qualities but its yellow tint made the gray paint normally used in crew compartments turn a very undesirable color. After much experimenting, designers found that using a lavender paint in the pilots' area gave the illusion of being gray when illuminated by daylight through the yellow windshield. The pilots' instrument panel was painted black, but all other panels were painted a very pale gray that made the compartment appear roomier. The seats were upholstered in light gray cloth, and the floors were covered in darker gray carpet. A curtain was installed between the pilots and the nuclear engineers to block sunlight.[5]

All portions of the aircraft exterior seen from the pilots' compartment were painted anti-glare black to diffuse direct sunlight. The initial design of a simple antiglare shield produced an unattractive pattern when combined with the black radome. The two areas were subsequently blended together and a small amount of trim extended upward and aft to provide a more appealing look.

Since the crew compartment was designed to be removable during maintenance, a method had to be devised to easily connect and disconnect the flight controls. Instead of the normal cables, a series of push-pull rods projecting from the bottom of the crew compartment were devised that could easily be connected to the cables in the lower fuselage. Push-pull rods were also used for the throttle and mixture control that connected to the normal cables underneath the crew compartment. The

The crew compartment could be completely removed from the NB-36H for maintenance or decontamination. The compartment was removed at least twice during the program. Here it is being loaded into the airplane on 27 April 1955. (Lockheed Martin)

Except for the new nose and the large scoops on the aft fuse-lage, the XB-36H looked like a B-36. All defensive armament and offensive systems were removed. (Lockheed Martin)

construction of the shielded crew compartment required the perfection of a method to bond rubber and lead to the metal alloys used in aircraft construction. The rubber, in its natural state, was procured from the Goodyear Rubber Company. The rubber was chemically cured and bonded to the alloys using special adhesives. Virgin lead was also bonded to the compartment using a technique that result-ed in the entire compartment – alloy, lead, and rubber – being a complete one-piece unit.[6]

The original XB-36 (42-13570) was turned over to the NTA program (called NEBO – Nuclear Engine Bomber – by Convair) in mid-1951 and was used for preliminary ground tests of radiation effects and shielding. The aircraft did not participate in any flights during its NEBO tenure, being strictly a ground-test article.

The NTA began its life as a B-36H-20-CF (51-5712) that had been damaged during the tornado at Carswell AFB on 1 September 1952. The estimated cost to restore the aircraft to an operational configuration was over $1 million – almost 50 percent of the cost of a new air-craft (minus the government-furnished equipment) – and had been deemed uneconomical. In particular, the nose of the bomber had been extensively damaged, and since a new crew compartment was part of the plan for the NTA, this airframe was a logical choice. The aircraft was for-mally assigned to MX-1589 in early 1953. By the start of 1955, the aircraft had received its new forward fuselage, and the wiring, tubing, instrument capsule, and crew compartment cooling systems had been installed. The air-craft was redesignated XB-36H on 11 March 1955, but was redesignated as NB-36H on 6 June 1955. The name "Convair Crusader" was painted on each side of the for-ward fuselage during the early portion of the test series.[7]

The NB-36H incorporated shielding around the reactor itself and there were also water jackets in the fuse-lage and behind the crew compartment to absorb radia-tion. A 4-ton lead disc shield was installed in forward

part of bomb bay No. 2. The 1,000-kilowatt, air-cooled ASTR weighed 35,000 pounds and was carried in bomb bay No. 4. A number of large air intakes and exhausts were installed in the sides and bottom of the rear fuselage to cool the reactor. The reactor could be removed from the aircraft while on the ground.

The first flight of the NB-36H was on 17 September 1955, with test pilot A. S. Witchell, Jr., at the controls. Flying alongside the NB-36H on every flight was a C-97 carrying a platoon of armed Marines ready to parachute and secure the area around the NTA in the event it crashed. An instrumented B-50D (48-058) also accompanied the NTA on most flights to gather data. Forty-seven flights were made up to March 1957, although the ASTR reactor was only critical on 21 of them. The flight program showed that the "aircraft normally would pose no threat, even if flying low." The principal concerns would be: (a) accidents which cause the release of fission products from the reac-tors, and (b) the dosage from exposure to leakage of radioactivity (in the direct-cycle concept). It was subse-quently decided that the risks caused by radiation under normal circumstances were no greater than the risks that had been incurred during the development of steam and electric power, the airplane, the automobile, or the rocket. The consequences of an accident, however, could be severe.

In the days before fly-by-wire systems, the idea of a removable crew compartment was fascinating. All of the cables for the flight controls, throttles, propeller controls, and tubing and electrics for instruments had to be connected. (Lockheed Martin)

The NB-36H was decommissioned at Fort Worth in late 1957 and was parked at the Nuclear Aircraft Research Facility pending final disposition. As the B-36 phase-out progressed, the Air Materiel Command (AMC, which was in charge of scrapping the B-36s) asked the Air Research and Development Command (ARDC, which owned the NB-36H) when it could be scrapped. No answer was forthcoming. This complicated the AMC's job since the agreement between AMC and ARDC required that AMC maintain sufficient spares on hand to support the NB-36H in case it was needed again. ARDC finally responded that flying activities had been curtailed due to the general FY58 defense funding constraints, and that ARDC planned to restart flight tests in FY59. ARDC requested AMC to take over the responsibility for storing the aircraft at Fort Worth, but AMC responded that estimated storage costs of $13,000 had not been budgeted. Air Force Headquarters subsequently directed ARDC to pay the storage costs since the aircraft was scheduled to be tested again the following

The twin radomes for the APG-41 fire-control radars remained on the tail, but the radars were absent and the 20mm cannon tail turret was removed and replaced by a fiberglass cover with a vent in it. (Don Pyeatt Collection)

This is not how the flight manual describes a take off – the upper hatch is supposed to be closed! On the fifth flight, 15 September 1955, the upper hatch suddenly opened during the takeoff run, resulting in a shaken crew and paperwork scattered everywhere. The aircraft safely landed 15 minutes later with no permanent effects. This was the shortest hop of the 47-flight test program. It is a testimony to the strength of the hinges that supported the heavily shielded hatch. (Lockheed Martin)

The atomic-powered X-6 aircraft was to be flight tested at the National Reactor Test Site near Arco, Idaho. A large arch hangar was built, but construction of the runway had not begun before the program was cancelled. (Department of Energy)

year when funds were available. As it turned out, FY59 funds for the NB-36H were not forthcoming, and in September 1958, the aircraft was scrapped at Fort Worth.[8]

Nevermore

However, in early 1953, the Eisenhower Administration determined that a nuclear-powered aircraft had no military value, and Secretary of Defense Charles E. Wilson did not include the ANP in the FY54 budget. After several weeks of negotiation and compromise, the ANP avoided complete cancellation, but the X-6 experiment was history. In the end, ANP had simply been around for too long while producing too few results. On 28 March 1961, President John F. Kennedy issued a statement cancelling ANP, "Nearly 15 years and about $1 billion have been devoted to the attempted development of a nuclear-powered aircraft; but the possibility of achieving a militarily useful aircraft in the foreseeable future is still very remote."[9]

An interesting shot of the Nuclear Aircraft Research Facility (on the spit of land at upper left) in Fort Worth. Note the large crane that lifted the crew module out of the airplane. The abandoned XB-36 is at the left of the photo, while the two YB-60s are in storage at the upper right. The B-36 at the lower center is positioned to test-fire its forward-facing 20mm cannon at the bunker directly ahead of it. Lake Worth is in the background. (National Archives College Park Collection)

APPENDIX D

COMPLETELY DIFFERENT
TRACK LANDING GEAR

Late in its career, the XB-36 (42-13570) was used for a series of tests of a track landing gear that would eliminate the need for the special runways required for heavy-aircraft operations. There was no intent to equip the B-36 fleet with the landing gear, and the XB-36 was used mostly because it was readily available. (Lockheed Martin)

The development of heavy bombers, and very heavy bombers, presented a host of problems unrelated to the aircraft themselves. One of these was the design of airfields, particularly paved taxiways and runways. Unlike the bombers (B-17 and B-24) that had served for most of World War II, the B-29 could not routinely use grass or dirt runways, although the Pacific airfields were often compacted, crushed coral as opposed to concrete or asphalt.[1] To put runway construction in perspective, consider that a 6,000-foot long by 100-foot-wide concrete runway for a B-29-type aircraft required approximately 18,000 tons of dry cement and 90,000 tons of aggregate. It was obvious that runways for the Northrop B-35 and Consolidated B-36 would need vastly more material.

Due to the sheer size of the B-36, the landing gear – and its effects on airfields – presented even more issues than previous aircraft. As part of the preliminary design for the XB-36, Convair investigated a variety of main landing gear concepts that included one, two, and four wheels per side. Ultimately, in order to fit the main gear into the wing when it was retracted, Convair decided to use a single 110-inch-diameter wheel per side. Another reason was the inability of industry to provide adequate brakes for a multi-wheel design. Unfortunately, this concentrated most of the aircraft's weight onto two relatively small contact patches, one on each side of the aircraft.

As of July 1946, only three runways in the world were capable of supporting the B-36 – Tarrant Field (Fort Worth AAF, later Carswell AFB), Eglin Field in Florida, and Fairfield-Suisun AAF (later Travis AFB)[2] in California; modifications to Patterson Field to accommodate the airplane would be ready in 18 months. However, plans had already been approved to modify one airfield per year to accommodate the new bomber (or other aircraft of similar weight).[3]

The 110-inch tires, each weighing 1,475 pounds, were the largest aircraft tires ever manufactured by the Goodyear Tire & Rubber Company. Each tire had a 225-pound inner tube pressurized to 100 psi, and at least 10 were manufactured. The 110-inch-diameter wheels were 46 inches wide and weighed 850 pounds each, and the dual multiple-disk brakes on each wheel added 735 pounds. Complete with the struts and ancillary equipment, each main gear weighed 8,550 pounds.

In mid-1945 the Maj. Gen. Edward M. Powers, Assistant Chief of Air Staff for Materiel, Maintenance, and Distribution, recommended that a new landing gear be developed to distribute the weight of the B-36 more evenly, thus reducing the need for specially built runways. As noted, one of the major problems encountered with designing a multi-wheel landing gear for the B-36 had been acquiring adequate brakes. These were finally developed and the production dual-tandem, four-wheel bogie-type undercarriage using 56-inch tires allowed the B-36 to use any airfield suitable for the B-29. The new

The track landing gear concept was initially developed by J. Walter Christie, the same man responsible for a highly successful Army tank track design. This is one of the A-20 testbeds. (National Archives College Park Collection)

landing gear configuration required "bumps" on top of the wing and on the landing gear doors to provide additional clearance when the landing gear was stowed, but the small increase in drag was compensated for by the 2,600 pounds the new landing gear saved.

However, the problems extended beyond the B-36 program. Until now, aircraft landing gear had consisted of a single axle on each strut, meaning either a single wheel (B-17 and B-24) or two wheels (B-29). In August 1944, the Army had issued requirements calling for "a new type airplane landing gear effecting maximum practicable weight distribution" suitable for use on average pavement and unprepared airfields. The requirement stated that the

The initial A-20C tests began in the spring of 1943, but a taxi accident in the summer of 1945 halted further efforts until a new A-20 was made available in 1947. Over 50 flights proved "very satisfactory." (National Archives College Park Collection)

weight concentration of future aircraft should not exceed that of the Douglas C-47. The use of either "multiple axle" or track gear was suggested. Ultimately, it was determined that meeting this requirement would prevent aircraft from fulfilling their military requirements, and the issue was dropped, but the basic premise nevertheless led to some interesting experiments, including the development of a workable (mostly) track landing gear for aircraft.[4]

The idea of applying track landing gear to aircraft was first proposed by J. Walter Christie, the inventor of the Christie suspension system for battle tanks, and the Dowty Equipment Corporation of Long Island, New York. After discussion between Christie and Gen. Henry H. "Hap" Arnold in November 1939, Christie was authorized to develop a track landing gear system for use on a Douglas A-20 Havoc.[5]

In June 1941, the Army awarded a $20,000 contract to Dowty for the design of a track landing gear, with Christie as the principle engineer. The Dowty design included a Goodrich air-inflated belt similar in cross-section to several "single tube" tires placed side-by-side and joined together at their sidewalls. Two main rollers with brakes were shaped so that the belt could roll on them without bunching the material. Two smaller, auxiliary rollers were sprung over the part of the belt that contacted the ground, while a smaller idler was mounted under the top span to provide

The Curtiss XP-40 was used to test the track gear concept on a fighter-type aircraft. This experiment was not completely successful since the small size of the tracks hampered their effectiveness. (Air Force Historical Research Agency Collection)

constant belt tension. The airplane would be supported by a lever suspension shock absorber and the entire installation was not expected to weight significantly more than a conventional wheel and tire gear.[6]

Dowty completed their design in February 1942 and was awarded a $100,000 contract to manufacture a single set of track landing gear for an A-20. The requirements included the ability to travel 140 mph on sod or concrete, to exert a ground pressure of less than 20 psi, and to surmount a 6x6-inch obstacle at 90 mph. The system needed to be delivered by January 1943. As a prelude to the A-20 system, Dowty and Firestone (who had replaced Goodrich as the belt supplier) installed a track landing gear on a Boeing-Stearman PT-17 Kaydet trainer. The system was later transferred to a Fairchild PT-19 Cornell trainer. The tracks, although heavier than wheels, functioned satisfactorily on both airplanes.[7]

By June 1942, the track gear was completed and sent to Wright Field where it was installed on an A-20C. The gear, which was not retractable, was used with a conventional nose wheel. Despite initial guarantees that the installation would add only 100 pounds to the A-20, in fact the track gear weighed 2,700 pounds compared to 900 pounds for the normal landing gear. Testing began in the spring of 1943 and after about 50 flights the gear was deemed "very satisfactory" in various soil conditions, including mud, sod, and sand. The fact that the A-20 installation weighed three-times as much as its conventional gear meant that take-off distances increased about 15 percent and adversely affected all other aspects of performance.[8] Nevertheless, these tests were sufficiently encouraging that the Army asked Firestone to provide design and cost data for a track landing gear for a Boeing B-17 and CG-4A Waco glider; apparently this idea went nowhere since no further information could be found in the archives.[9]

Unfortunately, the A-20C was irreparably damaged during a taxi test in the summer of 1945, and it took almost a year for another A-20 to be made available. In April 1947, the track gear was installed on an A-20H and service tests were completed in August. The final report concluded that the A-20 track installation had "proved the floatation principle of track gear entirely sound," and data from the A-20 tests were used as design criteria for subsequent efforts.[10]

In the meantime, the Army had awarded Firestone a $15,900 contract to develop a track gear for a Curtiss P-40 that would allow fighter aircraft to use sandy beaches in the Pacific. The P-40 installation used two (dual) tracks per side and was expected to exert only half the ground pressure as a conventional landing gear. The track gear was installed on an XP-40 at Wright field in September 1943, although the conventional tail wheel continued to be used. It was necessary to install 400 pounds of ballast in the tail to counteract the forward center-of-gravity shift caused by the heavier main track gear. The XP-40 with track gear, along with other P-40s modified with dual-wheel and

Initially the Air Force was going to use a Boeing B-29 to test the track gear on a large airplane, but ultimately selected the first B-50B (47-118), which had been retained by Boeing as a test ship, instead. Tow tests in May 1949 showed that belts constructed with all-rubber side reinforcements outlasted belts with metallic side reinforcements. When the B-50 began flight tests in Seattle, the track gear proved satisfactory. Note the temporary camera setup for initial taxi tests. (National Archives College Park Collection)

multi-wheel landing gear, was tested in sand (its primary target), snow, ice, mud, and sod. Prior to the tests being completed, the XP-40 was damaged beyond repair and further testing was abandoned since the P-40 track gear was considered "inefficient for fight operation because of excessive internal friction in the track, the inability of the track to get out of ditches and over obstacles, smallness of the units, and the inability of the gear to be sufficiently self-cleaning." The experiment had cost $44,391. Despite these unhappy results, as late as 1948 there was still some consid-

eration given to equipping Lockheed P-80s with a modified track landing gear system, although this never happened.[11]

Returning to large aircraft in late 1945, Fairchild and Firestone conducted a preliminary study of the feasibility of using track landing gear on a heavy transport aircraft, specifically the Fairchild C-82A Packet. This was in response to an Army dictate that required all future assault transports be capable of landing on unprepared or semi-prepared runways (depending on the weight of the aircraft). In April 1946, Fairchild made a $250,000 proposal

The B-50 installation was sized to fit into the wheel wells, but it is unclear if it was ever retracted in flight. Note that the nose gear (right) was steerable. The people give an indication of the size of the units. (Air Force Historical Research Agency Collection)

to install a track landing gear on a C-82. The Army accepted the proposal and specified the single-track gear was to include "sand chutes" to clear debris out of the track and a steerable nose track. Firestone manufactured the belt, but Goodyear and Goodrich were included in most discussions in case widespread production was forthcoming.[12]

Fabrication of the nose and main gear got underway in early 1947, and the installation increased the gross weight of the C-82A by 1,200 pounds. Taxi tests commenced in January 1948 and, although plagued by a variety of failures and problems, were generally successful. Unlike the earlier A-20 installation, the C-82 track gear was retractable, incorporated a steerable nose gear, and included hydraulic brakes. The tests revealed that the 9-inch bogie wheels and suspension springs needed redesigned and that magnesium bogies should replace the aluminum ones to save weight. On 18 May 1948, the Air Force awarded Fairchild a contract for 23 sets of track landing gear; 18 sets would be installed on production C-82s, while the other 5 sets would be used as spares.[13]

The production order was premature, and continued testing revealed more serious problems, including flaws in the belts and issues with the air and oil springs. Although the track landing gear performed satisfactorily on sod and some types of mud, it could not operate reliably on sand. It was determined that skis worked better on snow since they only exerted 3 psi rather than the 30 psi of the tracks. Nevertheless, the first production gear was accepted in February 1949 and, by the end of April, 11 track-equipped C-82s had been accepted and assigned to the 14th Air Force; the other seven planned aircraft were delivered with regular, wheeled landing gear. Eventually, the track-equipped C-82As reverted back to normal landing gear.[14]

Concurrently with the C-82 tests, the Army proceeded with the design of a track gear for the Boeing B-29. In May 1947 Boeing received an $87,204 contract to design a landing gear that could be installed on the B-29 or B-50. It was also hoped that the same track gear could be installed on the C-97 series of transports that were derivatives of the B-50. The track-equipped B-50 was to have a soil bearing pressure of 41 psi at a gross weight of 165,000 pounds, although the installation would reduce its combat range by 420 miles. The basic design was approved and in March 1948, the Air Force awarded Boeing a $509,315 contract for the construction, installation, and test of the landing gear on a B-29. The following month, the Air Force decided to forgo the B-29 installation in favor of going directly to a B-50.[15]

Serious problems soon arose. Goodyear experienced a great deal of difficulty fabricating a belt that could withstand the high tensile loads needed for the heavy, and fast, bomber. In fact, the first belt received from Goodyear could not be used above 70 mph. In addition, the track gear interfered with the defensive armament; the only solution appeared to be to stow and lock the nose turret with the guns facing aft instead of forward. The

track landing gear was installed on the first B-50B (47-118), which had been retained by Boeing as a test ship. Tow tests in May 1949 showed that belts constructed with all-rubber side reinforcements outlasted belts with metallic side reinforcements. Eventually the problems were overcome and, when the B-50 began flight-tests in Seattle, the track gear proved satisfactory.[16]

In November 1947, Air Force Headquarters directed the Air Materiel Command to obtain a cost estimate for installing a track gear on a Consolidated B-36. The manufacturer submitted sketches indicating a track gear could be fitted to the very-heavy bomber, but the Air Materiel Command preferred to wait until the C-82 and B-50 tests were completed. In April 1948, the XB-36 contract was amended to provide for the design, fabrication, and installation of a track landing gear. Sufficient funds were already available on the contract to cover the work. Confusingly, the following month this contract change was cancelled and Convair was ordered to install a track gear on the YB-36 instead. Eventually, this change order was also cancelled and the track landing gear work was moved to the B-36 production contract at a cost of $647,644, although the XB-36 was again the expected guinea pig.[17]

Some in the Air Force questioned the need for a track landing gear on the B-36 since it would always operated from well-prepared bases. The obvious exception was the Arctic bases to be used during pre-strike staging. It appears that there was never any intention of using the track-type gear on production B-36s, and the XB-36 was used as a testbed simply because it was a very heavy aircraft that was readily available. This did not stop several organizations (including the Air University) from proposing equipping production B-36s with track-style landing gear, but nothing came of the suggestions. However, the

At least 11 production Fairchild C-82A Packets appear to have been equiped with track landing gear from the factory. Eventually, all were converted to a conventional arrangement. (Air Force Historical Research Agency Collection)

Air Materiel Command believed that the new belt design being developed for the B-36 was the most promising undertaken up to that times, and that the entire design would tie in with the C-82 and B-50 programs to provide a complete set of data on the desirability of track gear.[18]

The Goodyear system of V-belts applied only 57 psi to the runway, compared to 156 psi for the production dual-tandem, four-wheel, bogie-type undercarriage. This would, in theory, allow very large aircraft to use unprepared landing strips instead of specially built runways. Each of the two belts on the main landing gear was 16 inches wide, 276 inches in circumference, and had a thickness of 1 inch except

for an additional 1-inch "V" in the center that fit into a slot on the bogie wheel to keep the track centered. Each belt was made of rubber reinforced with brass-plated steel cables and had a pull-strength of 150,000 pounds. The bogie wheels were made from a magnesium alloy that contained zirconium. Using 185 tapered roller bearings, weighing approximately 500 pounds, reduced friction. The track gear added approximately 5,000 pounds to the normal 16,000-pound landing gear. Nevertheless, this was only two-thirds of the expected increase when the project began.[19]

A strike at the Cleveland Pneumatic Tool Company delayed the fabrication of the track gear, and tests by the

The XB-36 made its first flight with the track gear on 29 March 1950. The main gear is shown at top left, and the nose gear at top right. There was never any intention of using the track gear on production B-36s, but this did not stop several organizations, including the Air University, from proposing B-36 variants that used track-style landing gear. (San Diego Air & Space Museum Collection)

Cold War Peacemaker

Air Force Photo and Equipment Laboratories delayed the availability of the XB-36 for the installation of the track gear until November 1949. A series of low- and medium-speed taxi tests were conducted during early March 1950 using the runways at Carswell. The first flight using the track gear came on 29 March 1950, and the resulting "screeching" sound was unnerving to those aboard the aircraft, including Beryl Erickson and Doc Witchell.[20]

The Air Force investigated the use of track landing gear on other aircraft, including the B-17, CG-4A, C-47, C-119 (C-82B), C-122, C-123, XP-87, and RB-49, but a lack of development funds and the questionable results of the C-82 and B-50 tests curbed the initial enthusiasm. As better wheels, tires, and brakes were developed and the Air Force conceded the need for well-provisioned operating bases, the need for the track landing gear receded and, other than the 11 short-lived C-82As, no production was undertaken. The concept remains a footnote of history.

There was one other experiment conducted to lower the footprint of the B-36. A single RB-36D was modified with an 8-wheel main bogie on at least the right main gear – essentially adding a second wheel next to each of the normal four wheels. Taxi tests were conducted on the grass next to the Fort Worth runways, but it is unclear if the aircraft ever flew in this configuration. If it did, it is obvious the landing gear would not fit into the wing, so it undoubtedly was not retracted.

Unrelated to the track landing gear experiments, a single RB-36D was modified with an 8-wheel main bogie on the right wing. Taxi tests were conducted in the grass, but the arrangement was obviously impractical for an operational airplane and was quickly dropped. (National Archives College Park Collection)

The XB-36 during taxi tests on a hard surface (most likely a taxiway) at Fort Worth. So far as is known, the few flight tests the airplane made were all conducted around Plant 4 – since the landing gear was not retractable it was unlikely the airplane went very far. (National Museum of the United States Air Force Collection)

APPENDIX E

STILLBORN CONCEPT
PRATT & WHITNEY VDT ENGINES

An all-wood mockup of the B-36 VDT installation was completed at Fort Worth. The B-36C used a tractor configuration, unlike the pusher configuration of the normal airplane. Note the stubs for four propeller blades and the cooling ducts situated on either side of the nacelle. (National Museum of the United States Air Force Collection)

The jet engine was beginning to make progress during the mid-1940s, but early models still suffered from numerous problems, most notably low power and high fuel consumption. This led engine designers to experiment using some jet-engine technology coupled with existing concepts. In the end, the most successful of these experiments was the turboprop – essentially a jet engine driving a conventional propeller. But along the way, several manufacturers explored ways of linking existing piston engines with turbines – usually called compounding.

When the original Wasp engine had been developed in 1926, it had an internal mechanically driven supercharger, and this became standard for all subsequent Wasp engines, including the R-4360. However, there was nothing new in the concept of supercharging outside the engine – exhaust-driven superchargers (at the time called turbo-superchargers; more often now simply turbochargers) had been used on the Liberty engines during World War I, and during World War II it became fairly common practice for some engines to use the exhaust gases to drive the supercharger. This arrangement provided a "cheap" source of power since the only mechanical power required was that needed to offset the nominal increase in exhaust backpressure created by the turbo-supercharger. This meant the pistons had to work a little harder to expel the exhaust gases from the cylinder on each stroke, but this was a small percentage of the power required to drive a mechanical supercharger. With the development of alloys capable of withstanding the high temperatures of the engine exhaust gases and the evolution of satisfactory controls, it was natural for power plant engineers to look for ways for the exhaust gases to do even more of the work.

However, the internal supercharging on the Wasp had demonstrated certain benefits. It helped to equally distribute the fuel-air mixture to each of a growing number of cylinders, and also allowed a more compact and self-contained power plant. This latter advantage was considered so compelling during World War II that when additional supercharging was required for combat at higher altitudes, various Wasp-family engines were developed with a second auxiliary stage of mechanically driven supercharging. These engines, with their elongated rear sections, were used in various models of F4F Wildcats, F4U Corsairs, and F6F Hellcats.

Nevertheless, even proponents of mechanical superchargers were aware of the drawbacks of the concept. The largest of these was that it took a considerable amount of the engine's power to drive the internal supercharger. The 600-hp Wasp engine required 44 hp to drive its supercharger – the 3,500-hp R-4360 required 435 hp. In theory, for the Wasp Major to produce 4,000 hp at 40,000 feet, it would need to divert more than 1,200 hp to the supercharger. The power required went up quickly as the altitude increased. There was another disadvantage to the internal supercharger – engineers could not cool down the

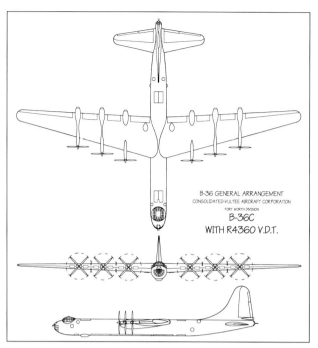

This three-view drawing shows the general arrangement of the VDT-powered B-36C. Note that the forward upper turret bays show the original B-model configuration with the life-boat island in the middle. The conversion from pusher to tractor was deceptively difficult. (Convair)

intake air prior to using it. On aircraft with external turbo-superchargers, it was already common practice to use intercoolers (or aftercoolers) to cool the compressed air before it entered the cylinders. The cooler the air, the less likely it would pre-detonate ("ping" or "knock"), allowing more spark advance and, hence, greater power.[1]

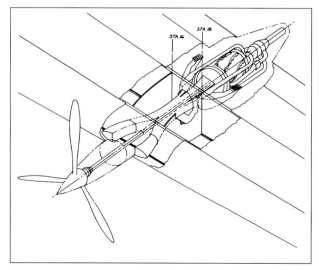

The R-4360-VDT was mounted in its normal location toward the back of the wing, but drove a long driveshaft forward to the propeller. Note the cooling ducts on either side of the shaft, one of the items that proved difficult to perfect. (Convair)

Compounding appeared to solve both of these problems. By eliminating the internal supercharger, the R-4360-VDT instantly gained 435 hp from the current production engine – unfortunately, it also lost the 1,930 hp that was provided by the supercharger. The engine itself would have to make up the resulting loss of 1,500 hp. In retrospect, it is hard to see how the engineers intended to accomplish this. Since compounding compressed the air outside the R-4360, it was possible to run the air through a large aftercooler prior to using it in the cylinders, providing much cooler air. This allowed the engine to run more efficiently, providing a few hundred horsepower boost. The jet thrust from the turbine could add another 300 hp or so, but this still left 1,000 hp unaccounted for.

As envisioned by Pratt & Whitney engineers, compounding had four major design goals: (1) provide more power for takeoff to get heavier loads into the air, (2) give more power for continuous operation at high altitudes, (3) fuel savings, and (4) be less complex.

To accomplish these goals, Pratt & Whitney investigated four "compounding" concepts. The simplest was one where the exhaust gases were passed through a conventional exhaust gas turbine that transmitted power back to the crankshaft through a suitable mechanical drive. This was the approach taken by Wright for the R-3350 Compound. As proposed for the R-4360, this type of compound was confined to low-altitude operation because its maximum-altitude performance was limited by the capacity of its internal-engine supercharger.

Another compounding arrangement was to add conventional exhaust-driven superchargers (turbochargers) to the combination just described. This partially compensated for the altitude restrictions of the first concept, but offered little advantage to the standard R-4360.

The third concept was to duct the hot exhaust gases from the R-4360 directly into the burner cans of a conventional jet engine. A compressor on the front of the jet unit supplied additional air to mix with the engine exhaust and complete the combustion of residual fuel. The resultant hot gas mixture was then passed through the turbine unit to produce power for operating the compressor. Excess power was transmitted back to the R-4360 through suitable shafting and the exhaust was discharged rearward to provide additional thrust.[2]

The fourth concept was the variable discharge turbo-supercharger (or turbine, depending on when the description was written).[3] In actuality, the VDT selected for development was the 17th configuration studied by Don Hersey and P. S. Hopper in an attempt to find the ultimate configuration for extracting more power from the R-4360. The Wasp Major VDT was made public on 2 August 1945 at a "semi" open house to celebrate the twentieth anniversary of Pratt & Whitney. At the back of the experimental hangar was a full-scale engineering model of the new R-4360-VDT[4] with a sign that indicated the engine was to develop "Combat, 4,360 horsepower; takeoff, 3,800 horsepower; normal, 2,800 horsepower." This claimed output was sort of the Holy Grail for engine designers – one horsepower per cubic inch.[5]

The development go-ahead for the new engine was received from the War Department in April 1946 with the expected applications being the B-36C, B-50C (later redesignated B-54), and the Republic F-12 (production version of the XR-12) Rainbow reconnaissance aircraft. An R-2800 Double Wasp was used as a proof-of-concept engine and completed a ten-hour endurance test in March 1947. Eight experimental engines were ordered, and by the end of 1948, they had accumulated 1,725 hours of test time. An additional 8,321 hours of testing was also accomplished on various partial test engines. A 150-hour qualification test was completed in August 1948, clearing the way for flight-testing to begin. An R-4360-VDT was installed at the

Not the best photo, but significant. This was the trailing edge of the VDT wing mockup showing the three engine locations, although only the one on the left has the complete nacelle installed. The R-4360 sat in, more or less, its normal location at the rear spar, and the jet-engine components were located in a streamlined nacelle that protruded past the trailing edge. Note the sculpted sections of the trailing edge where the flaps were located. (National Museum of the United States Air Force Collection)

No. 2 position (left wing, inside) on a B-50A (46-061) for the initial flight tests. In this installation, the R-4360 engine sat in its normal position, with the GE turbine below and behind it in the nacelle. This would be remarkably different from the installation planned for the B-36C.[6]

Conceptually, the VDT engine was fairly simple – all of the piston engine's exhaust gases were discharged through a turbine to provide jet thrust. This could, in the case of the R-4360, add several hundred pounds of thrust to each engine – the equivalent of adding about 300 hp. The R-4360-VDT engine included three primary components: the Wasp Major, a variable discharge turbo-supercharger, and an aftercooler. Engine exhaust gases were used to spin the turbine before being discharged through the variable-area nozzle. On the same axis with the turbine was a two-stage, centrifugal compressor that supercharged all of the intake air for the Wasp Major. A large air-to-air aftercooler (conceptually identical to the intercooler used by the non-VDT engines) reduced the temperature of the intake air. The cooled air passed through a metering unit into the engine, and fuel was injected into the individual cylinders and ignited.[7]

The VDT installation differed from the normal turbo-supercharged R-4360 mainly because there was no wastegate to divert part of the hot exhaust gases overboard at intermediate altitudes. Instead, the VDT passed all of its exhaust gases through the turbine at all times. The R-4360 itself, while appearing little changed externally, deleted the internal supercharger used by other R-4360s.

The General Electric CHM-2 turbine had all of the elements of a contemporary turbojet engine – air compressor, nozzle guide vanes, turbine rotor, tail pipe, and exhaust nozzle – except that the Wasp Major performed the function of the jet burners. As in a jet engine, the air was first compressed, but then, instead of being mixed with fuel and burned in the usual jet engine burners, the air was fed into the 28 cylinders of the R-4360. After fuel was injected and burned inside the cylinders of the piston engine, the exhaust gases were routed back to the turbine and directed by guide vanes through the turbine rotor and discharged out the tailpipe. The hot exhaust gases turned the turbine, which was mechanically connected to the compressor the fed the R-4360.

The discharge nozzle of the turbine could be varied in size to maintain the most efficient discharge speed regardless of altitude – a concept not used on most jet engines of the era. This nozzle was also used to control the power output of the Wasp Major since opening or closing the nozzle changed the difference in pressures of the exhaust gas forward and aft of the turbine and determined the amount of exhaust energy extracted by the turbine. The quantity of supercharged air delivered to the Wasp Major dictated its power output. The conventional throttle was used on the VDT only at slow speeds and low altitudes where the turbine was ineffective.

Convair aircraft had participated in jet engine development since the beginning. This B-24 (44-41986), based at the NACA Lewis Laboratory on 9 July 1946, was modified with a General Electric I-16 in the waist compartment, a large air scoop on top of the fuselage, and the exhaust exiting at the former tail-gunner's position. (National Archives College Park Collection)

Although the concept was appealing, difficulties in providing proper cooling eventually caused its demise. The problem lay more in the B-36 installation than with the engine itself – a similar R-4360-VDT performed adequately when tested in the B-50C configuration. The packaging of the B-36 caused the problem. In order to not seriously affect the center-of-gravity of the B-36, and also to reuse as much structure as possible, the R-4360 engine was installed near its normal position in the rear of the wing, with the turbine even further back. This made cooling both units difficult – a problem compounded by the rarified atmosphere at the expected 40,000–45,000-foot cruising altitude. Ground tests indicated that the new engine would actually provide less power than the basic R-4360-41, and the project was finally cancelled.

Not a VDT airplane, but an unusual model in any case. Note the extended propeller nacelles. This might have been yet another turboprop proposal. The NB-36H mockup is in the upper right corner. (National Museum of the United States Air Force Collection)

APPENDIX F

AHEAD OF ITS TIME
BELL GAM-63 RASCAL

The only known inflight photograph showing a Bell GAM-63 RASCAL missile under a DB-36H (51-5710, in this case). The retractable missile director is under the rear fuselage. The missile occupied the two aft bomb bays, with the electronics package occupying the forward bomb bay. (Convair via Richard Freeman via the Jay Miller Collection)

On 7 July 1952, the Air Force decided to equip some B-36Hs with the Bell B-63 (later GAM-63) "Parasite Pilotless Bomber," more commonly called RASCAL. The name RASCAL was actually an acronym that stood for RAdar SCAnning Link, named for the guidance system developed jointly by Bell Avionics, Radio Corporation of America (RCA), and Texas Instruments, and installed aboard the controlling aircraft. A Bell-designed 4,000-lbf liquid-propellant rocket engine made up of three vertical in-line thrust chambers powered the GAM-63. The missile was 31 feet long with a body diameter of 4 feet and could carry a 3,000-pound W-5 (later W-27) nuclear warhead up to 110 miles at a maximum speed of Mach 2.95. From the official RASCAL history, "The RASCAL mission is the destruction of peripheral targets having strong local defenses, thereby reducing losses of manned aircraft because of these defenses. The missile will be used as an initial attack weapon when time and the tactical situation permit. However, only those targets which present well defined radar returns can be attacked with RASCAL."[1]

In the DB-36H configuration, a retractable radio antenna was installed in the aft fuselage to provide a data link to the missile during flight. The missile was carried semi-submerged in the combined bomb bay Nos. 3 and 4 and the electronic guidance package was installed in bomb bay No. 1. Most of the RASCAL equipment was designed to be easily removable from the B-36, allowing the aircraft to return to its basic bomber configuration in less than 12 hours. Otherwise, the RASCAL carriers were expected to be identical to the Featherweight II B-36H configuration.[2] The standard crew of 15 was carried, except that the bombardier would have the added responsibility of launching and guiding the missile.[3]

A B-36H (51-5710) was converted into the YDB-36H prototype,[4] and the contract included an option to modify an additional 11 B-36Hs into the "director-bomber" configuration. The production option was exercised on 26 May 1953 and the original schedule was to deliver all 12 DB-36Hs by the end of 1954. However, delays in the development of the RASCAL and its guidance system quickly delayed the program.[5]

The operational mission was straightforward, and familiar to modern pilots using many precision-guided munitions. The RASCAL was dropped from the bomber approximately 100 miles from the target, and the engines were ignited by a lanyard pull after the missile was free of the carrier aircraft. If the lanyard or its associated switch malfunctioned, a timer started the engines a set time after release. The initial leg of RASCAL flight was controlled by a self-contained inertial system that obtained reference information from the K-3A bomb/nav system in the B-36 prior to launch. As the missile approached the target area, the bombardier in the B-36 took over guidance of the missile through the data link. Although the missile was flying

The YDB-36H (51-5710) shows the deployed director antenna under the rear fuselage and a RASCAL in the combined bomb bays Nos. 3 and 4. Note that the forward bomb bay doors are open. This airplane was a Featherweight II, meaning it still had all of its defensive armament. (Jay Miller Collection)

based on its own inertial guidance, the B-36 operator could make minor adjustments via the data link. The missile typically would reach 50,000 feet altitude and a speed of approximately Mach 2.5 during its flight. The operator in the B-36 controlled the terminal guidance portion of the missile's flight via a video data link. For airburst detonations, the missile would still be traveling at approximately Mach 1.29 at the time the warhead exploded.[6]

The first unpowered RASCAL drop test from the YDB-36H was on 25 August 1953, and the Bell-designed guidance system was installed before the aircraft was delivered to the Air Force on 22 July 1954. On 6 July 1954, the Air Force released the B-36H (51-5706) that had been used in the Tanbo XIV experiments to the RASCAL program. A week later, this became the first aircraft to enter the RASCAL production program, and was redelivered to the Air Force on 21 December. The next day it flew to Holloman AFB to participate in the RASCAL test program, and at least two live firings

The RASCAL was guided by a radio link from the mothership for much of its flight, and the DB-36H included a retractable direction antenna under the rear fuselage. Note that the doors resemble small versions of the bomb bay doors. (Lockheed Martin)

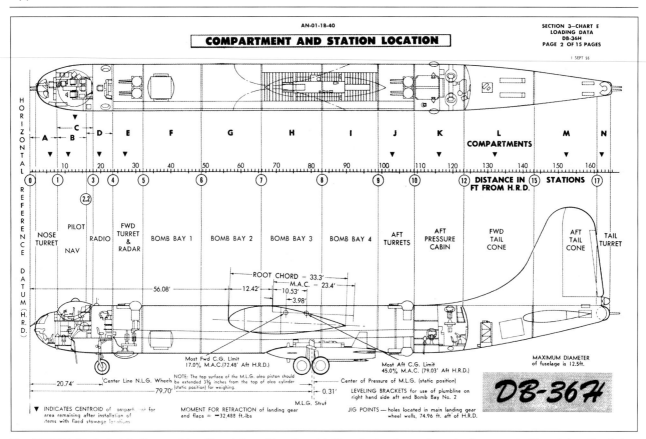

The RASCAL fit nicely into the combined bomb bays Nos. 3 and 4. The electronics package took up most of bomb bay No. 1, but this left No. 2 free to carry bombs or an additional fuel tank. (National Museum of the United States Air Force Collection)

The RASCAL was a sophisticated missile for the 1950s, and featured both internal and radio-relay guidance capabilities. The missile was 32 feet long and 4 feet in diameter, with a span over the aft wings of 16.7 feet. (Air Force Historical Research Agency Collection)

occurred in the first 6 months of 1955. The production program encountered numerous delays, all related to the missile itself and infighting between the Air Materiel Command and the Strategic Air Command over the choice of carrier aircraft and the relative merits of the entire RASCAL Program. Finally, on 12 July 1955, the Air Force cancelled the B-36 carrier aircraft program. By this time, all 12 of the DB-36H modification kits had been manufactured, although they had only been installed on two aircraft. It could not be determined how many missiles were launched before the DB-36/GAM-63 program was cancelled.[7]

In the meantime, by the end of 1951 the Air Force had decided to integrate the RASCAL onto the Boeing B-47. By this time it was evident that the B-36 would be retired in the not-too-distant future, and the B-47 was quickly becoming the most numerous bomber in the inventory. The Air Materiel Command decided to modify a B-47B (51-2186) as a RASCAL carrier under the designation YDB-47B. A single RASCAL was suspended from the starboard side of the fuselage below the wing – the RASCAL was a large missile for the medium bomber and could not be carried semisubmerged as it was on the B-36.

SAC, on the other hand, felt that equipping the B-47 fleet with the large and bulky externally mounted RASCAL would degrade the aircraft's performance to such extent as to make the whole concept of dubious value. SAC also feared that the guidance system would never work very well, and was reluctant to add even more complex electronic equipment to an already electronically packed B-47. Modification costs (about a million dollars per aircraft) were high, and personnel training demands were considerable. Nevertheless, the program continued and Boeing modified 30 B-47s at its Wichita, Kansas, facility as part of Project EBBTIDE. The 445th Bombing Squadron from the 321st Bomb Wing at Pinecastle AFB, Florida, accepted the first production RASCAL missile on 30 October 1957.[8]

A launch platform was installed in bomb bays No. 3 and 4 that provided aerodynamic protection for the rest of the bomb bay after the missile was fired. Note the hole to accommodate the cables used to hoist the missile. (Lockheed Martin)

The RASCAL turned out to be a fairly accurate and effective weapon, but the concept rapidly became obsolete in the face of new developments in the field of air-launched missiles. In October 1958, the Strategic Air Command recommended that the RASCAL program be terminated. Air Force Headquarters accepted this recommendation, and during the first week in December 1958 directed the Air Materiel Command to dispose of the 78 experimental and 58 production RASCAL missiles that had been accepted. By this time, the three DB-36s had already been scrapped.[9]

A RASCAL being loaded into the YDB-36H at Kirtland AFB, New Mexico. All RASCAL tests, except for some inert fit-checks, took place at Kirtland. Note that the bottom stabilizer fin folded to allow clearance under the B-36. (Jay Miller Collection)

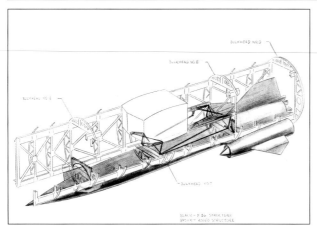
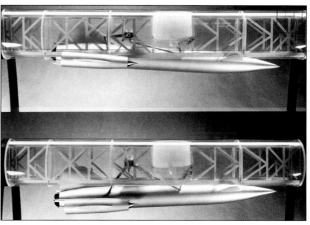

This early NA-704 concept (this page and top of next) for the North American Aviation B-64 (later SM-64) Navaho cruise missile took up all four bomb bays on the B-36. During the late 1940s and early 1950s the Air Force was certain that it wanted to develop long-range missiles, but was unsure if the resulting design would be a ballistic missile or a high-speed cruise missile. The Navaho was one of the latter. In the end the Atlas and Titan intercontinental ballistic missiles (ICBM) were chosen for further development. Nevertheless, later versions of the Navaho were the first large aircraft to fly at Mach 2 and provided an interesting technology base for high-speed winged flight. Note the tight clearance between the missile and the B-36 landing gear in the photo below; the model did not include landing gear doors to better observe the clearance issues. The final Navaho concept abandoned the use of a B-36 as a carrier and opted for a large rocket booster instead. Although linked directly to the Navaho program, this booster led directly to the creation of the of the Rocketdyne Division of North American that supplied rocket engines for many launch vehicles and ICBMs. (National Archives College Park Collection)

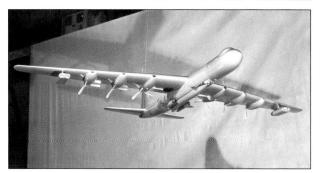

BOEING 497 DISPLAY MODEL - PARASITE VEHICLES   2-24-51   117265

Having absolutely nothing to do with B-36s, we present this interesting Boeing Model 497 that functioned as a missile carrier (note the three RASCALs and one Navaho), cargo carrier using the detachable pod at the far left, and mothership for a smaller aircraft with a V-tail. The Model 497 itself appears to be powered by six large turboprop engines. (Air Force Historical Research Agency Collection)

By 1953, the Air Force development agencies were leaning toward using the Boeing B-47 as a RASCAL carrier instead of the B-36. Given the comparably small size of the B-47, the RASCAL was carried externally, on a pylon attached to the starboard side of the fuselage. Two of the prototype YDB-47Es (53-2346 at left and 51-5219 at right) are shown. The plan got far enough that the 321st Bomb Wing was training with the missile before the program was cancelled. (National Museum of the United States Air Force Collection

The next airborne missile program was much more ambitious. The Douglas GAM-87A Skybolt was an air-launched ballistic missile (ALBM) developed during the late 1950s to provide mobile basing for the ICBM force by mounting them on heavy bombers rather than in fixed missile silos. The United Kingdom joined the program in 1960, intending to use it on their V bomber force. The U.S. platform was the Boeing B-52G/H (60-0008 shown). (National Archives College Park Collection)

The GAM-87A was powered by a two-stage solid-fuel rocket motor. Each B-52H carried four missiles, two under each wing on side-by-side pylons, while the Avro Vulcan carried one each on smaller pylons. (National Archives College Park Collection)

Skybolt was fitted with a jettisonable tailcone to reduce drag while on the pylon. First-stage control was by eight movable tail fins, while the second stage was equipped with a gimballed nozzle. (National Archives College Park Collection)

Skybolt was a large solid-propellant missile. It was 38 feet long, 3 feet in diameter, and weighed 11,000 pounds. The missile had a top speed of 8,500 mph, a range of 1,150 miles, and used a W-59 thermonuclear warhead with a 1.2-megaton yield. This test round was launched at Eglin AFB, Florida, in 1962. The first fully successful Skybolt flight occurred on 19 December 1962, but on that same day the program was cancelled. Note the nose art on the B-52 in the background. (National Archives College Park Collection)

APPENDIX G

BIZARRE CONCEPT

PARASITES AND OTHER COUPLING IDEAS

One of the ten GRB-36Ds (49-2692) with a Republic RF-84K (52-7266). Except for the reconfigured bomb bays, the only external change to the carriers was the addition of an AN/APX-29A IFF/rendezvous beacon on the upper fuselage just ahead of the wing. Surprisingly, the FICON concept proved to be quite workable, although its service-life was fairly short. (National Museum of the United States Air Force Collection)

The concept for parasite aircraft was not new by the 1950s. Although several countries had investigated the idea, perhaps the most successful application was the U.S. Navy's Curtiss F9C Sparrowhawk biplanes from the 1930s. First ordered in June 1930, the F9C was less than 20 feet long with a wingspan of only 25.5 feet. A single 420-hp Wright R-975 engine could propel the 2,000-pound fighter to a top speed of 175 mph. When the Navy began building two large airships – *Akron* and *Macon* – it was decided that each airship would be equipped with a small hangar deck that allowed up to five Sparrowhawks to be carried. The original XF9C-1 prototype was modified with a hook device in front of the canopy and tests were conducted using the airship *Los Angeles* beginning on 23 October 1931. Six production F9C-2 Sparrowhawks had been ordered a week earlier.[1]

By all accounts, the little fighters were quite successful as parasites. Unfortunately, the *Akron* was lost on 4 April 1933, followed by the *Macon* on 12 February 1935, effectively ending the program. A decade later, the U.S. military would try again.

XP-85 Goblin

The first jet fighters introduced near the end of World War II had insufficient range to escort the long-range B-35 and B-36 bombers then on the drawing boards. As one possible solution to this problem, the Army Air Forces revived the parasite fighter idea of the early 1930s, and proposed that the long-range bombers carry their protective fighters right along with them.[2]

On 29 January 1944, the Army Air Forces invited the industry to submit concept proposals for parasite jet fighters. The McDonnell Aircraft Corporation was the only company to respond, and proposed a small fighter aircraft to be carried partially inside a parent B-29, B-36, or B-35 heavy bomber. However, the AAF rejected this plan in January 1945, concluding that the fighter would have to be carried entirely inside the B-35 or B-36.[3]

On 19 March 1945, McDonnell submitted a revised proposal for an even smaller aircraft with an egg-shaped fuselage, a triple vertical stabilizer, a horizontal stabilizer with pronounced dihedral, and vertically folding sweptback wings. A single 3,000-lbf Westinghouse 24C (XJ34) axial-flow turbojet used a nose intake and a straight-through exhaust. The airplane was only 15 feet long, with a wingspan of 21 feet, an empty weight of 3,984 pounds, and a gross weight of 5,600 pounds, making it, by far, the smallest jet fighter. In fact, the airplane was smaller than the F9C, although it weighed twice as much. The aircraft had a pressurized cockpit, an ejection seat, and the eventual armament was to be four .50-cal. machine guns in the sides of the forward fuselage. The top speed was over-optimistically estimated at 648 mph. It would be launched and recovered from a trapeze that extended from its parent aircraft at

The first McDonnell XF-85 (46-523) and its Bell-built Boeing B-29B (44-84111). This shows the diminutive size of the Goblin. This is a fairly late photo, evidenced by the winglets on the XF-85. (National Archives College Park Collection)

altitudes up to 48,000 feet. The airplane had an endurance of about 80 minutes and the parasite could be refueled from the bomber fuel system while tucked in the bomb bay.[4]

The Army Air Forces liked the proposal, and ordered two XP-85 prototypes (46-523/524) and a static test article on 9 October 1945. The Army Air Forces

Given the timing, this is probably a mockup of the XF-85, shown at the St. Louis airshow on 17 October 1948. Since this was in the middle of the flight-test campaign, it is unlikely this is a real airplane. The B-36, missing armament, is likely an A- or B-model. (National Archives College Park Collection)

specified that the 24th (the first B-36B) and subsequent B-36s would be capable of carrying a single P-85 in addition to the usual bomb load. It was even planned that some B-36s would be modified so that they could carry three P-85 fighters and no bomb load, and some popular press accounts mentioned carrying four fighters. It appears that the first few B-36Bs actually had the mounting brackets for the trapeze included in their bomb bays.[4]

Since the XP-85 was to be launched and recovered from a retractable trapeze underneath its parent bomber, no conventional landing gear was installed. A retractable hook was installed on top of the fuselage in front of the cockpit. During recovery, the XP-85 would approach its carrier bomber from underneath, and the hook would gently engage the trapeze. Once securely attached, the aircraft would be pulled up into the bomb bay. If an emergency landing were necessary, the aircraft was provided with a retractable steel skid underneath the fuselage, and steel runners protected the wingtips.

A B-36 could not be spared for the project, so a B-29B (44-84111) was modified with a special launch-and-recovery trapeze for use in the initial testing. A few test flights were made with the XP-85, but the recovery operation proved to be much more difficult than expected, forcing several emergency landings using the retractable steel skid. The Air Force concluded that recovering the Goblin was probably far beyond the capabilities of the average squadron pilot. In addition, it was projected that the performance of the XP-85 would likely be inferior to that of foreign interceptors that would soon enter service. Furthermore, a budget crunch in the autumn of 1949 led to a severe shortage of funds for developmental projects. Consequently, the Air Force terminated the XP-85 program on 24 October 1949.[6]

FICON

The FICON (FIghter CONveyor) project was essentially a follow-on to the earlier XP-85 experiments. It was reasoned that many of the difficulties encountered with the XP-85 were due to that aircraft's unique shape, largely dictated by the requirement that it fit entirely into the bomb bay of a B-35 or B-36. If that requirement was relaxed, a more conventional fighter configuration could be used. Since the straight-wing Republic F-84 Thunderjet was proving to be fairly successful in service, an F-84E was chosen as the subject of the next round of experiments.

On 19 January 1951, Convair was authorized to modify an RB-36F (49-2707) to carry a modified F-84E. The bomb bay of the JRB-36F was extensively modified, and a retractable H-shaped cradle that was securely fastened to the rear wing spar replaced the usual bomb racks. A single F-84E (49-2115) was modified to carry a hook on the upper nose ahead of its cockpit. During the recovery operation, the F-84E was to fly up underneath the B-36 and use its hook to engage a slot in the cradle. The cradle would then rotate down over the fuselage of the F-84E and engage hardpoints on the rear fuselage. Once attached, the F-84E would be pulled upward and nestle semi-submerged in the bomb bays of the JRB-36F. Launch was carried out by reversing this process.

The JRB-36F/F-84E combination began its first tests on 8 January 1952 and the first complete cycle of retrieval, retraction, and launch took place on 23 April 1952. The tests were remarkably trouble-free, and demonstrated that a good pilot should have no particular difficulty performing the operation.

By this time, there was less emphasis on using the FICON concept for fighter escorts, but a new need had

The YRF-84F (49-2430, it used to be the YF-84F), attached to the trapeze on the JRB-36F (49-2707). The photo was taken from the lower aft dighting blister. Note the heavily framed canopy on the fighter. (National Archives College Park Collection)

The FICON control panel in one of the GBR-36Ds during 1955. The window at the lower left looks into the bomb bay. There were other control panels at the bombardier's station and some on the flight deck. (National Archives College Park Collection)

developed. Increasing Soviet air defenses were making it more difficult for the large strategic reconnaissance aircraft to penetrate Soviet airspace. The Air Force was not as worried about bomber penetration since by that time the two nations would be at war and fleets of bombers could assist in protecting each other. But reconnaissance aircraft penetrated one at a time, hopefully without being detected. The FICON concept offered a way to transport a relatively small reconnaissance aircraft close to Soviet borders. It could then be released, make its reconnaissance run, and return to the waiting carrier aircraft. The new Republic RF-84F Thunderflash would be perfect. And it could carry a small atomic weapon if the need ever arose.

In 1953, the first swept-wing YF-84F (51-1828) was modified in much the same manner as the F-84E, except that its horizontal stabilizer (which had been relocated in the swept-wing version) was sharply canted downward to clear the bottom of the B-36 during launch and recovery.

Contracts awarded Convair and Republic in the fall of 1953 called for modifying 10 RB-36D-IIIs and 25 RF-84Fs (52-7254/7278), respectively. This was far below the number of aircraft the Strategic Air Command originally had in mind – 30 RB-36s and 75 RF-84s – but yet another budget crunch had arrived. The first GRB-36D-III carrier was delivered in February 1955, six months ahead of the first GRF-84K.

The parasite could be picked up in midair en route to the target area, or by ground hook-up prior to takeoff. Night operations were also possible. In a typical mission, the GRF-84K was carried out to a 2,810-mile radius and launched at an altitude of 25,000 feet. After completing the mission, the fighter would be recovered by the GRB-36D and returned to base. The parasite would be released about 800 to 1,000 miles from the target and within a relatively

safe area. The pilot of the RF-84 would continue on to the target, obtain high- or low-level photography, as desired, then return to the carrier.

The GRB-36Ds were modified with special plug-and-clearance doors instead of bomb bay doors, the FICON trapeze, a trapeze operator's station in the camera compartment, and two independent hydraulic systems for trapeze and door actuation. The clearance doors fit tightly around the parasite during flight, while the plug doors filled the hole that remained when the GRF-84K was not being carried. Special night and rendezvous lighting was installed on the GRB-36D horizontal stabilizers and under the fuselage, and an APX-29A IFF/rendezvous set was installed on top of the fuselage. The bomb bay was equipped with a catwalk, safety wires, and handholds so that the GRF-84K pilot could ingress/egress during flight. Since the B-36 did not normally carry jet fuel (the jet engines were modified to run on aviation gas), an 1,140-gallon fuel tank filled with JP-4 was carried offset to the left side (to clear the GRF-84K's tail) in bomb bay No. 4 so that the GRF-84K could be refueled while mated.[7] The GRB-36D could also supply electrical power, preheat air, and pressurization air to the parasite during flight.

The operational Air Force crews began training at Convair during late 1955 when 13 pilots from Fairchild AFB arrived. After initial daylight training at Convair, the pilots returned to Fairchild where more extensive training, including night and high-altitude operations continued. The GRB-36D carriers saw limited service with the 99th Strategic Reconnaissance Wing (SRW) based at Fairchild AFB, operating with RF-84Ks from the 91st Strategic Reconnaissance Squadron of the 71st SRW initially based at Great Falls AFB, Montana, then moved to Larson AFB, Washington (now Boeing's Moses Lake facility).[8]

The RF-84K was extremely close to the ground (note the fuel tanks) when it was mounted in the bomb bay of the GRB-36D. This pair as photographed on 3 April 1956 at Edwards AFB. (National Archives College Park Collection)

A typical GRB-36D (49-2694) – not much different than any other RB-36 except for the RF-84K in the bomb bay. The most telling feature was the APX-29A beacon installed in the blister on top of the fuselage. (National Archives College Park Collection)

In at least one case, the GRB-36D proved to be an adequate emergency landing field. On 12 December 1955, an RF-84K piloted by Capt. F. P. Robbinson was practicing night operations when his hydraulic system began to fail. The pilot suspected he did not have sufficient time to return to base, but radioed a GRB-36D that was nearby and explained the situation. Maj. Jack R. Packwood, the pilot of the bomber, arranged to rendezvous with the fighter and a hookup was made without incident. The mated pair returned to Fairchild AFB without further incident. The Air Force quoted Capt. Robbinson: "The GRB-36 was the best emergency alternate I ever heard of. If it hadn't been there, it's a cinch I would have had to bail out." The same bomber crew had made 19 other hookups and drops earlier in the day during routine practice. The bomber belonged to the 348th BS of the 99th Bomb Wing.[9]

Other stories have circulated about new operations personnel at Larson being confused by RF-84K pilots that filed 48-hour long flight plans with no stopovers listed.

No details have been released concerning the missions flown by the FICONs, but rumors have persisted that the RF-84Ks made several overflights of the northeastern Soviet Union on reconnaissance missions prior to the U-2 becoming available. No available documentation supports these rumors, but not a great deal has been released about the operations of the 99th SRW during that time period. Once the U-2 had proven its ability, the FICONs were quickly phased out of service.

Tom-Tom

Several other bizarre experiments were performed during the late 1940s and early 1950s to test the feasibility of extending the range of jet fighters by having them carried into the combat zone by bombers. Perhaps the most unusual of these range-extension experiments were Projects TIP TOW and Tom-Tom where jet fighters were attached to the wingtips of B-29s and B-36s.

An operational GRB-36D (49-2692) and RF-84K (52-7269) at Fairchild AFB, Washington, on 13 February 1956. Note the configuration of the "air plug doors" that replaced the standard bomb bay doors. These fit tightly against the Thunderflash when it was tucked inside the bomb bay. To aid clearance, the horizontal stabilizers on the RF-84K were canted downward, but reportedly had no adverse effect on the handling characteristics of the aircraft. (National Archives College Park Collection)

Dr. Richard Vogt, a German scientist who came to America after World War II, had first put the concept forward. Dr. Vogt intended to use the idea to increase the range of an aircraft by attaching two "free floating" panels to carry extra fuel. This could be accomplished without undue structural weight penalties if the extensions were free to articulate and were self-supported by their own aerodynamic lift. In addition, the panels would effectively increase the aspect ratio of the overall wing, providing a significant reduction in wing drag. Therefore, as the theory went, the extra fuel was being carried "for free" by the more efficient wing and the extra fuel increased the range of the aircraft. Other potential uses for this concept quickly became apparent. The one that sparked the most interest was for a bomber to carry two escort fighters, one on each wingtip. The Germans had apparently experimented with the concept during late 1944 and early 1945.[10]

During 1949, initial U.S. experiments had successfully used a Douglas C-47A and Culver PQ-14B. These tests involved a very simple coupling device that was a single-joint attachment that permitted 3 degrees of freedom for the PQ-14. A small ring was placed on a short boom attached to the right wingtip of the C-47. Only local structural reinforcement was required since the PQ-14 would be supported by its own lift. A lance was mounted on the left wingtip of the PQ-14, and by facing the lance rearward, no locking mechanism was required since drag would keep the aircraft in place. The PQ-14 would position itself slightly ahead of the C-47 and essentially "back" the lance into the ring. To uncouple, the PQ-14 would simply speed up. The first attempt at coupling was made on 19 August 1949 over Wright Field, Ohio. Problems with wingtip vortex interference were encountered, forcing the engineers to reevaluate the concept. The solution was to move the ring further away from the C-47's wingtip, and on 7 October 1949 a successful coupling was made with Capt. Clarence E. "Bud" Anderson at the controls of the PQ-14B.[11]

One of the RF-84Fs (51-1847) bailed to Convair for the FICON test programs being loaded into the first GRB-36D (49-2696) at Plant 4. Note the close-fitting seal between the F-84's vertical stabilizer and the B-36. Once the technicians are finished, the air-plug doors will be closed tightly around the fighter, minimizing the drag of the mated pair. This Thunderflash was displayed for years at the Citadel, but was scrapped in 1996 when severe corrosion was discovered on the airframe. (Lockheed Martin)

One of the RF-84Fs (51-1849) mated to the right wingtip of the JRB-36F (49-2707) on 8 June 1956. Note that both wingtips on the B-36 are modified to tow F-84s, but all three aircraft were seldom together. (Lockheed Martin)

At the same time as the C-47/PQ-14 experiments, a full-scale program was initiated using a B-29 to tow two straight-wing F-84 fighters. Republic Aviation was awarded a contract to design, build, and evaluate the combination under Project TIP TOW.

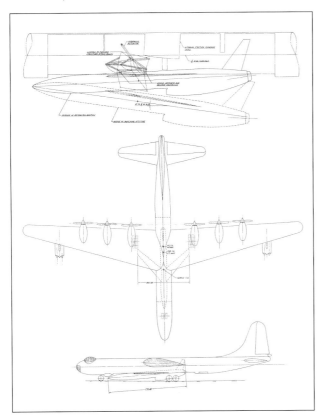

One of the more bizarre concepts involved mating a Northrop SM-62 Snark cruise missile to a B-36. The 50,000-pound Snark was a large turbojet-powered missile that was 64.5 feet long with a 42.5-foot wingspan. (45th SW History Office Collection)

Two F-84Ds (48-641 and 48-661) were modified for the initial TIP TOW tests under the designation EF-84D. The wingtips of the EF-84Ds were modified so that they could be attached to flexible mounts fitted to the wingtips of a specially modified EB-29A (44-62093). This idea proved to be highly dangerous, although successful linkups were made, resulting in almost 15 hours of wingtip coupled flight. Tragically, on 24 April 1953, during a test of an advanced autopilot system that was supposed to make coupled-flying easier for the pilots of the F-84s, one of the fighters rolled up and over onto the wing of the B-29. The left wing of the bomber failed, and both aircraft crashed, killing the pilot of the EF-84D and four of the five crew aboard the EB-29A. TIP TOW was immediately cancelled.[12]

A similar project was undertaken with a pair of RF-84Fs (51-1848 and 51-1849) attached to wingtip hook-up assemblies on the JRB-36F (49-2707 – the initial FICON testbed). The B-36 was formally assigned to the Tom-Tom project on 8 May 1954. Interestingly, the Tom-Tom moniker was derived from the first names of two men – Maj. Gen. Thomas P. Gerrity and Convair contract manager Tom Sullivan – which is why it is not written in all caps.

The B-36 system included provisions to launch and retrieve the fighters in flight, and to provide fuel, pressurization, and heating air to the parasites while coupled. The wing structure of the B-36 and F-84s were substantially strengthened to tolerate the expected stress of coupled flight. Interestingly, the Thieblot Engineering Company accomplished the actual design of the Tom-Tom mechanisms under subcontract to Convair. A fixed mockup of the coupling mechanism was attached to the wing of the JRB-36F and one RF-84F and 7 hours of proximity flight tests were completed on 30 September 1954. Each of the F-84s was equipped with an articulating jaw that was designed to firmly clamp onto a retractable member on the wingtip of the B-36. Once a firm attachment was made, the B-36 would retract the member into a streamlined fairing where fluid, electrical and air connections would be made to allow the F-84 to shut down its engine.[13]

Most sources indicate that only a few hookup attempts[14] were made, and wingtip vortices and turbulence made this operation a very dangerous affair. The first hookup – using only the left-hand fighter – was made on 2 November 1955. In what became the final Tom-Tom flight, on 26 September 1956, Beryl Erickson found the F-84 he was piloting oscillating violently up and down while attached to the B-36 wingtip. Fortunately, part of the attachment mechanism broke and the F-84 fell away from the bomber before any serious damage was done. Since experiments with midair refueling techniques seemed to offer greater promise for increased fighter ranges with far less risk to the lives of aircrews, the Tom-Tom experiments were cancelled.[15]

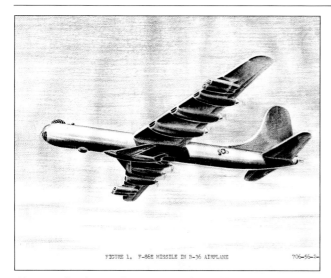

FIGURE 1. F-86E MISSILE IN B-36 AIRPLANE

706-56-2

Okay, maybe the Snark was not all that odd. This B-36 is carrying an unpiloted offensive-missile F-86 variant. Again, it was to be used as an cruise missile, allowing the B-36 to stay out of enemy air space. (National Records Center St. Louis Collection)

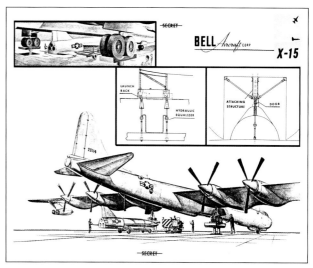

Three of the four X-15 rocket-plane proposals used a B-36 mothership (the fourth used a B-50). This is the Bell D171 concept being loaded into the bomb bay. Note the hydraulic jacks lifting the bomber. (Benjamin F. Guenther Collection)

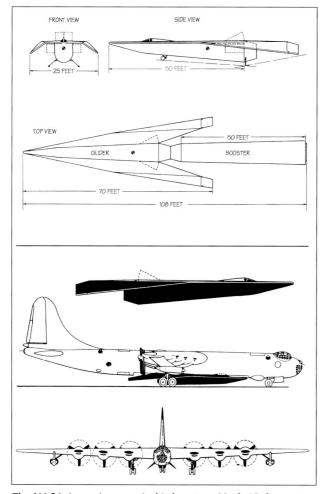

The NACA Ames Aeronautical Laboratory Mach 10 demonstrator was an early precursor to the Space Shuttle. Like many research proposals from the late 1950s, this one was carried by a B-36. (National Archives College Park Collection)

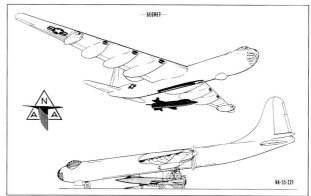

The North American ESO-7487 concept eventually won the competition and became the X-15. The Air Force authorized modifying a B-36 to carry the airplane, but before this happened the program switched to a pair of Boeing B-52s. (Benjamin F. Guenther Collection)

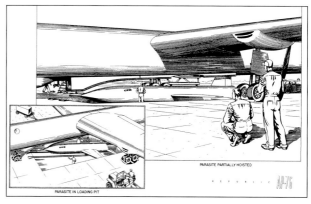

The Republic AP-76 was the largest and heaviest of the X-15 competitors. Republic already had experience using the B-36 as a carrier aircraft, having built the RF-84K FICON aircraft. (Benjamin F. Guenther Collection)

ENDNOTES
CITATIONS AND POINTS OF INTEREST

An early B-36 model being tested in the NACA Ames Aeronautical Laboratory 16-foot wind tunnel. Note the arrangement of the cooling ducts on the engine nacelles. The final configuration brought the lower ducts all the way to the leading edge of the wing instead of being cut back like those on the model. This significantly improved cooling. (National Archives College Park Collection)

Preface

1 The first words out of many people's mouths when viewing the aircraft for the first time were, "Jesus Christ, it's big," or something similar. Several other aircraft, particularly the Hughes HK-1 "Spruce Goose" elicited the same reaction.

2 Lee Van Atta, "Single B-36 Will Replace Nine B-17s In Globe-Girdling Atom Bomb Force," *Fort Worth Star-Telegram*, 30 August 1946.

3 "B-36 to Carry Own Fighter Protection in Bomb Bays," *Fort Worth Star-Telegram*, 13 September 1946.

Chapter 1 – Cowboys to Cockpits

1 When the Air Force became a separate service in 1947, the nomenclature was changed to Air Force Plant 4.

2 *Dallas News*, 10 August 1948. ("Tin Lizzie" was a colloquial term for Ford Motor Company's first production automobile, the Model T. Lizzie was slang for horse, so the Tin Lizzie replaced the Iron Horse (the railroads).

3 "B-36 to Carry Own Fighter Protection in Bomb Bays," *Fort Worth Star-Telegram*, 13 September 1946.

4 Women in the Air Force (WAF) was a United States Air Force program which served to bring women into limited roles in the Air Force. WAF was formed in 1948, when President Truman signed the Women's Armed Services Integration Act, allowing women to serve directly in the military. The WAF was distinct from the Women's Auxiliary Ferrying Squadron (WAFS), a small group of female transport pilots that was formed in 1942 and folded into the Women Airforce Service Pilots (WASP) in 1943; WASP was disbanded in December, 1944.

5 Walter C. Hornday, "Washingtonians in Dither As Inauguration Day Nears," *Dallas News*, 16 January 1949.

6 See www.fortworthclub.com

7 *Handbook of Texas Online*, s.v., http://www.tshaonline.org/handbook/online/articles/WW/fwo28.html

8 Carter's birth name was Giles Amon Carter.

9 Jerry Flemmons, *Amon: The Texan who Played Cowboy for America*, (Lubbock, TX: Texas Tech University Press, 1998).

10 Louis J. Wortham (1858-1927) represented Tarrant County in the House of the Texas Legislature from 1909 to 1915. He was co-founder and editor (until 1923) of the *Fort Worth Star-Telegram*.

11 Carter wisely retained Louis Wortham as editor of the *Fort Worth Star-Telegram*.

12 Jerry Flemmons, *Amon: The Texan who Played Cowboy for America*, (Lubbock, TX: Texas Tech University Press, 1998).

13 Committee members included W. G. Turner, W. G. Burton, A. G. Carter, W. Monnig, W. C. Stripling, and G. C. Clifford.

14 The aircraft were transported by rail on the same track that was finished by Fort Worth residents 35 years earlier.

15 In preparation for Garros' flight, Edmond Audemars tested the gusty winds by raising his Demoiselle a few feet off the ground in three consecutive runs within the confines of the Driving Club.

16 Rodgers (12 January 1879–3 April 1912) was a pioneer American aviator who was the first civilian to purchase a Wright Flyer and the first to make a transcontinental flight.

17 Interestingly, the Vin Fiz Bottling Company was a subsidiary of the Armour Meat Packing Company.

18 The *Vin Fiz Flyer*'s original destination was the State Fair of Texas at Dallas but a contract with Cal Rodgers' promoters was declined due to what was considered by Fair officials an excessive fee. Dallas then contracted a well-known aviator, J.A.D. McCurdy, to fly instead of Rogers and Fort Worth eagerly paid Rodger's fee. When McCurdy's airplane crashed during the first day of the Fair, Dallas officials hurriedly hired Rodgers to fly in McCurdy's place, but not before Rodgers had flown to Fort Worth.

19 Wortham was still editor of the *Fort Worth Star-Telegram* at that time.

20 From a study of the life of Dermott Lang Allen by Gp Capt. H. Neubroch, 2005.

21 Water supply for the bases was readily available from a series of lakes on the Trinity River that were completed in 1916, only one year earlier.

22 B. B. Paddock, *Fort Worth and the Texas Northwest*, (St. Louis, MO: The Lewis Publishing Company, 1922).

23 Petroleum supplies would become a central requirement in the selection criteria for Consolidated's bomber plant. Large fleets of aircraft – and a mile-long air-conditioned assembly building – would consume huge quantities of petroleum products. As aircraft became larger, the demand for fuel would increase even more.

24 Capt. B.B. Paddock, *Fort Worth and the Texas Northwest*, Volume II, (Chicago: The Lewis Publishing Company, 1922), p. 672.

25 *The Columbia Encyclopedia*, Sixth Edition (New York: Columbia University Press, 2001).

26 From the correspondence files of the Fort Worth Chamber of Commerce via C. Roger Cripliver.

27 William Wagner, *Reuben Fleet and The Story of Consolidated Aircraft*, (Fallbrook, CA: Aero Publishers, 1976).

28 For more information, see, *"Brother, Can You Spare a Billion?" The Story Of Jesse H. Jones, Head of the Reconstruction Finance Corporation*, documentary video production of www.HoustonPBS.org

29 From a 2005 telephone interview by Don Pyeatt with Charles Holloway, grandson of Reuben Hollis Fleet.

30 E. C. Barksdale, Professor of History, Head, Social Science Department, Arlington State College, *The Genesis of The Aviation Industry in North Texas*, (Austin, TX: Bureau of Business Research, The University of Texas, Austin, 1958).

31 From the correspondence files of the Fort Worth Chamber of Commerce via C. Roger Cripliver.

32 E. C. Barksdale, Professor of History, Head, Social Science Department, Arlington State College, *The Genesis of The Aviation Industry in North Texas*, (Austin, TX: Bureau of Business Research, The University of Texas, Austin, 1958).

33 William Wagner, *Reuben Fleet and The Story of Consolidated Aircraft*, (Fallbrook, CA: Aero Publishers, 1976).

34 Ibid.

35 Joel Davidson "Building for World War II: The Aerospace Industry," (Washington, DC: National Building Museum. 2008). See also www.nbm.org

36 Jerry Flemmons, *Amon: The Texan who Played Cowboy for America*, (Lubbock, TX: Texas Tech University Press, 1998).

37 Smith, a former resident of Fort Worth and president of American Airlines since 25 October 1934, joined the Army when the war began and helped organize the Air Transport Command.

38 From a public exhibit, Fort Worth Museum of Science and History

39 Bowmar had originally lured Consolidated to San Diego, and his role was to buffer Fleet from the pressures of local Chambers of Commerce promoters as the group inspected prospective plant sites.

40 William Wagner, *Reuben Fleet and The Story of Consolidated Aircraft*, (Fallbrook, CA: Aero Publishers, 1976)

41 Also referred to as "cabled" or "wired," was communication by telegraphy. Younger readers are urged to perform an internet search for descriptions of this obsolete technology.

42 Jerry Flemmons, *Amon: The Texan who Played Cowboy for America*, (Lubbock, TX: Texas Tech University Press, 1998).

43 "Bomber Plant To Be Located At Tulsa," *Dallas News*, 22 December 1940.

44 Jerry Flemmons, *Amon: The Texan who Played Cowboy for America*, (Lubbock, TX: Texas Tech University Press, 1998).

45 Government Aircraft Plant No. 1 was in Omaha, Nebraska; No. 2 was in Kansas City, Kansas; No. 3 was in Tulsa, Oklahoma. See http://www.airforcebase.net/usaf/afp_list.html for a complete list of plants.

46 "Fort Worth's Bomber Plant Contract Let," *Dallas News* (AP), 9 March 1941.

47 "Fort Worth, Tulsa Plant Contracts Let," *Dallas News* (AP), 16 March 1941.

48 Felix R. McKnight, staff correspondent, "Dirt Broken In Rain for Plane Plant," *Dallas News*, 19 April 1941.

49 "2 Vital Army Bureaus Go To Fort Worth," *Dallas News*, 6 May 1942.

50 From the memoirs of Mr. Joe Jopling, former conductor on the transport trailers and a retired Convair employee.

51 Although the first B-24 was completed on 17 April 1942, it was not formally accepted by the Army until 1 May.

52 Printed in *The Eagle*, Official Publication of Consolidated Vultee Aircraft Corporation, Fort Worth Division, Friday, 10 August 1945.

53 "Tarrant Airfield To Be Converted For B-29s, B-32s" *Dallas News*, 18 July 1945.

54 Stalin knew about the atom bomb before Truman hinted its existence through spies working within the U.S. nuclear development program.

55 Before World War II began, the Soviet Union's borders were threatened on the west by Nazi Germany and on the east by Japan; both countries hoped to claim territories for their natural resources and military values. Stalin was eager for Truman to decimate Japan's military.

Chapter 2 – The Consolidated B-36

1 *Liberator*, issued by General Dynamics for the Fiftieth Anniversary of the first flight. The breakdown was 1,804 B-24D/Js, 939 B-24E/Hs, 291 C-87s, and 114 B-32s (in addition to a single example built in San Diego).

2 As with many things in the Air Force, the first few models use Roman numerals, and subsequent versions use Arabic numbers. So it was with nuclear weapons; Arabic numbers were used beginning with the Mk 4.

3 Marcelle Size Knack, *Post-World War II Bombers*, (Washington DC: Office of Air Force History, 1988), p 3. It should be noted that until the early 1950s, the range and speed of military aircraft were usually shown in statute miles. Afterward, the Air Force began to measure speed in knots and range in nautical miles.

4 Bill Leary, *Flyers of Barron Field*, (Fort Worth, TX: Yrael Publishing Company, 2003), pp 59-67. Greenville, Texas native Ormer Leslie Locklear (28 October 1891 – 2 August 1920), famous aerial daredevil and barnstormer, conducted several in-flight refueling experiments in 1918 while an instructor pilot at Fort Worth's Barron Field, one of three World War I Army flight-training schools in the area. He first transferred fuel from one Curtiss JN-4 to another by strapping a gas can to himself and climbing from the lower wing of one aircraft to the upper wing of another, down to the lower wing and then to the fuselage to pour the fuel into the aircraft's tank. (Source: *Aircraft Journal, 3 May 1919*. This feat was later performed several times by "copycat" daredevils such as Wesley May who duplicated it in 1921.) Locklear later refined the process to lowering a hose from the upper aircraft to the lower, but still requiring an extra-cockpit maneuver to place the hose into the tank. Soon after his Army discharge in 1919, Locklear was poised to fly the first non-stop transcontinental flight from New York to San Francisco by staging his cadets along the route to ferry fuel to him in-flight. In addition to the transcontinental flight, Locklear had firm plans to win the Daily Mail Prize for being first to cross the Atlantic from Newfoundland to Ireland – and possibly to England – in an aircraft provided for him for the feat by Glenn Curtiss (Source: *The Evening World*, 2 June 1919).

5 The Boeing XB-15 (Model 294) first flew on 15 October 1937, and was the largest aircraft built in the United States at the time. The experimental bomber looked much like the early B-17s, but had a wingspan almost half again as long (149 feet) and was 20 feet

longer (87.5 feet). It had a maximum weight of just over 70,000 pounds. The airplane was used to haul cargo during World War II under the XC-105 designation, and its wing design was used successfully on the Boeing 314 Clippers. The XC-105 was scrapped at Kelly Field in 1945. The Douglas XB-19 dwarfed all previous U.S. aircraft, with a wingspan of 212 feet and an overall length of 132 feet. Maximum weight was 162,000 pounds – about 20,000 pounds more than the B-29. Despite advances in technology that made the XB-19 obsolete before it was completed, the Army Air Corps felt that the prototype would be useful for testing. Its construction took so long that competition for the contracts to make the XB-35 and XB-36 occurred two months before its first flight. The airplane finally made its maiden flight on 27 June 1941, more than three years after the construction contract was awarded. In 1943, the original Wright R-3350 air-cooled engines were replaced with Allison V-3420-11 liquid-cooled engines and the designation changed to XB-19A. After testing was completed, the XB-19A served as a cargo carrier until it was scrapped in 1949.

6 "Case History of XB-36, YB-36, and B-36 Airplanes (Revised)," Historical Office, Air Materiel Command, 28 May 1948, p. 1. The compensation arrangement was not unusual at the time. The rationale was that the winner received a large development and production contract and would eventually recoup expenses and make a reasonable profit. The loser was essentially reimbursed for expenses plus a small fee. In today's world, the government provides "bid and proposal" funds to each contractor that allows them to compete for new contracts at no (or little) cost to themselves. Between 1934 and 1947, Boeing was the Boeing Aircraft Co.; in 1947, it changed its name back to the Boeing Airplane Co.

7 The word "range" is often qualified with good reason. In this context, it indicates how far an aircraft can fly under given operating conditions, from takeoff until fuel exhaustion. This differs from "combat radius" which is the distance an aircraft can fly, then turn around and return to its point of departure, with a given payload at a given speed and altitude with specified reserves. The combat radius is usually a great deal less than half of the maximum range of the aircraft for a variety of reasons.

8 "Case History of XB-36, YB-36, and B-36 Airplanes (Revised)," pp. 1-2.

9 "Case History of XB-36, YB-36, and B-36 Airplanes (Revised)," pp. 2-3; "History of B-36 Procurement," Air Materiel Command, 12 July 1949, p. 1-2.

10 "Case History of XB-36, YB-36, and B-36 Airplanes (Revised)," p. 3; Meyers K. Jacobsen, "Design Development of the XB-36," *AAHS Journal*, Winter 1970, p. 227.

11 "Case History of XB-36, YB-36, and B-36 Airplanes (Revised)," pp. 5-7.

12 Ibid, p. 11.

13 *Aviation Week*, 28 January 1952, p 47.

14 "Case History of XB-36, YB-36, and B-36 Airplanes (Revised)," p. 11; Knack, *Post-World War II Bombers*, p. 8; The map in *Convairiety*, 1 September 1948, p. 5 provides the distance between San Diego and Fort Worth.

15 "Case History of XB-36, YB-36, and B-36 Airplanes (Revised)," p. 11.

16 Convair promotional literature, and a large sign by the main gate to the plant, usually said, "Convair A Division of General Dynamics Corporation."

17 A Letter of Intent was not, technically, a legally binding document and committed no funds. It was essentially a gentleman's handshake. A Letter Contract, on the other hand, was legally binding, committed funds, and made the U.S. Government liable for default.

18 "Case History of XB-36, YB-36, and B-36 Airplanes (Revised)," p. 14; "Story of B-36 Dates Back to Early in 1941," *Convairiety*, 11 August 1954.

19 "Case History of XB-36, YB-36, and B-36 Airplanes (Revised)," p. 3.

20 Letter, Maj. Gen. Bennett E. Meyers, Air Materiel Command, to

Harry Woodhead, no subject, dated 7 July 1944, in the archives at the San Diego Aerospace Museum.

21 Knack, *Post-World War II Bombers*, p. 11.

22 "Case History of XB-36, YB-36, and B-36 Airplanes (Revised)," pp. 24-25

23 These were Tarrant Field (Fort Worth AAF), Eglin Field in Florida, and Fairfield-Suisun AAF in California, although modifications were proceeding at Patterson Field, Ohio, to accommodate the new airplane.

24 "Case History of XB-36, YB-36, and B-36 Airplanes (Revised)," p. 10.

25 Ibid, p. 13.

26 Until the 1960s, it was normal practice for business correspondence to only use first and middle initials, not first names. Nevertheless, where possible, first names have been provided.

27 The quote is from Hearings before the Subcommittee on Appropriations, House of Representatives, Military Establishment Appropriations, 1947, 79th Congress, 2nd Session, 8 May 1946, p. 23; "Case History of XB-36, YB-36, and B-36 Airplanes (Revised)," p. 13.

28 "Investigation of Workmanship on the XB-36 Airplane," report from the AAF Air Technical Services Command, Engineering Division, 3 August 1945; "Case History of XB-36, YB-36, and B-36 Airplanes (Revised)," pp. 9 and 12; Walton S, Moody, *Building a Strategic Air Force*, (Washington DC: Air Force History and Museums Program, 1996), p. 100; "Case History of XB-36, YB-36, and B-36 Airplanes (Revised)," p. 33; Move under power data from *Convairiety*, 30 January 1952, p. 1; *Convairiety*, 29 May 1957, pp. 1-2.

29 "Case History of XB-36, YB-36, and B-36 Airplanes (Revised)," pp. 7-8 and 12.

30 "Development of Airborne Armament: 1910-1961," Volume II, Historical Division, Aeronautical Systems Division, October 1961, pp. 192-193.

31 Ibid, pp. 193-194.

32 "Case History of XB-36, YB-36, and B-36 Airplanes (Revised)," pp. 32-33.

33 Wright Field became Wright-Patterson AFB on 13 January 1948.

34 *Convairiety*, 5 January 1949, p. 5.

35 AN-01-5EUB-1, "Flight Operating Instructions, USAF Series B-36B Aircraft," 16 November 1948, p. 22.

36 Test conducted during 1951 found that even on a 103 degF Texas day, the airframe could experience temperatures as low as –100 degF at 40,000 feet.

37 Delivery data in *Convairiety*, 15 June 1955, p. 1.

38 "Eighth Air Force Due Delivery On First B-36 of 100 Ordered" (UP) 23 March 1948.

39 TSgt. Gregory S. Byard, "7th BMW B-36 Chronology," 7th Bomb Wing History Office, undated, pp. 4-5, in the files at the Air Force Historical Research Center.

40 Convair report FZA-36-091, "Summary Report of B-36A Airplane Long Range Simulated Tactical Mission Flight Two," 4 June 1948; *Convairiety*, 5 January 1949, p. 5; "7th BMW B-36 Chronology," pp. 5-6.

41 "7th BMW B-36 Chronology," pp. 7-8.

42 See chapter four for additional information.

43 Knack, *Post-World War II Bombers*, pp. 21. The other two B-36As – 44-92004/005 – were delivered as test aircraft to the Air Materiel Command; 004 was tested to destruction at Wright Field and 005 was later converted into an RB-36E.

44 "Development of Airborne Armament: 1910-1961," pp. 47-48 and 198-199.

45 *Aviation Week*, 18 October 1948, p. 12; Walton S. Moody, *Building a Strategic Air Force*, (Washington DC: Air Force History and Museums Program, 1996), p. 238.

46 "Development of Airborne Armament: 1910-1961," pp. 51-52.

47 "7th BMW B-36 Chronology," p. 9.

48 *Convairiety*, 16 February 1949, p.1 and p. 8.

49 *Convairiety*, 13 April 1949, p.1 and p. 8; *Aviation Week*, 15

August 1949, p. 14; "Crippled B-36 Sets Down With New Distance Record," (AP) 13 March 1949.

50 Moody, *Building a Strategic Air Force*, p. 267.

51 Streets in Carswell's base housing addition were named for victims of this crash. The $5.25 million housing addition was built by attorney Raymond E. Buck's construction company, the Buccoo Corporation, starting in July of 1950.

52 Summary of the Air Force accident report as shown at: http://www.air-and-space.com/b-36%20wrecks.htm#44-92035.

53 Moody, *Building a Strategic Air Force*, p. 268.

54 The original 100 aircraft contract did not specify models, but resulted in 22 B-36As and 73 B-36Bs – 5 aircraft were cancelled to cover the costs of the stillborn B-36C project.

55 There seems to be some confusion over whether this was "discharge" or "displacement" with contemporary literature using both terms. Most Pratt & Whitney documentation, however, uses "discharge" so that is what will be used in this book.

56 Letter, Maj. Gen. Lawrence C. Craigie, Chief of the Research and Engineering Division, Wright Field, to the Commanding General, Air Materiel Command, 10 September 1947; Letter, Lt. Gen. Nathan F. Twining, Commanding General, Air Materiel Command, Wright Field, to the Chief of Staff of the Air Force, 30 September 1947.

57 Letter from Gen. Joseph T. McNarney, Commanding General, Air Materiel Command, Wright Field, to the Air Force Chief of Staff, 21 April 1948.

58 Robert Hotz, "Why B-36 Was Made USAF Top Bomber," *Aviation Week*, 15 August 1949, p. 13.

59 "Soviet 'Aid' Reported In B-36 Production" (AP) 10 August 1949. In the same article, Maj. Gen. Frederick H. Smith, Air Force Requirements Chief, told of efforts to keep Air Force Plant 4 in operation by merging Convair's operations with those of Northrop Aircraft, Inc., maker of the B-49 jet-powered "Flying Wing."

60 *Aviation Week*, 15 August 1949, p. 14; AF-WP-O-APR 61 250, Index of AF Serial Numbers Assigned to Aircraft 1958 and Prior, Part 1: Numerical Listing; Prepared by the Procurement Division, Programmed Procurement Branch, Reports Section, MCPPSR, p. 125, in the files at the Jay Miller Collection.

61 A reproducible photo of the first flight could not be found, but see *Convairiety*, 13 April 1949, p. 1.

62 Bell also manufactured the pods for the B-47. The B-36 pods were under subcontract to Convair, while the B-47 pods were under subcontract to Boeing.

63 The fact that Bell manufactured the pods, instead of Boeing, came from *Convairiety*, 15 February 1950, p. 4; *Convairiety*, 23 May 1951, p. 8.

64 "Red Noses Not From Moonshine But Sign of B-36 in Flight Test," Convairiety, 11 January 1950, p 2.

65 "Development of Airborne Armament: 1910-1961," Volume I, Historical Division, Aeronautical Systems Division, October 1961, pp. 50-51.

66 Marcelle Size Knack, *Post-World War II Bombers*, Office of Air Force History, 1988, p 34.

67 All of the B-36Bs that were converted after production became B-36Ds; none were converted into RB-36Ds.

68 Cannon data from *Convairiety*, 6 December 1950, p.1 and p. 8; *Convairiety*, 10 January 1951, p. 5; Building 3 data from *Convairiety*, 9 May 1951, p. 8.

69 Report from Col. A. A. Fickel, USAF, Assistant to the Commanding General, ARDC to Gen. Schlatter and Gen. Cook (HQ, ARDC, Wright-Patterson AFB), 19 March 1951.

70 Or perhaps over the Soviet Union. Nevertheless, despite persistent rumors, no records could be found to indicate that the RB-36s ever conducted overflights.

71 *Convairiety*, 4 January 1950, p. 1; Flight logs belonging to Berton L. Woods, who flew on almost every B-36 at Fort Worth – his entry on 14 December 1949 for 44-92088 indicates it was a "10-engine" reconnaissance model; other entries around it indicate B-models as "6-engine."

72 Wayne Wachsmuth, "B-36 Peacemaker," *Detail & Scale*, Volume 47, (Fort Worth, TX: Detail & Scale, 1997), p. 20.
73 *Convairiety*, 14 March 1951.
74 Bulkhead 5.0 was the front of bomb bay No. 1; bulkhead 6.0 was the front of bomb bay No. 2; bulkhead 7.0 was the front of bomb bay No. 3; bulkhead 8.0 was the front of bomb bay No. 4; and bulkhead No. 9.0 was the pressure dome between bomb bay No. 4 and the aft pressurized compartment.
75 "Phase II ECM Manufacturing Plan," Convair Fort Worth ECP-678AH and ECP-678AG, 14 July 1954, pp. 28-29; "ECP 2308 Phase X ON TOP Manufacturing Plan," Convair, 13 September 1954; RB-36 Aircraft Weather Reconnaissance Manufacturing Plan," Convair, 12 August 1954; "Phase II ECM and Phase X ON TOP Manufacturing Plan," Convair Fort Worth, 22 October 1954, (no page numbers)
76 Order/quantity data comes from *Convairiety*, 4 January 1950, p. 3; Convair Field Service Letter No. 56, 11 June 1951; "7th BMW B-36 Chronology," pp. 22-23. Although 36 B-36Fs were ordered, two were diverted to the YB-60 program prior to delivery.
77 Knack, *Post-World War II Bombers*, p. 41.
78 Convair Field Service Letter No. 56, 11 June 1951.
79 "7th BMW B-36 Chronology," pp. 22-23.
80 Ibid, pp. 26-28.
81 *Convairiety*, 1 August 1951, p. 5.
82 Mock-up inspection from *Convairiety*, 30 August 1950, p. 1; "Drag Evaluation of the YDB-36H," AFFTC report 53-31, October 1953, originally classified SECRET, declassified on 31 December 1972, Appendix I, p. 3 ; "Development of Airborne Armament: 1910-1961," pp. 199-203.
83 "Development of Airborne Armament: 1910-1961," pp. 199-203; Mock-up inspection from *Convairiety*, 30 August 1950, p. 1.
84 Order/quantity data comes from *Convairiety*, 4 January 1950, p. 3; *Convairiety*, 12 September 1951, p. 1.
85 Knack, *Post-World War II Bombers*, p. 51; *Convairiety*, 25 August 1954, p. 1.
86 At the time, this was always written in all caps – FEATHERWEIGHT.
87 SAC Programming Plan 10-54, "Featherweight Modification for the B-36 Fleet," originally classified Top Secret, 28 January 1954; "History of the Fifteenth Air Force," 1 January 1954 to 30 June 1954, Top Secret Supplement, Project Featherweight, 3 December 1954, p. 1, in the files of the AFHRA as K670.01-15. All declassified in 1972.
88 "History of the Fifteenth Air Force," p. 3; "Featherweight Project Manufacturing Plan," Convair Fort Worth, 1954.
89 "Featherweight Project Manufacturing Plan," p. 9.
90 Ibid, pp. 9-10.
91 "History of the Fifteenth Air Force," pp. 3-4.
92 Ibid, pp. 4-6.
93 Ibid.
94 Notes and documentation supplied by C. Roger Cripliver, who was responsible for writing many of the TCTOs used in these programs.
95 *Convairiety*, 17 June 1953, p. 1 and p. 8.
96 "Long Range Bombardment Airplane, MCD-392," Aircraft Laboratory, Engineering Division, no date (but sometime in 1941).
97 T.O. 1B-36J-1, "Flight Handbook: USAF Series B-36J-III aircraft; Featherweight – Configuration III," revised 6 April 1956, pp. 810-812 "Mission C."
98 Maximum continuous power was 2,650-bhp for the R4360s and 96-percent for the J47s.
99 Thanks to fellow Specialty Press author Tommy Thomason for the F9F story.
100 Navy Department, Board of Inspection and Survey, "Report of Service Acceptance Trials on Model F2H-1 Aircraft," TED No. BIS 21112, 31 July 1951; "Report on the Performance Phase of Service Acceptance Trials for the Model F2H-1 Airplane, BuNo 122541," 6 June 1950, Appendix E, Plate I, Appendix E, Plate IV. The service ceiling is defined at the altitude were the rate of climb drops below 500 feet per minute.
101 Navy Department, Board of Inspection and Survey, "Report of Service Acceptance Trials on Model F2H-1 Aircraft," TED No. BIS 21112, 31 July 1951, p. 10.
102 Yefim Gordon, *Mikoyan-Gurevich MiG-15*, (Leicester, UK: Midland Publishing, 2001).
103 It is not certain why some parts of the Air Force continued to voice this since it seriously undercut the rationale for massive expenditures by the Western Allies on the DEW line, the Pine Tree line, BMEWS, and any number of other expensive radar projects to protect Europe and North America.

Chapter 3 – The Bleeding Edge

1 SAC Manual 50-30, "B-36 Gunnery," November 1954. Interestingly, the –50 degF limit meant the system would likely not work above about 30,000 feet altitude.
2 A detailed history of the defensive systems may be found in Meyers K. Jacobsen, et. al., *Convair B-36: A Comprehensive History of America's "Big Stick,"* (Atglen, PA: Schiffer Military History), pp. 246-287; see also "Development of Airborne Armament: 1910-1961," Volume II, Historical Division, Aeronautical Systems Division, October 1961, pp. 169-206.
3 "Convair Development Department Annual Report 1953," 27 May 1954, p. 7; "Convair Development Department Fourth Annual Report," 8 September 1955, p. 23.
4 AF-WP-O-APR 61-250, "Index of AF Serial Numbers Assigned to Aircraft 1958 and Prior," Part 1: Numerical Listing, prepared by the Procurement Division, Programmed Procurement Branch, Reports Section, MCPPSR, p. 125.
5 Werrell, The Evolution of the Cruise Missile, p. 236; Forrest E. Armstrong, "From New Technology Development to Operational usefulness – B-36, B-58, F-111/FB-111," a paper written for an AIAA conference, no date.
6 SAC Manual 50-30, "B-36 Gunnery," November 1954.
7 AN 01-5EUB-1, "Flight Operating Instructions for the USAF Series B-36B Aircraft," 16 November 1949, p 94.
8 Ibid, p 13.
9 *Aviation Week*, 12 September 1949, p 37.
10 AN 01-5EUC-2 (1B-36D-2), "Erection and Maintenance Instructions, USAF Series B-36D Aircraft," 3 June 1954, p 637.
11 *Aviation Week*, 18 October 1948, p 12.
12 The bombs had been built and were controlled by the Manhattan Engineering District, which became the Armed Forces Special Weapons Project after the war. Eventually the manufacture and control of nuclear weapons passed to the Atomic Energy Commission and later to the Department of Energy.
13 Walton S. Moody, *Building a Strategic Air Force*, (Washington DC: Air Force History and Museums Program, 1996), pp. 167-170.
14 The first three nuclear weapon designations used Roman numerals; subsequent weapons used Arabic numbers.
15 Moody, *Building a Strategic Air Force*, pp. 167-170.
16 "History of Project Saddletree," Air Material Command, Wright-Patterson AFB, May 1963.
17 Moody, *Building a Strategic Air Force*, pp. 244-245.
18 A more in-depth, albeit somewhat confusing, look at the various early bomb modifications to the B-36 may be found in Jacobsen, et. al., *Convair B-36*, pp. 235-240. Other data from AN01-5EUE-2 (undated), T.O. 1B-36D-2-1 dated 23 March 1956, and T.O. 1B-36D-4 dated 16 November 1956.
19 AN 01-5EUC-2 (1B-36D-2), "Erection and Maintenance Instructions, USAF Series B-36D Aircraft," 3 June 1954, p 519.
20 1B-36H(III)-1, "Flight Handbook for the USAF Series B-36H-III Aircraft," 26 November 1954, p 229.
21 "Phase II ECM Manufacturing Plan," ECP-678AH and ECP-678AG, 14 July 1954.

22 See Graham White, *R-4360: Pratt & Whitney's Major Miracle*, (North Branch, MN: Specialty Press, 2006) for the complete history of the engine.

23 The terminology of the time called mechanical devices "superchargers" and exhaust-driven devices "turbo-superchargers." Today, the latter devices are called "turbochargers."

24 SAC Manual 50-35, "Aircraft Performance Engineer's Manual for B-36 Aircraft Engine Operation," 1953.

25 AN 01-5EUC-2 (1B-36D-2), "Erection and Maintenance Instructions, USAF Series B-36D Aircraft," 3 June 1954. 13 SAC Manual 50-35.

26 SAC Manual 50-35, passim; 1B-36H(III)-1, p. 1-13; AN-01-5EUB-1, p. 4.

27 "High-altitude propeller" comment from Mike Moore in conversation with the author, 11 May 2001.

28 *Aviation Week*, 12 July 1948, p. 21.

Chapter 4 – Conflict Unfinished

1 It should be noted that the atomic bombing of Hiroshima and Nagasaki, the establishment of the United States Air Forces in Europe, and delivery of the first operational B-36s to the Air Force were initially scheduled for about the same time in 1945. Had the coincidence of these three events actually occurred, the United States would have achieved undeniable military supremacy over the Soviets before the Cold War had even begun.

2 "United States Air Forces in Europe," http://en.wikipedia.org/wiki/United_States_Air_Forces_in_Europe

3 Winston Churchill's 5 March 1946 "Sinews of Peace" speech at Westminster College in Fulton, Missouri: "From Stettin in the Baltic to Trieste in the Adriatic an 'iron curtain' has descended across the Continent. Behind that line lie all the capitals of the ancient states of Central and Eastern Europe. Warsaw, Berlin, Prague, Vienna, Budapest, Belgrade, Bucharest and Sofia; all these famous cities and the populations around them lie in what I must call the Soviet sphere, and all are subject, in one form or another, not only to Soviet influence but to a very high and in some cases increasing measure of control from Moscow."

4 The status of the Strategic Air Command and its relationship to the JCS remained in flux until early 1949. See http://www.dtic.mil/doctrine/jel/history/ucp.pdf

5 In reality, there were many differences between the airplanes, mostly because the Soviets used the metric system, not Imperial units. This drove thicker skin (since that is what Soviet industry manufactured), resulting in a 3,100-pound increase in empty weight. In addition, the Shvetsov ASh-73 engines were considerably different than the Wright R-3350s used by the B-29. Nevertheless, the airplane was certainly a reverse-engineered version of the B-29.

6 Ironically, the Army Air Forces technically no longer existed at the time of the open house, having been replaced by the independent Air Force.

7 Newspaper images of this lettering lead the authors to conclude it was hand-painted specifically for the ceremony. None of it remained on the aircraft when it made its two flights in August 1947, nor while it was being tested at Wright-Patterson AFB.

8 World attention focused on Gen. Ramey in July of 1947 after a news report alleged the crash of an unidentified flying object – a Flying Saucer – had crashed near Roswell, New Mexico. Army intelligence officers at Roswell sent the object to Wright Field, Ohio, for closer inspection. The debris was flown in a B-29, making a stop at Eighth Air Force headquarters at Fort Worth Army Air Field where Ramey identified the remains as a RAWIN high altitude radar-reflecting device and ordered them "to be thrown away." Base intelligence officer Maj. Edwin M. Kirton, speaking for Ramey, said it would not be necessary to forward the objects to Wright Field. Source: "Suspected 'Disk' Only Flying Weather Vane" *Dallas News*, 9 September 1947.

9 "Forerunner of Vast Fleet is Named 'CITY OF FORT WORTH,'" *Fort Worth Star-Telegram*, 5 August 1947.

10 Ibid.

11 The 7th Bombardment Group (Very Heavy) had been activated on 1 October 1946, consisting of the 9th, 436th, and 492nd Bombardment Squadrons. On 17 November 1947, the 7th Bombardment Wing (Very Heavy) was established as an overarching organization encompassing the 7th BG plus various support and maintenance groups. On 1 December 1948, the 11th Bomb Group (Heavy) was organized under the 7th Bomb Wing. The 11th was elevated to Wing status on 16 February 1951. This left the 7th BG with no real task since both the 7th Bomb Wing and 11th Bomb Wing acted as independent entities. However, it was not until 16 June 1952 that the 7th Bomb Group was officially inactivated. In addition, during this period, the term "Bombardment" was replaced with "Bomb" and "Very Heavy" become "Heavy." To ease possible confusion – even though it is technically incorrect – this text will simply refer to the 7th Bomb Wing and 11th Bomb Wing regardless of their Group relationships.

12 http://www.afhra.af.mil/factsheets/factsheet.asp?id=9628. In Air Force lineage, to establish a unit is "to assign a designation" while organize means "to assign personnel." See http://www.maxwell.af.mil/au/afhra/rso/guide_usaf_lineage_honors.html

13 In September 1948 the Rome Air Depot, New York, was renamed Griffiss AFB in honor of Lt. Col. Griffiss, who was originally from Buffalo, New York.

14 "Leaders Tell Plans for New U.S. Might," (AP), 18 March 1948.

15 "Eighth Air Force Due Delivery On First B-36 of 100 Ordered," (AP), 23 March 1948. Calling the B-36A "war ready" was pure propaganda since the aircraft were not equipped with defensive systems, nor any meaningful offensive systems and were ultimately used mostly for service tests and training.

16 "7th BMW B-36 Chronology," TSgt. Gregory S. Byard, 7th Bomb Wing Historian, undated, pp. 4-5, in the files at the Air Force Historical Research Agency.

17 "Alaska Base Will House Giant B-36's," (AP), 27 March 1948.

18 Eielson AFB was named for Carl Ben Eielson, an Alaska aviation pioneer who was killed, along with his mechanic Earl Borland, in the crash of their Hamilton aircraft in 1929. Eielson and Borland were attempting a rescue flight to an icebound ship in the Bering Sea when they were killed.

19 "7th BMW B-36 Chronology," pp. 7-8.

20 Felix R. McKnight, "Texas Seen by Johnson as U.S. Air Heartbeat," *Dallas News*, 19 July 1948. The numbers, or course, were part of the greater propaganda campaign conducted by the United States and the Soviet Union and were completely fictitious. For instance, the USAF alone procured more than 1,300 aircraft in 1948, and the Navy built a similar number. Those numbers would triple in 1949. Meanwhile, the Soviets built fewer than half Johnson's claimed number.

21 "'Utmost Asked to Meet Urgent B-36 Goal: Must Build 18 by End Of the Year." *Convairiety*. 10 November 1948.

22 "Here's Chance to Name B-36." *Convairiety*. 8 December 1948.

23 According to the 7 December 1947 *Dallas Morning News*, the Air Force considered individually naming each B-36 after States of the Union. "Military planes usually carry a popular-type name, like Flying Fortress or Thunderbolt, but have never been christened separately." Given that many more B-36s were built than there are States, this would have been an interesting exercise.

24 Fairfield-Suisun was renamed Travis AFB in 1951 for Brig. Gen. Robert F. Travis, who was killed when a B-29 crashed on 5 August 1950; the ensuing fire caused the 10,000 pounds of high explosives in a Mk 4 nuclear weapon to detonate, killing Travis and 18 others. On 13 June 1953, Rapid City AFB was renamed after Brig. Gen. Richard E. Ellsworth, who was killed when an RB-36H crashed in Newfoundland on 23 March 1953, killing Ellsworth and 22 others.

25 Although there was little alarm from the announcement, there was considerable surprise that the Soviets had developed a nuclear weapon so quickly, nearly five years faster than projected. Unknown to the U.S. was the long-term passing of nuclear secrets to the Soviets by key U.S. atomic scientists Klaus Fuchs and Theodore Hall – and unidentified others.

26 The Air Force maintained possession of the bomb itself – the casing, fuzing, and delivery system (parachute, etc.), but not the fissionable material in the bomb core (implosion assembly).

27 In 1941, the War Department purchased the area known as Sunset Field from Spokane County for a World War II B-17 and C-47 training facility. Following the acquisition, they renamed the facility Geiger Field in honor of Major Harold C. Geiger, a pioneer in Army aviation and ballooning. In 1946, a portion of the airfield was designated a municipal airport, and commercial airline operations were moved from Felts Field to Geiger Field. In 1960, the facility was renamed Spokane International Airport.

28 Amon Carter was a frequent guest of political and military leaders at Carswell. Soon after the annual air inspection in 1950, Carter was awarded the Exceptional Service Award, the highest award given to a civilian by the military, for his support of the Air Force at Carswell. On 5 December 1950, he received the prestigious Frank M. Hawks Memorial Award from American Legion Air Service Post 501 of New York City as "one of the true pioneers of American aviation." Vice-Admiral Charles E. Rosendahl, (ret), himself a former award winner, presented the award to Carter. Previous winners included Fiorello LaGuardia, Randolph Hearst, Gen. Hoyt S. Vandenberg, Igor Sikorsky, and William Lear.

29 From a 31 July 1998 interview of the copilot of this flight by Don Pyeatt.

30 In later years, sensationalists and conspiracy theorists have distorted the events surrounding the crash of 2075 by accusing the Air Force of covering up the loss, and even a detonation, of a live nuclear weapon on Canadian territory. The conspiracy advocates ignore the facts that nuclear bomb cores were in the possession and control of the Atomic Energy Commission at the time and could be released to the military only by presidential directive during a national emergency, and the bomber's mission profile called for practice bombings of American cities on its return to Carswell. These two facts alone make the speculative claims of a "live" nuclear device onboard the aircraft blatantly absurd.

31 "House Group Approves Military Base Build-Up", (UPI), 24 March 1950.

32 While war was raging in Korea, a potential threat to world peace was developing in the Mideast due to a challenge by Egypt of Britain's control of the Suez Canal. Egyptian president Nasser closed the Suez Canal to Israeli shipping in an attempt to evict Britain from the area. Egypt then threatened the annihilation of Israel with massive amounts of war materiel bought from the Soviet Union via Czechoslovakia. The ensuing Suez Crisis (or Tripartite Aggression, depending where one sat) marked the beginning of numerous 7th Bomb Wing peacekeeping deployments to the United Kingdom and North Africa. These developments further explain why the B-36 was withheld from the Korean Conflict and placed on standby in the Mideast throughout most of the 1950s. Beyond the scope of this book, readers are urged to research the Suez Crisis using authoritative sources such as Selwyn Troen and Moshe Shemesh, *The Suez-Sinai Crisis, 1956: Retrospective and Reappraisal*, (New York: Columbia University Press, 1990).

33 Gen. Fairchild (1894–1950) was a native of nearby Bellingham, Washington. The general entered service as a sergeant with the Washington National Guard in June 1916 and died while serving as the Vice Chief of Staff in March 1950.

34 Bases on U.S. territory are called Air Force Bases (AFB); on foreign soil they are called Air Bases (AB).

35 *Convairiety*, 31 January 1951, p. 1; *Convairiety*, 19 December 1951, p. 1. Sidi Slimane is in the western center of Morocco, located

between Kenitra and Meknes. Nouasseur is located near Casablanca and is now known as Mohammed V International Airport. With the destabilization of French government in Morocco, and Moroccan independence in 1956, the government of Mohammed V wanted the US Air Force to pull out of the SAC bases in Morocco, insisting on such action after American intervention in Lebanon in 1958. The United States agreed to leave as of December 1959, and was fully out of Morocco in 1963.

36 Historic American Engineering Record, Loring AFB, Weapons Storage Area, Northeastern corner of base at northern end of Maine Road, Limestone vicinity, Aroostook County, ME. On file with The Library of Congress.

37 Walker AFB was named after Brig. Gen. Kenneth N. Walker (1898–1943), a native of Los Cerrillos, New Mexico. He was killed during a bombing mission over Rabaul, New Guinea on 5 January 1943 and was posthumously awarded the Medal of Honor. Roswell AFB was renamed in his honor on 13 January 1948, and the base was permanently closed on 30 June 1967. Borinquen AAF was built in September 1939 at Aguadilla, Puerto Rico. On 18 September 1948, it was renamed Ramey AFB in honor of Brig. Gen. Howard K. Ramey (1896–1943), who was killed on a reconnaissance mission in the South Pacific during World War II. The base was closed in 1973 and is now used by the U.S. Coast Guard.

38 Just outside El Paso, Texas, the original Ft. Bliss airfield was established in 1916 for the 1st Aero Squadron. On 25 January 1925, the field was named for Lt. James Berthes "Buster" Biggs from El Paso killed in World War I. In 1920, Camp Owen Bierne opened on the site of the current airbase as a base for airship operations but the units were soon disbanded and on 1 July 1926, Biggs Field was moved to the former Camp Bierne location and the older field closed. Biggs Field served primarily as a refueling site until World War II, when it became a primary heavy bomber Operational Training Unit location for the Army Air Forces. After World War II, the OTU was inactivated and the base housed fighter operations for two years. On 1 February 1948 the base was re-dedicated as Biggs AFB as a base for heavy bombers. The runway at Biggs was the third largest runway in the United States at the time. The base was closed in 1966, but was subsequently reopened as a permanent U.S. Army Airfield.

39 Greater Southwest Airport was closed on 13 January 1974 when the new Dallas-Fort Worth International Airport opened. The old main runway at Greater Southwest is now named Amon Carter Boulevard.

40 The U.S. government referred to the atoll as "Eniwetok" until 1974, when it changed its official spelling to "Enewetak" (along with many other Marshall Islands place names) to more properly reflect their proper pronunciation by the Marshall Islanders.

41 Chuck Hansen, *U.S. Nuclear Weapons: The Secret History*, (Arlington TX: Aerofax, Inc, 1988); http://www.cddc.vt.edu/host/atomic/atmosphr/ustests.html#Ivy

42 Stated in the April 1949 "Name The Plane" contest.

43 Morgan made his screen debut using the name "Henry Morgan," before switching to "Henry 'Harry' Morgan" and eventually "Harry Morgan," to avoid confusion with the then-popular comedian of the same name on radio and TV.

44 Shannon Cannard, "Another Day, Another Crusade," *Fort Worth Business Press*, Volume 16, Issue 32, Monday, 1 March 2004.

45 This B-52 arrived at Carswell on 19 February 1958 and was assigned to the newly organized 4123rd Strategic Wing. During a ceremony when it arrived, the B-52 was named "City of Fort Worth." This aircraft is now on display at Pima Air & Space Museum.

46 For excerpts from Mr. Carter's speech see the Epilog.

47 See Ed Calvert, Don Pyeatt, and Richard Marmo, *B-36: Saving the Last Peacemaker*, at http://www.prowebfortworth.com, for the complete saga of the last B-36.

48 "7th BMW B-36 Chronology," p. 10. The Revolt of the Admirals and the controversy surrounding the National Security Act of 1947 and subsequent development of the Strategic Air Command are outside the scope of this book. Several good studies have been done on these events. See, for instance, Jeffery G. Barlow, *Revolt of the Admirals: The Fight for Naval Aviation, 1945-1950*, (Washington D.C.: Naval Historical Center, 1994) and Walton S. Moody, *Building a Strategic Air Force*, (Washington DC: Air Force History and Museums Program, 1996).

49 *Aviation Week*, 12 September 1949, p 37.

50 Louis Arthur Johnson (1891–1966) was the second United States Secretary of Defense, serving in the cabinet of President Harry S. Truman from 28 March 1949 to 19 September 1950. He had been an Assistant Secretary of War from 1937 to 1940, but was not selected as Secretary of War in favor of Henry Stimson. After a series of conflicts with Defense Secretary James V. Forrestal over defense budget cutbacks, President Truman asked for Forrestal's resignation, replacing him with Johnson early in 1949.

51 "Navy, Air Force Urged To Wage 8-Mile-Up Duel," (AP), 19 May 1949.

52 Drew Pearson, *Dallas News*, 30 June 1949.

53 Marcelle Size Knack, *Post-World War II Bombers*, Office of Air Force History, 1988, p 27; Keith D. McFarland and David L. Roll, *Louis Johnson and the Arming of America: The Roosevelt and Truman Years*, (Bloomington, IN: Indiana University Press, 2005).

54 http://www.afhra.af.mil/factsheets/factsheet.asp?id=9628

55 Walton S. Moody, *Building a Strategic Air Force*, (Washington DC: Air Force History and Museums Program, 1996), pp. 412-414.

56 From an interview with Lt. Col. Frank F. Kleinwechter, Jr. USAF (ret).

57 *Convairiety*, 10 September 1952, pp. 1-2.

58 *Convairiety*, 24 September 1952, p. 1.

59 Extrand was the Director of Maintenance for the 7th BW; Tibbetts was the SAC Deputy Chief of Staff for Materiel.

60 Letter to Don Pyeatt from Ben Fay, former Convair contracts
    Ibid.

62 *Convairiety*, 24 September 1952, p. 1; "7th BMW B-36 Chronology," TSgt Gregory S. Byard, 7th Bomb Wing Historian, undated, pp. 30-31, in the files at the Air Force Historical Research Center.

63 "7th BMW B-36 Chronology," p. 29; Moody, *Building a Strategic Air Force*, pp. 412-414.

64 http://en.wikipedia.org/wiki/Cold_War, which cites Walter LaFeber, "Cold War," an essay in *A Reader's Companion to American History*, Eric Foner and John A. Garraty, eds. (Boston, MA: Houghton Mifflin Company, 1991).

Epilog – Political Ideology

1 Uttered by "Joshua," the personality used by the War Operational Plan Response (W.O.P.R.) computer after it achieved sentience in the 1983 movie *War Games*. The conclusion was reached after simulating all possible scenarios for a nuclear war and discovering the outcome was the same in each: everybody loses.

2 To read Mr. Carter's entire speech, see http://www.b-36 peacemakermuseum.org/Articles/agcjr.htm

Appendix A – The First Wide Body

1 "Model 37," *The Eagle*, 25 May 1945.

2 Marcelle Size Knack, *Post-World War II Bombers*, Office of Air Force History, 1988, p 8.

3 Convair report ZD-37-004, "CVAC Model 37 for Pan American Airways," 15 February 1945.

4 Convair report ZH-026, "A Comparison of Performance Between the Model 37 and a Flying Boat Version of the Same Airplane," 17 August 1945.

5 Convair XC-99 Press Book, undated, p 1.

6 *Aviation Week*, 2 June 1952, p 12.

7 Convair XC-99 Press Book, undated, p 18.

8 Ibid, p 20.

9 Ibid, p 28.

10 *Aviation Week*, 5 December 1949, p 14.

Appendix B – Unworthy Competitor

1 *Aviation Week*, 29 January 1951, p 13.

2 Ibid.

3 Mockup Inspection of the Model YB-60 Airplane, Convair, Contract No. AF-33(038)-2182, 20 August 1951, p 3.

4 "YB-60 Standard Aircraft Characteristics," 21 September 1951, classified SECRET, declassified 16 December 1966. In the files at the Air Force Museum; "Phase II Flight Test of the YB-60 Airplane," AFFTC report 53-10, April 1953, originally classified SECRET; declassified on 29 March 1977, Appendix II, p. 4.

5 "YB-60 Standard Aircraft Characteristics;" "Transition to Swept Wing B-36," a small paper published by Convair and classified Secret at the time (undated). Copies are in the files at the San Diego Aerospace Museum, Air Force Historical Research Agency, and the National Archives; "Phase II Flight Test of the YB-60 Airplane," p. 1.

6 Mockup Inspection of the Model YB-60 Airplane, Convair, Contract No. AF-33(038)-2182, 20 August 1951, p 11. This represented the inclusion of MCRs 5009-5012, 5014-5016, and 5020-5022.

7 Ibid, p 22.

8 Ibid, p 22.

9 The XB-52's wing had been damaged during a ground test, so the YB-52 was the first B-52-type to fly.

10 *Fort Worth Star*, various dates in July 1954.

11 Convair report FZP-36-1001, "YB-60 Commercial Transport," 4 April 1953.

Appendix C – Dream Unrealized

1 For a much more complete description of the X-6 aircraft, see Jay Miller, *The X-Planes, X-1 to X-45*, (Hinckley, England: Midland Publishing, 2001).

2 Convair report XM-566, "Short History of the Design and Development of the Nose Section and Crew Compartment Mock-Up for the XB-36H," 20 March 1956; *Convairiety*, 12 September 1951, p. 1; "Convair Development Department Fourth Annual Report," 8 September 1955, p. 19.

3 *Convairiety*, 25 August 1954, p. 1; "Convair Development Department Fourth Annual Report," p. 19.

4 "Convair Development Department Fourth Annual Report," p. 19.

5 "Short History of the Design and Development of the Nose Section and Crew Compartment Mock-Up for the XB-36H," Convair report XM-566, 20 March 1956.

6 "Convair Development Department Fourth Annual Report," p. 20.

7 Ibid.

8 "Conclusion of B-36 Aircraft Phase-Out," Historical Monograph Nr. 1, Headquarters, San Antonio Air Materiel Area, Kelly AFB, Texas, March 1960.

9 "Review of the Manned Aircraft Nuclear Propulsion Program."

Appendix D – Completely Different

1 Ardath M. Morrow, "Case History of Track Landing Gear," Historical Office, Air Materiel Command, September 1950, p. 1

2 Interestingly, Fairfield-Suisun had been the terminus for Convairways, an airline run by Convair during World War II.

3 "Case History of XB-36, YB-36, and B-36 Airplanes (Revised)," pp. 10 and 24-25.

4   Military Requirement A-1-1, 24 August 1944; Morrow, "Case History of Track Landing Gear," pp. 1 and 9.

5   Morrow, "Case History of Track Landing Gear," pp. 1-2. The Christie suspension is a suspension system developed by Walter Christie for his tank designs that allowed considerably longer movement than conventional leaf spring systems then in common use. This allowed his tanks to have considerably greater cross-country speed and a lower profile. The system was first introduced on his M1928 design, and used on all of his designs until his death in 1944.

6   Morrow, "Case History of Track Landing Gear," p. 2.

7   Morrow, "Case History of Track Landing Gear," p. 3.

8   Morrow, "Case History of Track Landing Gear," pp. 3-4; Memorandum Report ENG-51/AD-801, "Endless Track landing gear on A-20C Airplane," 5 July 1943.

9   Letter, Aircraft Laboratory to Firestone, 31 August 1943, subject: Request for Design and Cost Data for Track Landing Gear for B-17 Airplane and CG-4A Glider.

10 Morrow, "Case History of Track Landing Gear," pp. 3-4.

11 Morrow, "Case History of Track Landing Gear," p. 4; Memorandum Report TSEAC9-4528-3-2, "P-40 Track Gear Test," 13 January 1947.

12 Morrow, "Case History of Track Landing Gear," pp. 5-6.

13 Morrow, "Case History of Track Landing Gear," pp. 6-7.

14 Morrow, "Case History of Track Landing Gear," pp. 7-8.

15 Morrow, "Case History of Track Landing Gear," pp. 9-11.

16 Morrow, "Case History of Track Landing Gear," pp. 9-11; http://home.att.net/~jbaugher2/b50_2.html.

17 Morrow, "Case History of Track Landing Gear," p. 12.

18 Morrow, "Case History of Track Landing Gear," p. 13.

19 Memorandum, subject: Track Landing Gear, to the USAF Chief of Staff from the Engineering Division, AMC, 1948; *Convairiety*, 29 March 1950, p. 8.

20 Morrow, "Case History of Track Landing Gear," p. 13; "7th BMW B-36 Chronology," TSgt Gregory S. Byard, 7th Bomb Wing Historian, undated, p. 16, in the files at the Air Force Historical Research Center.

Appendix E – Stillborn Concept

1   *Pratt & Whitney Bee-Hive*, January 1949, pp. 8-9.

2   *Pratt & Whitney Bee-Hive*, January 1949, pp. 10-11.

3   This originally meant variable discharge turbo-supercharger, but later became variable discharge turbine in order to sound more "modern."

4   The B-50C (B-54) and F-12 (XR-12) would have used R-4360-43 engines, while the B-36 would have used R-4360-51 engines.

5   *Pratt & Whitney Bee-Hive*, January 1949, p. 10.

6   *Pratt & Whitney Bee-Hive*, January 1949, p. 11.

7   *Pratt & Whitney Bee-Hive*, January 1949, p. 7.

Appendix F – Ahead of its Time

1   "Bernard J. Termena, "History of the RASCAL Weapon System," Air Materiel Command, September 1959.

2   "Drag Evaluation of the YDB-36H," Appendix I, p. 3; "B-36 Rascal Mock-up Inspection," a brochure released on 18 November 1952 in support of the mockup inspection, originally classified SECRET. Declassified in 1972. A Standard Aircraft Characteristics was issued for a Featherweight III version, but close examination shows that the data is for a Featherweight II (as were the drawings, etc.) – it appears that the cover is misidentified. It could not be ascertained if there was ever intent to use Featherweight III aircraft as B-63 carriers.

3   Standard Aircraft Characteristics, Consolidated Vultee DB-36H, 20 April 1954; Standard Aircraft Characteristics, Consolidated Vultee DB-36H-II, 3 October 1955.

4   The AFFTC test report and some other Air Force documentation lists this as a YDB-36H, but the aircraft history card does not confirm this. Still, it will be used here since it seems appropriate.

5   Aircraft History Cards supplied by Mike Moore, Lockheed Martin, Fort Worth; "Drag Evaluation of the YDB-36H," Appendix I, p. 3; "B-36 Rascal Mock-up Inspection," p. 25.

6   Termena, "History of the RASCAL Weapon System;" "B-36 Rascal Mock-up Inspection"; "Semi-Annual Progress Report," Holloman Air Development Center, 8 July 1955.

7   Termena, "History of the RASCAL Weapon System;" "Convair Development Department Fourth Annual Report," p. 9; "Semi-Annual Progress Report," Holloman Air Development Center, 8 July 1955; "Weekly Test Report Status," Holloman Air Development Center, 19 June 1955. Both were originally classified SECRET and were declassified in 1966.

8   Termena, "History of the RASCAL Weapon System;" "Convair Development Department Annual Report 1953," 27 May 1954, p. 27; "Convair Development Department Fourth Annual Report," p. 25.

9   Termena, "History of the RASCAL Weapon System."

Appendix G – Bizarre Concept

1   Ray Wagner, *American Combat Planes*, third edition, (New York: Doubleday and Company, 1982), pp. 141-142.

2   "Case History of XB-36, YB-36, and B-36 Airplanes (Revised)," p. 13

3   "Historical Data on Aircraft Designed But Not Produced: 1945-Present – Fighters;" "Air Force Developmental Aircraft," p. 25.

4   "Air Force Developmental Aircraft," a report prepared by the Air Research and Development Command and the Air Materiel Command, April 1957, pp. 26-27.

5   Ibid; *Aviation Week*, 18 October 1948, p. 12; Walton S. Moody, *Building a Strategic Air Force*, (Washington, DC: Air Force History and Museums Program, 1996), p. 238; "B-36 to Carry Own Fighter Protection in Bomb Bays," *Fort Worth Star-Telegram*, 13 September 1946.

6   "Air Force Developmental Aircraft," pp. 25-27; conversation between Scott Crossfield and Dennis R. Jenkins, 12 June 2005.

7   1B-36(R)D(G)-1 FICON Flight Manual, 17 June 1955.

8   Training data from *Convairiety*, 16 November 1955.

9   *Convairiety*, 28 December 1955, p. 1 and p. 8.

10 Clarence E. "Bud" Anderson, "Aircraft Wingtip Coupling Experiments," a paper prepared for the Society of Experimental Test Pilots.

11 Ibid.

12 Brian Lockett, "Flying Aircraft Carriers of the USAF: Wing Tip Coupling – Section 2: EB-29A/EF-84D," *AAHS Journal*, Vol. 53, No. 4, Winter 2008, pp.302-303. Everybody else has gotten this wrong, including us in previous books, saying that all three aircraft in the array were lost. Lockett finally got it right.

13 "Convair Development Department Fourth Annual Report," 8 September 1955, p. 22.

14 Some reports say as many as 50 hookups were made, but no confirmation of this could be found.

15 The TIP-TOW and Tom Tom experiments played, indirectly, a major role in the early conceptual development of the WS-110A (what became the North American XB-70) that relied on the concept of wingtip coupling for massive fuel tanks.

INDEX
WHERE TO FIND THE INFORMATION

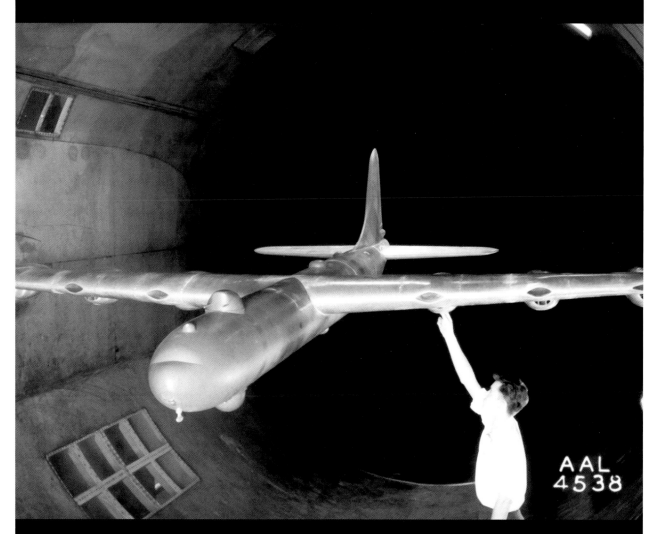

This is the same model as seen on page 228 being tested at NACA Ames. Initially, the XB-36 was going to carry several large, manned turrets instead of the remote-control turrets that eventually emerged. The manned turrets would not have been retractable, causing significant drag, resulting in reduced speed and range. The retractable turrets solved these issues, and great expense in complexity. (Nick Veronico Collection)

Another example of the rapid technological revolution that took place in the immediate post war years. The Convair XF-92 (46-682) was an aerodynamic prototype of a rocket-powered interceptor that never materialized, but led directly to the F-102 Delta Dagger and F-106 Delta Dart interceptors, and also paved the way for the B-58 Hustler. Next to it is a B-36D (44-92064) that provides a good view of its nose armament and details of the windscreen and canopy. (National Archives College Park Collection)